ROCK AND ROLL
BUSKER

GRAHAM FORBES

Published by McNidder & Grace
Bridge Innovation Centre,
Pembrokeshire Science and Technology Park,
Pembroke Dock SA72 6UN

First Published 2013

A catalogue record for this work is available from the British
Library.

ISBN: 978-0-85716-018-8

Designed by Obsidian Design

Printed and bound in England by CPI Group (UK) Ltd,
Croydon CR0 4YY

For my daughters-in-law
Xinzi and Lorraine.

By the same author:

Rock & Roll Mountains
Rock & Roll Tourist

Contents

Thanks and Acknowledgements

It is a magical thing to make music with other people. In addition to those mentioned in the book, there are so many that I have been privileged to play with and I would like to thank them all for the days they gave me. Most recently these have been: Gordon and Shona Martin, Hazie Martin, Alan Mathers, Roddy Wilkie, David Storey, Robert Calder, Cameron Lewis, Fiona Green, Lisa McCormick, Kari Green, Charlotte Marshall, Tim Clarke, Fraser J Lyndsay, Colin Robertson, Stuart Morrison, Jade Lezar, Eric Stewart, Les Barrett, Brian McFie and Alisdair Dingwall.

In America: Rick Fass, Wendy Joffe, Buster Coles, Larry Yunker, Jimmy Purcell, Peter D Straw, RJ Howson, Tom MacKnight, Greg Slusher, Sudie Brattli, Geno and Julie Anne Marino, Carolyn Davis, Kara Nally, Katt Graeber, Pete Aravelo, Andrew Lacroix, Mitch Minx, Brandon Bennett, Bobby Ray Bishop, "English" Willie, Dave Sakelaris, Kevin Nikirk, Andrew Gohman, Brian Ellingson, Mitch Clark, Theresa Nichols-Wimer, Skip Metheny, Michael Dempsey, Rebecca Bird, Jimi Gee, Tom Carrano, Mack Black, Bert Dellarmi, Rusty Cage, David Robbins, Dave Talkovic, Joe Bruno, Jeremy Egglefield, Eddie James Liashek, Sandi Grecco and Kerri Collins.

I would also like to thank for editorial assistance and encouragement: Armorel Allan, Ryan Praefke, David Fletcher, Alex Mayes, Andy Peden Smith, Linda MacFadyen, and especially Graham and Alan Forbes, without whom this book would probably have only a few chapters.

I live in Glasgow half the year, where everyone plays louder than me, and Florida the other half, where everyone plays quieter. I'm always pleased to hear from like-minded people. My email address is: write2g@hotmail.com, and on Facebook, grahamforbes01.

Forewarned

Most rock biographies are about pampered superstars. They tell tales of sex and drugs and rock and roll. We've heard them all before. In the real world, millions of ordinary musicians like me are playing in bars, dance halls, hotels and restaurants. We do it for little pay; most of us know we will never play the big stadiums of the world. We are not impressed by whining multi-millionaire rock stars bleating about their addictions and hard lives... *aye right*. These guys really piss us off even if they do play great riffs that we'll spend hours slavishly copying.

Rock And Roll Busker is a tribute to all working muzos. The guys who will drag their gear through snowdrifts to play *Brown Eyed Girl* one more time if that's what the dancers want. We are what we are, and we do what we do. Without us, Saturday nights would be much quieter. For some it might seem a Highway to Hell but we have a whole lot of laughs on the way. It *is* only rock and roll, but we love it.

Introduction

About 20 years ago in Nashville, Tennessee, a very renowned hit songwriter named Harlan Howard told me the following: "Son, do you realise that, statistically speaking, you have a better chance of being killed by lightning while riding a bicycle than you do of ever, in your entire lifetime, having a Top 40 record?" I was a green upstart in my mid 20's at the time, swimming naively in a sea of countless other would-be singers and players all desperate just to get a foot or a toe into any door, and I suppose he was mercifully trying to put me off pursuing a career as a professional musician.

But for all of the reasons Graham Forbes so eloquently describes in this book, Howard's cautionary words to me only strengthened my resolve. With the decline of sales revenue from recorded music over the past decade, and the subsequent consolidation of media industries worldwide, I'd reckon that one's chances of having a hit record now have decreased even further in favour of death by lightning and bicycles. But the Truth, known and felt in ways that certainly pass understanding by every true musician, has always been that anyone who pursued the music business in the hopes of earning a fortune was in it for the wrong reasons, and was almost certainly setting themselves up for monumental disappointment. A writer writes. A player plays. We do what we are – or we suppress it at great psychological and spiritual costs. This is true for the financially successful and unsuccessful alike.

Recently, I heard Bob Dylan – clearly an artist who falls firmly on the "successful" end of the financial scale – interviewed. He was asked whether, at his age, he was still happy to be touring constantly, playing shows all over the world, dragging himself through a endless litany of airports and hotels and venue dressing rooms. Wouldn't he be happier spending more time in comfort at home these days? His answer was beautiful and pinned me like a bolt of recognition: He said that the point of life was not to be "happy," but rather the point of life was to figure out what one is supposed to be doing and then to spend as much of one's time as possible doing it! Last week, I was told essentially the same thing by a completely unknown guitar player in his early 60's working for tips in a tiny honky tonk bar on Nashville's Lower Broadway.

So this book is definitely for any and all of our kindred musician spirits out there who want to share in the experience and passion of another musician; you will see yourself reflected in Graham's words over and over. And it is also a book for those folks out there who know and/or love a musician or an artist but simply cannot understand what drives them so fiercely against all reasonable odds. Hell, it's a book for everyone really, because it's just a damn good story, wonderfully told.

Most importantly, this book is a story of hope. It's a story of how fulfilment and satisfaction are often found in unexpected places and how one must be open to recognising and embracing them. And it's a story of coming to terms with one's own nature. I found myself continuously chuckling and nodding knowingly throughout reading it. As for me, the highest any of my records has ever charted is number 39, but hey – I beat the odds! And I haven't been killed by lightning yet. And neither has Graham Forbes. Join him for this part of his journey. See you down the road, G!

John Wheeler, Hayseed Dixie

1

BODIE VALDEZ AND FRIENDS

No one decides to become a musician.

You either are or you aren't. You're born one, your DNA or brain circuits or whatever it is that makes you a bit weird are wired that way. There really isn't a choice. You have to play. But here's where it gets tricky. From the outside it looks like a really cool life. And for a few it is. Very cool. Who wouldn't want to play a shiny Fender Stratocaster, prance in front of beautiful women, and, just to end the day perfectly, get paid and laid too?

Millions try, but few are asked to give up their day jobs.

All that guff peddled by LA get-rich-quick gurus, all that baloney they preach that we can achieve anything, anything at all if only we put our mind to it, has brought crushing disappointment to many, but makes wonderful TV entertainment. True believers queue to be canon fodder on *American Idol* and *X Factor*, croaking out their hopeful songs and wondering why everyone is peeing themselves laughing.

If they really were musicians, *X Factor* would simply have been another stop on the road; definitely a milestone, but just one more gig. If a national talent show is the first time someone has appeared onstage, then what have they been doing all their life? They see rock stars making it look so easy and think they can do that, but they don't realise it took years and hundreds of gigs to get that kind of confidence and professionalism. No amount of thinking positive thoughts or motivational hugging will make someone a musician. Simon Cowell can X-Factory the final product and mass-market a new star, but the winner had to have real talent in the first place.

In Texas, there's a mega-successful TV preacher called Joel Osteen. He's a very convincing speaker; a good-looking white boy with a gentle voice and charming smile. He says interesting things, positive words of encouragement that offer hope, comforting thousands, perhaps millions of troubled souls adrift on these stormy waters of life. Every week 17,000 followers pack the former basketball arena where he has his church; countless more tune in on Sunday morning TV.

He promises abundance in all things and knows no one is likely to disagree; who doesn't want to pay off their credit cards? And who can deny we could do more than perhaps we thought possible if we get rid of our negative thoughts? If the nodding believers really want something, no matter how seemingly impossible, Joel assures them that God would not have given them that desire without the means to achieve it. Suddenly, for his thousands of trusting followers, life becomes simple; they close their eyes and raise their outstretched hands to the heavens. It all makes sense! Joel promises them that they are children of the Most High God and He will reward them in supernatural ways. All they need is faith.

If only it were so easy.

As teenagers, most of us posed in front of our bedroom mirror, imagining a future playing packed stadium gigs, signing autographs and hanging out with the Stones, but the majority wisely accepted that there was far more chance of winning the lottery and sensibly readjusted their expectations, hopefully at a young age when there was still time to forge an interesting career in worthwhile and useful employment. Some never quite accept that they were not destined to stand beside Bono, playing guitar to adoring millions, and are usually to be found working in music shops, with cynical and bitter smirks on their faces.

Then there are guys like me, perhaps had a little taste of success here and there, maybe landing lucky occasionally, but never becoming a household name, at least not beyond hearing distance of our homes. We play because we love it. Most of the time. And whatever happens, whatever disappointments, heartless betrayals and cruel rejections we endure we keep coming back for more, like happy little puppy dogs. Just takes one round of applause, one pat on the back and, yippee, life is good again.

There are millions of us all over the world. We're not impressed by biographies ghost-written for multi-millionaire rock stars whining about their addictions and hard lives... *aye right*. These guys really piss us off even if they do play great riffs that we'll spend hours slavishly copying. And I don't want to single anyone out, but we loath those rock stars that preach love and peace but hate their bandmates so much they can't bring themselves to travel in the same private jet, although they are not slow to pocket the re-union tour loot. You know who I'm talking about.

There was some well-faded ex rock star on TV the other day, bleating about how they never wanted to be a star in the first place, sigh... They were whining about how they'd never been comfortable being recognised everywhere they went and so it wasn't their fault they became addicted to heroin. And they had battled against alcoholism too; life had been so tough at the top. Then they told us how they'd been cured, but became hooked on sleeping pills and so had gone to the only place that would understand, Eric Clapton's rehab retreat in sunny Antigua. *And you know what*, they breathlessly explained, like we gave a shit, *it was there they discovered that all their lives they'd actually been depressed and....*

Spare me.

3

All over the world, in every city, in every bar, dancehall, wedding reception room, wherever there is a corner to set up a little Fender amp and a few twiddly bits and pieces, you'll find real musicians, men and women who play for the love of it. Maybe only a few have God-given talent, maybe we're just too dumb to quit, but we like it. In cafes and restaurants, guys with acoustic guitars and backing tracks bravely playing *Brown Eyed Girl* for munching salad-eaters, or in the corners of little wooden beach-front bars singing *You can almost taste the hot dawgs and French fries they sell* to margarita-slurping sunset watchers.

We may be in steamy bars coaxing silky blues riffs out of battered old Stratocasters, or we could be still-slim small-town rockers occasionally getting to play in the opening band for someone famous, enjoying being able to turn up our amps for a change, and feel, for half an hour or so, like a genuine big-stage rock star.

Why do we do it?

It would be nice if I could offer a simple explanation. Because there are no limousines, no helping hands to unload the beat-up car at 2am, no one to lift our tattered old amplifier as we carefully lug our gear back into the house on a freezing night after playing a 5-hour wedding, no antidote for the bone-deep fatigue that awaits us at our day job next morning. There are no supermodel groupies, money is always scarce and what we have is often blown on yet another bit of equipment that we hope will finally give us the guitar sound that we have been searching for all those years. Many of us are divorced, or in our second or third marriages. A few lucky ones have wives who somehow know why their husbands trail off night after night in all weather to play the same old songs; who understand why their men prefer belting out *Mustang Sally* rather than sit at home watching this week's CSI, or maybe having a nice early night for a change. A few even know why, to a musician, a warm valve amp working perfectly is such an elusive thing of joy.

The hopeful hordes queuing for TV talent shows have never imagined the possible harsh reality that their dreams of a career in music could be a lifetime trek round small town bars and hotel function rooms. But if you had told most working musicians that this is how their lives would unfold, they'd still jump in with both feet. Of course, some of them will get hooked on drugs or drink, but it sure isn't out of wallowing in self-pity about the torment of being loved by millions of devoted fans.

Some people are born to build things, or perform root canal work, or stir endless pots of pasta in sweating kitchens, or paint walls, or do the countless other tasks that make life liveable. Some fail to find anything honest or productive to do and become politicians or bankers – don't get me started. Musicians are born to play. We only feel right when we're playing. It's something we just have to do.

I don't really understand it. But I was playing guitar in a blues bar in Bradenton, Florida last night and the house band had Doc Mambo, a terrific New York-Cuban bass player, and his pal from Macon, Georgia on keyboards. They'd toured the world as sidemen for some big names back in the day so they really knew their stuff. Doc always listening, playing close to the bass drum, playing the right notes to lift or soften just when the music needed it, not like those robots who trot out the same old boring scales and plodding runs no matter what the rest of the band is playing. Always simple, never flash, none of that slappy, flashy, arty-farty, demented, all-over-the-damn-fretboard nonsense that some guys think makes them look clever. No, this guy knew how to build atmosphere, emotion. He breathed music.

The keyboard player – oh, it was great to watch this big grinning black guy teasing out the notes so gently, then when he got excited slapping the keys like they were congas, and the rhythm making everyone want to move, to sway with him.

Bodie Valdez is singing;
Ah went down to the crossroads, fell down on ma knees.
Asked the Lord above for mercy, save me if you please.

He left home with a broken heart many years ago, and gradually travelled the Greyhound routes south, searching out old bluesmen to teach him his craft, even finding guys that had played beside Robert Johnston. He's blowing and sucking on his harmonica, it rises and falls and wails and growls and moans and howls, just like it did when he was jamming with Buddy Guy back home in sweet Chicago.

And they gave me a tweed covered cigarette-burned 1959 Fender Bassman amp to play through, with four 10-inch speakers and all the right valves and stuff, and hanging from my shoulders was a beautiful sunburst Strat with great pickups and, I tell you, there are some nights when the amp sound is just so good that the guitar will do any damn thing that you want it to. It's like it was wired straight into your brain. And yes, it was one of those so-rare nights when I could get every sound locked up in my head to come out of this steaming little amp, you know what I mean? As if it knew how we should sound, like it was part of me, my hands, my body.

And we're playing like we'd been on this stage together a thousand times, me and these guys, although I'd never met them before, but tonight we sounded like one person, one mind. And the guitar was so responsive, my hands were sweating, the warm rosewood neck smooth and slinky and damn, I was making that guitar scream. I stroked it gently, squeezing out a few Memphis-blues chords, then hit a high A on the third string and bent the thing until it was like a wail of pure pleasure, then dropped back down to a low uneasy growl then back up to a howl of sheer pain like something from the swampland outside in the hot Florida backwoods. We all knew why we were playing, what Bodie was singing about. *Have You Ever Loved A Woman?*

And everyone in that bar could see, could hear, could feel that something really special was happening here tonight. Even the tattooed denim and leather bikers at the back stopped aiming down their pool cues and paid attention, 50-dollar grudge bets on hold. The bartender stood and stared, arms folded, towel resting on his shoulder. No-one was asking for Jackie D's or Coors anyhow, not now, not when these guys with that skinny Scottish stranger were playing like that. *Damn that's good!*

And the short-skirted waitress, legs still smooth and long as in her high-school cheerleader days all those years ago, her stomach bare and flat, oh ok, maybe a little saggy, just a little, but sure good enough to pick up some nice tips later on when one or two of those guys leaning on their usual lonesome spots at the bar started thinking about their cold and empty beds back in the trailer park just around the corner. Even they stopped nursing their warm shots and looked up from the memories that churned in their brains, for a moment forgetting missed sure-things and might-have-beens, nodding their heads as the bluesmen on the little stage played like the whole world was here tonight.

The crowd loved it. It's amazing how much applause, how much cheering, how much happiness 31 people can give you.

2

THE ECHOS

From the very start, I imagined how cool it would be to be famous. As soon as I was old enough to know there was such a thing as famous, I wanted it.

I had just started wearing long trousers when I first heard the Beatles and the Stones. Until that moment I had fantasised about being a footballer. I wanted to score goals, sign autographs, be recognised wherever I went. Then, as soon as I heard Mick sing *Route 66* I forgot all about kicking a ball. I wanted to score girls, sign autographs, be recognised wherever I went.

I'd love to be able to say that something about music deeply inspired me, that one haunting note in those churning guitar chords moved me in a spiritual way, or that it connected all my dormant neural circuits together, and that I knew right then I'd be a slave to the Stratocaster for the rest of my days. Perhaps that's what happened. But there was a far more important reason.

Rock music made me feel incredibly horny. And at 14, that's really all that matters. *Well I'm a king bee, buzzing round your hive* – of course! Now I knew what girls were for and what I wanted to do with them. I managed to save four quid by doing some odd jobs, marched into a local music shop and bought my first guitar, my first real six-string and played it, as someone said, 'til my fingers bled. Glasgow was a tough city on a skinny kid, so they weren't the best days of my life. But they sure weren't the worst.

The Stones called themselves an *RnB* band. I loved that: *RnB* – what a name for music. The Beatles were a *beat* group, but *RnB* sounded far nastier. Even if he didn't like their music, your father would happily wave your big sister off on a date with a Beatle, knowing they'd have her back by ten. But never with one of the Stones – they would just have her. The Beatles were friendly moptops, especially Paul with his big brown angel eyes; they were nice lads even if they did need their hair cut, and at least it was clean, you could tell that by the way it bounced when they sang *oooo* and *ahhh*. The Stones were dirty. They pissed in garage forecourts. They looked like girls, ugly ones. The *Daily Mail* trumpeted that a spell in the army would sort them out. There had never been anything like them.

RnB conjured up images of packed sweaty cellar clubs, blue smoke curling up from the cigarette the guitar player had wedged at the top of his strings, skinny, pale guys on stage, wearing dirty jeans and with dirty Jeans gazing up at them, harmonica wailing, the crack of snare with the thud of the bass drum, and the sweet smell of hot valves. At the corner of Byres Road and Great Western Road, the north-most outpost of Glasgow's posh West End, just a couple of miles from where I lived, there was a club like that in a long-disused train station at the entrance to the Botanic Gardens. The Candlelite Club.

Even the spelling *lite* looked so cool to me. I'd walk there every Sunday night to stand in front of the stage with a wee notebook in my hand, writing down the chords the band were playing – I'd do anything to learn these songs. The band was called the Poets. They were great. They were eventually signed by Andrew Loog Oldham, the Stones manager, but they never quite made the big-time. To me they were gods. They were everything I wanted to be.

It's amazing the beefy bouncer let me in because the place was dangerous, was always packed with headcases from the *Maryhill Fleet*, one of Glasgow's biggest gangs. These nutters were very proud that they were all *pure mental*. Walls were daubed with the words *Fleet Ya Bass*, an expression that academics spent months trying to figure out. Some pontificated it was from Gaelic. It meant only this: if the mad bastards caught you then you could expect to be nutted senseless. Or *ripped*, which meant a piece of street surgery would be carried out on your face. In the worst case, if you gave the *Fleet* reason to think you might be one of their rivals, the equally pure mental *Partick Cross*, they might deliver their ultimate service guarantee. I saw it spray painted on derelict tenements: *Maryhill Fleet kick to kill*. Sometimes they did – a pal's older brother was booted to death at a club very like the Candelite. He was 17. Going anywhere in Glasgow meant keeping your wits about you at all times. You learned to smell trouble. It was fucking terrifying.

I remember squeezing into the club among the drunk and drooling hooligans. They were all a lot older so they left me alone. I was wearing my school blazer, my only jacket. I'd managed to unpick the stitching that held on the badge; my exasperated mother was constantly sewing it back on again. In those days clothes were made in good, solid British factories that had outlawed child labour a century before, so they were expensive. Kids my age just didn't have many clothes and what they had was built to last.

I stood at the front of the stage, as close to the band as I could, staring at their black leather jackets – what I would have given for one of those. And their long sideburns – their 'image' was based on a picture of Robert Burns. It would be many years before the bum-fluff on my face could look like that. They played earthy songs like *Little By Little, Fortune Teller*, and a terrific wailing version of the Animals' *House of the*

Rising Sun using harmonica instead of an organ. Every so often the packed crowd would surge wildly when a fight broke out and a well aimed head butt found the bridge of someone's nose: the girls in that club were fearsome.

The band always took a break around nine and I would leave then – I had an angry father wanting to know where the hell I had been to this time at night. I'd rush home, carefully avoiding any sneering gang members on the hunt for prey, grunt hello to my parents then disappear into my bedroom and quietly play as many songs as I could remember. If I had spent half as much time studying, as my father was always telling me to do, I'd probably have ended up going to university and wasting my life as a lawyer or accountant.

I really had to work hard learning guitar. Some guys have a great 'ear'. They can hear when a guitar is in tune, for a start. I kind of couldn't, at least not at the start. It took a while. My confidence wasn't helped when our psychopathic music teacher lined all the boys up, played a note and told each of us in turn to sing it. Alone. When you are 14 and faced with a room full of smirking girls, there are few greater terrors. He might as well have ordered us to show our dicks to the class.

I went rigid, my face burning. I croaked and tried to hum the note for the bald, bony old bastard who I hated more deeply than anything else, and who ended his days crippled with lingering cancer, boils, piles and a thousand bitter regrets, or at least he did if my wishes counted for anything. A horrible noise came from my throat, like a horse choking. He glared at me. *Tone deaf! Next!* Judgement made. I could probably have learned guitar in a school music class, but I was condemned. Tone Deaf. If I wanted to play guitar, I was on my own.

He was an arsehole. I'm not tone deaf, although compared to some of the really good musicians I worked with years later, I certainly didn't hear as clearly as they did. Even average musicians usually hear a lot more in music than most people who usually focus on the vocals; after a bit of practise it is quite easy to listen to a record and concentrate on any of the instruments, blocking out the rest, in the same way that someone who has taken the time to learn a foreign language can hear words that just sound like gibberish to anyone else. Especially if the language is Dutch, or Gaelic – although I don't believe these are actual languages, they are just grant-grabbing scams to get money out of Tourist Boards, are they not?

Some lucky musicians have what is known as perfect pitch. They can hear the slightest error in tuning, which makes a lot of 60s and 70s guitar solos pretty painful for them to listen to. I have met guys that could listen to a damn dial tone and tell you what note it is. I know a musician who used to remember telephone numbers by the little sounds they made on her keypad. Some of these people go nuts because in cities we are surrounded by so many discordant sounds, their brains get overloaded trying to block them out. This might be one reason why some musicians take drugs. It also might be the reason why some less talented musicians take drugs – it is not easy working with someone who has perfect pitch and a personal vision of how every friggin note should be played by every band member on every single tune. There is such a visionary in many well-known bands, which is why they can be very successful groups but miserable people.

When I heard the Stones I knew what I wanted to do with my life. Suddenly everything made sense. I had a pal in school called Gordon Miller who told me he had a guitar and we decided to form a band. Everyone called him Wee Millsy, because he was. He wore specs, had a pigeon chest, skinny legs and was very clever, especially with foreign languages. He was an odd character, with a sense of drama. When I first met him he was wearing a broad bandage round his forehead that made him look like a First World War soldier. He just loved spending afternoons in the Casualty ward of the Western Infirmary.

Wee Millsy was a good footballer, having learned to play with boys who lived in his street but, unlike him, went to a Catholic school. Surviving among these guys was quite an achievement; they were cruel and hard little bastards, most of them belonging to the feared *Partick Cross* gang. If wee Millsy hadn't been so good at darting up the right wing with the ball at his feet they would have used him as a punchbag because he went to Hyndland School, as I did, and it was a Protestant school. Glaswegian politicians have always demanded religious apartheid.

Football in those days was a man's game, and every week, it seemed, wee Millsy would get clattered, especially if he had nipped round a big defender and made him look clumsy. When that happened wee Millsy would turn up at school with impressive sticking tape and bandages swathed around various parts of his body or on one unforgettable occasion, hirpling along with two walking sticks that belonged to his old granny. The dear old lady depended on the sticks to make her daily walk to the local dairy to buy milk for her cup of tea, so I guessed she was drinking it black that day. Actually, she wasn't really a dear old lady, she was one of those crabbit old buggers that complained about everything. The people at the dairy were probably glad to get a few days' peace.

So wee Millsy and I decided we would be pop stars. Or at least I did. When I was practising guitar, he amused himself conjugating Latin verbs, or reading the sort of books that would guarantee him a place at Glasgow University. I spent far too much time reading about the Stones and drawing guitars on my jotters. I'd draw wee Millsy and myself on a big stage standing in front of a wild drummer, singing to a sea of heads, cables snaking behind us to Selmer amps just like the Stones had, all of us with long hair and ever so slightly scowling. This was important.

I would stand in front of the mirror practising my 'look'. I had to seem as though I was too cool to want fans so couldn't appear to be interested, but at the same time needed to look interesting. It was good to give the impression that I had opinions on things like the Atom Bomb, and so was slightly angry, but not annoyed. The key was to look bored but not boring. It was not an easy task. I just wished my father wouldn't keep making me get a haircut – he was convinced that anyone with long hair was a 'pansy'. The minute mine touched my ears he would glance up from his newspaper then loudly bark one word. *Hair!* He lived in morbid fear that if it were allowed to grow, the next stage would be a mincing walk and an interest in flower arranging.

His worries were made even worse when I started to buy a girls' weekly pop magazine called *Jackie*. He could have saved himself years of torment; I was obsessed with girls. Buying *Jackie* was part of a plan; the mag had a problem page where the very wise Cathy and Claire would give advice to girls confused about the problems of teenage dating. There were men's magazines that offered similar counselling, but from a male perspective. I already knew how teenage boys thought. I wanted to understand what females wanted so that I would know exactly what to say to my fantasy girl, which was pretty much anyone in a skirt.

I learned that girls respect guys who didn't make a fevered lunge to grasp their tits on the first date. This was well worth knowing, because the power of female breasts was almost unbearable, I longed to touch them. I thought I would get somewhere if I held doors open for girls and casually drop into conversation how I much I disliked the guys in school who bragged to everyone about what they did to their girlfriends. Of course, all this was in vain. The only guys at school who had cool girlfriends were Neanderthals, guys on the rugby team, great hulking brutes that looked ridiculous in school blazers and treated all girls like shit. Some of them even shaved for chrissake.

Deep down, I knew that only playing guitar in an RnB band would get me a *chick* who wouldn't deck me when I tried to unbutton her blouse. My dad's constant pointing to the front door and telling me not to come back until I'd been to the barber was the torpedo that always sank my ship. It was impossible to look like Keith Richards when your nut was trimmed to the nut. If Mick Jagger had a short back and sides, would the girls be screaming at him? No, I thought not.

And so I continued to dream and draw on my school jotters. I knew it was only a matter of time. I would draw the bass drum and on the front was the clincher, the final wonderful touch, the thing that would make every guy in the school envious and every girl want us. There it was for the world to see, the band name: *the Echos*. I said the name over and over, I could 'hear' us being announced on *Top Of The Pops. And now, with their latest toppermost of the poppermost chart hit, the ECHOS*! How could we fail with a name like that?

When wee Millsy invited me to learn some songs in the two-room-and-kitchen council flat he shared with his mother, sister and brother, I messed up my hair as much as possible and rushed there, excited as never before. This would be the start. After tonight I could say I played in a band. *In a band*. The doors that would open! Everything was about to change, finally my life was about to begin.

Wee Millsy was limping like someone with a badly fitted artificial leg as he took me into his tiny bedroom, which was almost filled with the bunk beds in which he and his brother slept until they were in their early 20s, when they finished university and moved out. His mother slept in the kitchen in an alcove that tenement dwellers called a bed recess, while his sister had the luxury of a fold down couch in the 'front' room of the house. She was older, studying English and Politics at

Glasgow Uni, and glanced at me as though I was a dog turd.

Gordon's father had died of lung cancer many years before. Despite this, his mother smoked with total dedication and, at only 14 years old, wee Millsy was getting through a 5-pack of Bristol most days, plus as many as he could whip from his mother's supply. He could even skilfully 'nip' the glowing end of his cigarette when he wanted to save it for later. My father would have murdered me if I smoked. I preferred to save my money for guitar-related things, even though I thought Keith Richards looked so damn good with a glowing filter tip dangling from his mouth.

I took my guitar out of its nylon case. Here we go. Wee Millsy grimaced at the awful unseen pain in his injured leg then we played our first song together. I think it might have been *My Girl*, the Otis Redding version. I had carefully memorised the guitar part after watching the Poets do it the previous weekend.

In a few minutes one thing became clear: I couldn't sing and he could barely play guitar. It was a good start.

3

THE FORBES BROS

I spent every moment practising guitar. My favourite place was in the bathroom. In the same way that would-be Sinatras love to hear their voice gently echoing back to them from their lavvy walls, so too did my guitar sound warm and sweet as it harmonised with my exuberant teenage farts, in those wonderful years when you can let rip completely confident that there will be no unintended outcome. I'd practise playing chords and scales until the pan had etched a deep red ring round my arse.

And then at 14 came the opportunity to actually play a gig. I was on holiday with my family, at a campsite in Ayrshire. Somehow all seven of us had crammed into a wee car driven by a pal of my Dad. This saved the bus fare. Compared to somewhere like Butlins, which we thought was the dream vacation destination of the wealthy, the campsite was truly awful, a grim few rows of wooden huts quickly thrown up by some cash-strapped farmer on a field too barren to produce any kind of crop. In fertile Ayrshire, famous for delicious potatoes and smiling cows, that means a really bad field. Perhaps it had nuclear waste underneath or the hastily bulldozed remains of an open cast coal mine. Something terrible must have lurked beneath the surface or the farmer, I am sure, would have grown turnips instead of the annual hassle of being overrun by impoverished Glaswegian holidaymakers. It looked like a former POW camp, and, judging by the ancient, creaky beds in the huts, it might well have been. Even the name of the place was full of foreboding: *Drongan.* Nobody could make that sound like a nice, carefree holiday spot. It promised grey sky and forlorn winds. But we loved it.

My family was not wealthy. Very few people were in those days, but we owned our own flat, and my mother did not have to work. We were 'comfortable', which meant that the money we would not have to spend on coal during the two-week holiday could be used for renting just such a hut as this. All we had to do was get there.

I loved holidays at the huts because I would forage in the nearby woods. In those innocent times, children were encouraged to go off to play by themselves in places such as dense woodland and not return until nightfall, sufficiently exhausted to sleep peacefully until the next happy sunrise. I discovered a waterfall one day, and somehow this summed up everything wonderful about remote countryside. A waterfall. It looked to me like something out of Africa. I remember suddenly coming into a small clearing in the trees and there it was, the most amazing sight I had ever seen. It was probably about 10 feet high, not exactly the Victoria Falls, but something about the way it tumbled down what seemed like a giant rocky cliff and into a deep pool of sparkling water made me feel as if I were deep in the jungle. I just knew there would be huge fish in that pool. Maybe even the ones I'd read about that could eat human flesh.

A few older boys appeared and I backed off. If you grew up in Glasgow you knew you must not appear scared of bigger boys or they would home in on you with all sorts of tortures, but you had to balance this bravado against making sure you would have a good start in case you had to run like fuck. The trick was not sprinting until it was necessary. Wild dogs will always chase someone running in fear and this rule applied equally to Glaswegian teenagers, especially Celtic fans.

The possibility of piranha did not deter one of the boys from stripping off and jumping into the pool. I watched, hoping he would be pulled below the surface by some thrashing unseen denizen of the deep, but after a while he stopped swimming and just squatted with the water up to his waist. His face took on an odd look, as though he was straining, and suddenly a great huge shit triumphantly bobbed to the surface. His pals laughed and started throwing stones into the water beside him, trying to hit the Glaswegian brown trout and splash their pal with it. I decided to bugger off at that point in case they threw me in too.

It often rained, great windswept deluges sweeping in off the cold and moody Irish Sea, like revenge for years of cruel colonialism, turning the site into a thick quagmire from which there was no escape. To provide a diversion and relieve the happy Glasgow working folk of their saved coal money, the farmer offered entertainment. At the top end of the campsite was a large two-room community hut that had a bar of sorts – a rickety wooden table with an old lady arthritically opening and pouring cans of McEwan's Pale Ale into grimy pint glasses. Her fingers were curled and misshapen, the brutal cost of a lifetime of milking cows on freezing winter mornings so that we city folk might have something creamy to pour on our Corn Flakes. There was a carefully dispensed bottle of whisky too.

The menfolk would hand over a few coins and eventually be given their glass of dark, frothy, sour-smelling beer. They would lounge around cheerfully, as though they were in the VIP bar of the QE2, smoking and talking about the great football players of the post war years. I knew the names of many legends that had retired before I was born, and if they had passed me in the street I would easily have recognised George Young, Jimmy McGrory, Alan Morton and others.

When I looked at old photographs of these players, I noticed that they never smiled, they had hardened faces and grainy skin as if they had spent many years working down coal mines, and wore big clumpety boots. They looked far older, even in their best playing years, than wee Willie Henderson, slim Jim Baxter and the other stars I could see every week at Ibrox or Firhill, the home of Partick Thistle. Well, at Ibrox anyway.

With something to drink at the makeshift bar, the men of the camp were content to be on holiday in the countryside, away from the dirt and noise and crowds of the city. Even if it was pissing with rain, it was far better to be here than working in the freezing docks and shipyards of Glasgow, as many of them did. Holidays had been unknown when our parents were children. Did we know how lucky we were?

All the kids below drinking age, from squalling babies to surly young teenagers bored because it was too wet outside to play football or shit in pools beneath waterfalls, were in the strict charge of their mothers who would lead them into the other room in the community hut, collect a cup of tea and a glass of flat lemonade and a saucer of digestive biscuits, then settle down on wooden chairs to watch the evening's spectacle: the talent contest. Plump motherly arses in floral printed skirts bulged out the backs of the chairs. The women always seemed to wear the same summer dress, as though they only had one, and they carefully kept them free of drips from their teacups. There was a small stage at the far end of the room, and it would be from this dizzying height I would first look out at a crowd. This was to be my very first public appearance. I was crapping myself.

It's always best not to over-think these things. If you do you will always talk yourself out of it. Far better to barge ahead before the fear takes hold, like a snowboarder soaring over a crevasse in the hope he will be safely across before it realises he is there. A woman was on the stage, first blowing loudly then speaking into a silver microphone that seemed to shrink from her grasp. In a thick, excitingly exotic Ayrshire accent, she invited anyone who wanted to come up and 'do a turn' to write down their name on a board at the side. The grand prize tonight was a hamper of groceries. She pointed proudly to a table at the side of the stage; on it posed a small, embarrassed-looking cardboard box. In it were a tin of beans, a brown paper bag of Ayrshire *tatties* still dirty from the field, and half a dozen eggs.

I casually glanced at the other hopeful contenders. They were all adults, except for a couple of snotty little kids I just knew would recite a poem or something equally childish. I quickly realised I would be the only one playing an instrument and felt a sudden surge of confidence. How could I fail to win? I quickly scrawled my name on the board. This would be easy.

I had persuaded my younger brother to sing a Dylan song with me and we had been practising it all week. I could hear it, constantly running through my head: *How many roads must a man wa-alk down*. We sat stiffly near the front, nervously waiting for our turn. So far the acts had been dire. The two kids came and went with not a word. As soon as they stood on the stage their heads dropped and they turned their backs and stayed silent. Then it was the turn of some old guy chirping out a Harry Lauder song. He had clearly enjoyed his 'wee refreshment' at the bar too much and could hardly stand. Like all the men, he was wearing old brown sandals with thick dark socks, long grey trousers and a white shirt with the collar open. He was a terrible singer and his quivering voice sounded thin and weedy. I doubted the judges would be impressed. Yes, this was going to be easy.

At last our names were called and my brother and I stepped confidently onto the stage. All of a sudden we saw all the faces stare up at us, some curious, others clearly hostile, rooting for their own family or friends to win. My brother stepped to the microphone stand, his 13-year-old knees knocking. He glanced at what seemed to be a massive crowd.

"Aw fuck."

He muttered it, or thought he did, but he was too close to the microphone. His young voice boomed through the room. Everyone heard him and some of the older kids began laughing. Some instinct made us start playing; I strummed my guitar and we warbled, *How many* streets *must a man wa-alk down?* There was a loud guffaw from an older boy who must have known the song, and knew, to a Glaswegian, a road is the same as a street. Soon the laughter spread, but we sang on, as I defiantly hammered out my carefully learned chords.

We didn't win the spuds.

4

THE BOWMEN

It was great to be in a band in the 60s and, more than anything in this world, it was what I wanted. It was the key to everything. One Saturday afternoon I saw a few goofy looking guys carrying a couple of drums, a mic stand and a proper electric guitar along Dumbarton Road in Glasgow to a church hall they were playing in. They were pushing an amplifier in a pram. The guy holding the guitar didn't have a case for it, and it gleamed in the sunshine, all glorious metallic silver and red and black. It looked, to me, the most wonderful thing on earth, and I knew right then I had to have one, I would do anything to possess such a thing. And here was the clincher, as dorky and bumbling as these guys were, there were a few giggling girls following them, asking for autographs, and did they know any of the Beatles?

Without the band equipment, these guys would have been duffed up in a heartbeat in any Glasgow school playground, but their guitars transformed them into gods. There has never been anything as powerful as the 'beat boom' in the 60s. God alone on his throne up high must have had the faintest idea what it must have been like to actually *be* a Beatle back then. Even mummies' boys like this lot – where else would they have got the money to buy their equipment? – were like stars. As it happened they went on to sell millions of records under the name Middle of the Road.

Being in a group – any group – was all I wanted. I would happily have swapped a leg for a three-minute spot on *Top Of The Pops*. Nowadays almost everyone plays in some band or other but then it was the domain of beings from another planet. Or so it seemed. Strumming my Spanish guitar along with wee Millsy had been a start, but studying and football seemed far more important to him. I couldn't imagine why. Knowing Latin verbs would never get you laid. I had to get an electric guitar.

I was quite good at making money. Instead of breaking my back doing a newspaper round for a shop, staggering miles with a bulging sack for a few shillings as many of my pals did, I discovered that if I could find my own customers I could buy newspapers at a discount direct from the Evening Times, the main paper in Glasgow. And so I chose four streets near where I lived, and set about convincing the neighbours how good it would be to have their paper delivered every night. Within a week, I was collecting a large bundle of newspapers. The profit on each one was mine; I soon had enough money saved to buy an electric guitar. The Evening Times is still going, and although I faithfully delivered thousands of copies for the five years I was at secondary school, they have never as much as reviewed one of my books. I'm just saying...

And then I saw a postcard in a shop window selling a Hoffner Colorama guitar, one of the better of the crappier guitars of the time. The student selling it accepted my offer of £7.00 and showed me how to plug the guitar into the back of my radio, since I didn't have an amplifier.

When my father saw me sticking bare wires into the radio he nearly threw it, and me, out of the window. When he calmed down, he sighed and arranged for me to buy a little amplifier on hire purchase from a guy he knew who owned a little music shop. He didn't approve of me playing guitar, not in the slightest, but if I was going to muck about it would be best not to electrocute myself.

At last…

I was 16 years old. I'd been practising every day. Now I had a proper electric guitar and an amp I managed to join a wee band with a couple of older guys from school. Actually, they weren't much older, I was in third year and they were repeating their fourth year, so there would only be a couple of years in it. But at that age it's a lot. They looked much older, they were even shaving – I was only just out of short trousers. They had played proper gigs before; I hadn't. They way they talked they had done a lot of things I hadn't. We were booked to play at a wee bowling club and I felt like one of the Stones. I also had an invite from a girl to go with her to an all-night party, and that might have meant another first, but when I told her I would be playing a gig instead she stormed off in a huff. I didn't care.

We were playing to what seemed very old people. The men all had matching blazers with the club's badge on the chest pocket, even some of their wives were wearing them. I'll never forget how good it felt plugging my red Hoffner guitar into my little amplifier, playing alongside another guitarist, a bass player and a drummer, and the way I forgot about everything else, all the teenage worries, all that stuff. As long as I was playing nothing else mattered.

And then we got a gig playing for the Girl Guides. A dream come true. If someone offered me a world tour today I doubt I would be more excited. I knew a guy in a proper band who was playing at their Christmas dance in a church hall just a few streets away. In those days it was common to have an 'interval group' – another band that would play for half an hour or so – giving the main band a break. Yes, we could be the interval band. I could hardly sleep all week, the thought of playing to girls my own age, the after-gig fantasies I imagined…

When I arrived at the church hall, the main band was there but their bass player hadn't turned up. He'd been at a Christmas night out and was unconscious at home, well pished. They asked us to start the gig and they would go on as soon as they'd sobered him up.

I couldn't get on the stage fast enough.

We played our songs. We were pretty awful, but I loved it. As soon as we finished the other guys in my band rushed off to the pub – they reckoned they were too cool to hang around here with all these kids. The Girl Guides were having crisps and cola and starting to become restless – the main band hadn't started playing, their bass player still hadn't appeared. Their guitarist came up to me.

"Don't suppose your bass player could play with us?"

"He's away, he's gone out drinking."

He nodded to the bass amp and guitar set up on stage.

"Don't suppose there's any chance you can play bass, heh heh? Otherwise we'll have to play without one".

I knew the pub where our bass player had gone was just around the corner, and I could have got him in a few minutes, but there was no way I'd pass up this chance, even though I'd never played a bass before.

"Sure, no problem."

I managed to busk along fine, just concentrated on playing what seemed like the right notes in more or less the correct places. I knew all their songs: Tamla Motown, Beatles, Stones. I'd spent the last two years in my bedroom learning all those tunes. Standing on the big wooden stage in the church hall, in a real band playing to loads of people made me feel like I'd just won the World Cup. I knew I never wanted to do anything else.

On Monday at school, I was still feeling great when I met up with one of the guys from my own band. I noticed he hadn't shaved that morning and I wondered if I would ever have to start. I couldn't wait to grow long sideburns like he had. It felt terrific to be playing in a band with someone so much older, even though he was in the same class at school.

"We've decided you're out of the band."

I felt like I'd been kicked in the stomach.

"What..? Why..?"

"I said you're out the band. Nothing personal, but that's it. You're out."

I could feel hot tears burn my eyes. But I couldn't let him see that.

"But...why...we had a great time playing at the weekend... what's wrong?"

"Sorry, but we've decided we're going to play in pubs. You look too young. You'd never get in."

5

ROCKY PEBBLE

I was feeling really down, then the guy who owned the little music shop I'd bought my amp from offered me a Saturday job. This was very exciting – I knew I'd get to meet lots of bands. On my first day someone who worked at the Odeon Cinema handed in a couple of free tickets to see the Stones. It was the first big gig I ever went to. I immediately forgot all about the guys in school who'd dumped me.

One of the things I've always loved about playing in bands is the number of real characters you meet. The guy who owned the shop was a singer/guitarist who played working men's clubs all over Central Scotland. He was a comedy act, sometimes unintentionally, and well known because he was slightly eccentric, barking mad in fact. He called himself Rocky Pebble, and usually had another guitar player beside him named Sandy Beach, Big Jim Boulder or Chucky Stone, always something geological. He was a funny man. I got some guitar lessons from him, he could read music and had learned his trade well.

I got to meet many of the biggest names in the Glasgow music scene, guys that were like gods. Some of the older musicians were very interesting and easy to talk to; one had toured all over the place playing guitar with Lonnie Donegan. There was a tiny fat guy who had the purple face of someone with a serious heart condition and wore glasses like the bottoms of milk bottles. He also had a terrible speech impediment – he sounded as though he had no mouth and had taught his nose to speak. He had the shortest, stubbiest, fattest fingers I had ever seen, yet he could play blindingly fast Django Reinhardt jazz guitar solos.

Every week a guy with Downs Syndrome would come in to buy a harmonica. We used to call him the Merry Mongol, but we didn't mean it badly. He would walk round the pubs of Partick sucking and blowing the same two notes until the drinkers would good-humouredly give him coins to fuck off. Rumour was that his mother sent him out collecting and they lived in a fancy house on the takings.

Rocky was married to a nice, attractive but long-suffering woman, and they had a few kids, but when he was in his 40s he met a 17-year-old singer from a tough part of town who had a terrific voice. They became Glasgow's Sonny and Cher. Within days he had moved into a little rented flat with her. This caused a lot of muttering because even in Glasgow people just didn't walk out on their families, but it didn't embarrass Rocky in the least.

A few weeks later, the Daily Record was tipped off that a crazy man was painting the outside of his shop all sorts of psychedelic colours – Rocky had told me to call them. Nobody would give it a second glance now, but they sent a photographer and printed a half page picture. He loved that. Customers trooped to the shop and in no time he had opened two others. None of them ever made any money, but to Rocky this was a minor detail.

Rocky and his new girlfriend toured all the workingmen's clubs and were making quite a name for themselves. He was an optimistic soul, usually cheery, especially if he had managed a full week without one of his shops being broken into. His business stuttered on, he never really grasped that you have to pay your bills. He was no fool, he had raised the money to open his first shop by doing some moneylending in the docks where he had once worked; that took nerve. He survived that without being separated from his teeth, but his natural optimism and disregard for consequences made him an obvious target for salesmen.

He would never speak to one inside the shop, he figured that he was paying the rent and he would be the one to do the selling, but once he was in the open air he was fair game. I lost count of the number of times he would set off on the short walk to the bank to deposit the takings and he would return, excited as a kid at Christmas, all happy and grinning over some extravagant new purchase he'd made. Once again, he'd parted with the money before he'd got anywhere near the bank.

Although he and his 'fancy woman' were shacked up in a backstreet tenement flat someone had persuaded him an expensive dinghy would bring undreamed pleasure to his life. Or it would be a thousand bottles of an exotic skin care product, as his stake in a get rich quick venture. His tough young girlfriend would not be amused and they would have screaming rows, but nothing could dampen his enthusiasm for an irresistible buy or sparkling new pyramid scheme.

Some days it seemed the salesman were standing in line outside the shop, waiting to pounce. Soon debt collectors began to outnumber customers. He closed two shops and heroically tried to salvage his remaining flagship, a tiny little one-room store in a busy spot beside Partick Underground.

Then he became a Scientologist and immediately adopted strange, staring eyes. He told everyone how happy he was, and he did seem to be very content, even one dark night when thieves broke in and stole a Fender Stratocaster. Actually he maintained that the thieves ran out with nothing, it had been the cop that disturbed them that nicked the guitar. It was Partick after all.

He became fanatical about his new religion and began telling everyone who came into the shop that in a previous life he had been a giant spider adrift in the darkest reaches of outer space and that this accounted for his asthma, or something equally bizarre. The good people of Partick crowded into the shop to see this strange spaceman. Glasgow loves peaceful nutters.

Years later I got to play a few gigs with Rocky – his favourite song was *May The Bird of Paradise Fly Up Your Nose*. I was very pleased to be on stage with him and thank him that he had been my guitar teacher. He enjoyed that moment. He remained a devoted follower of L Ron Hubbard, however, which made normal conversation with him almost impossible, but always entertaining. L Ron had bought a ship and formed his own wee navy, and Rocky took to wearing the uniform of a professional Scientologist: grey, razor-pressed trousers, a blue blazer with a big golden badge on the breast pocket, some sort of gold braid on the shoulders, and a sea captain's hat. He proudly wore this everywhere he went, even to collect his Corn Flakes from the supermarket. He announced that he had signed a billion-year contract with the Sea Organisation, Commodore Ron's chosen elite, and his task was to help him clear this part of the universe of insanity, crime and war. Rocky seemed like just the man for the job.

He split up with his girlfriend and singing partner, I think when she reached the old age of 30. He found a new young girlfriend who was also a Sea Org member and they moved to Switzerland. I often wonder what they made of him there as he raced around in his sailor suit on his newest impulse buy, a big fat BMW motorbike, carrying out the work of the organisation he had dedicated the unimaginable future to serving. Unfortunately he only completed a tiny part of his billion-year contract; a truck coming the opposite way nipped through a red light, two universes collided and he never regained consciousness.

People still talk about his gigs in the old clubs around Glasgow. And I miss his happy, insane laugh.

6

GREENFLY

I was 19 and reckoned London was the best place to go to find a rock and roll band that might need, as the song goes, a helping hand. My brother was living there in a small bedsit with two other guys. One of them was back home in Ireland for a couple of weeks, so I could have his bed. I bought a ticket, and managed to pile my guitar, amplifier and speaker cab onto the train south.

My brother was surprised to see me appear at his door in Bayswater with my load of gear and wondered how the hell I'd managed to drag it all the way from Glasgow. He hadn't expected me to bring any more than an overnight bag but crammed it into the room, a tiny damp basement with three single beds. In no time we were out getting pished at the nearest pub. Somehow that led to a party in another part of London, I have no idea where. Around midnight, and totally blotto, I realised my brother and his flatmate had buggered off with some girls; they'd forgotten I was there. I had not a penny. A cab pulled up outside and two men and a woman were about to get into it. They were even more steaming than me – they could hardly stand. I saw my chance. I quickly jumped into the cab with them and told the driver to head for Bayswater.

As the taxi raced through the quiet late night streets, the men were muttering in thick Irish accents about some plan for causing fookin mayhem at Parliament. They were so drunk they seemed to think I was with the woman and didn't take any notice of me. When the cab stopped at the traffic lights outside Queensway Tube Station, I opened the door and jumped out. Suddenly it dawned on the people in the cab that this was not where they wanted to be.

"What the fook ur we doing here? We're going to Camden. What the fook ur we doing here?"

I ran like hell and was gone before they realised what I'd done. By the time I'd woken with a crippling hangover next morning I'd pretty much forgotten about it. Later in the week, though, there were front-page headlines when some IRA members threw CS gas canisters onto the floor of the House of Commons.

I found casual work as a security guard, sleeping on a camp bed during 62-hour weekend shifts watching empty factories, and another job collecting money for deck chair hire in Hyde Park. The main music weekly, *Melody Maker*, had ads for musicians wanted, but whenever I called one the first thing they asked was what equipment I had. At the time, London bands were very fussy; the very least they expected was a Gibson Les Paul and towering Marshall stack that cost about £1000 – a fortune. My gear was a pile of junk I'd picked up in old electrical stores and second hand shops, and the Hoffner guitar I'd bought for seven quid. It sounded great though, or at least I thought so.

If you don't believe how sniffy the ads were look at old issues of the *Melody Maker*: *Keyboard player wanted for prog rock band. MUST have split Hammond, Moog etc.* Or – *Guitarist wanted for original rock band, excellent gear and own transport essential.* I mean, it was hard enough to buy a decent guitar, but many of these bands expected you to have your own bloody van as well. A few years' later young musicians got fed up with all this nonsense and bought cheap guitars and amps from Woolworths. They started playing fast, noisy couldn't-give-a-shit music that someone called *punk*. The safety pins and Mohican hair all came later.

So the nearest I got to finding a gig was a couple of jam sessions at a pub near a factory I was supposed to be guarding, and a job working as a stagehand at the Palace Theatre, which wasn't exactly what I had in mind. Eventually I got sacked and, penniless as usual, I decided to hitch back to Glasgow.

This was not easy since I had my guitar, amp and speaker cabinet with me, but I used my last few quid to get a cab to a roundabout on the North Circular Road, where the motorway to Scotland started. I piled up my gear at the kerb and stuck my thumb in the air. A truck stopped almost immediately. He told me when he realised I was trying to hitch a lift with all that equipment he couldn't stop laughing and had gone right round the roundabout to come back and get me. He dropped me off at a service station near Preston and I managed to drag my stuff in for a cup of tea.

Luck plays a big part in the music business, and sitting in the café was a drummer who was also on the road back from London, his kit in the back of his old estate car. He told me later that when he saw me staggering in to the café with all my gear he thought I was insane. But he gave me a lift to Glasgow; by the time we got there we had decided to put a band together, and call ourselves *Greenfly*. We found a keyboard player who brought along a friend that played guitar. He was really good and I decided to switch to bass. His name was Brian Robertson and he later joined Thin Lizzy. We befriended some guy who had been given a big pay out after an accident at a nuclear plant or somewhere and he put up the money for us to record a hopeful demo, my very first time in a studio. I was very excited.

I was desperate to do some gigs, but the band never played anywhere. The drummer was 25, which seemed to the rest of us to be very old, and said he'd played all over London, including the Marquee, but all he wanted to do now was to get a recording contract. He wasn't interested in playing anywhere unless we would be paid, which seemed stupid since we spent most nights sitting in his shitty little rented room, trying to scrape together the money for a packet of cigarettes and talking about the big things we would do one day. When he refused to take a gig supporting Hawkwind in Glasgow I was broken hearted. I couldn't believe anyone would turn down the chance to play to a huge crowd in a big venue just because there was no cash in it. We all fell out and he buggered off forever.

I was beginning to wonder if I'd ever find a proper band to play in.

7

BAY CITY ROLLERS

When one is desperate to make the big time, as one was – that sounds posh doesn't it? Like I know a thing or two about grammar? Anyway, it can be difficult to know what band to put your dreams in. Sorry, should have said, into what band to put your dreams. Opportunities knock; will this one get somewhere or will it be another bunch of time wasters? Will you be a star this time next year, or will you forever regret just saying no? In every town, lonely backstreet bars have tables worn smooth by the elbows of guys who have lived a lifetime of bitter anguish, rueing the day they turned down the chance to play with the young bands that became Pink Floyd or Coldplay or U2.

One day I saw an ad in the Evening Times for a new band looking for a guitarist. I 'phoned them. They said they'd be playing pop music. I was skinny and young and – don't laugh! – looked it in an angelic sort of way, like John Keats or someone. I really wanted to play with a full-tilt rock band, but, yeah, I could see myself as a pop star prancing on *Top Of The Pops*.

The band was called the Bay City Rollers.

They were based in Edinburgh and they told me I'd be met at Waverley Station in Edinburgh. I headed to Glasgow Queen Street Station with my guitar, not sure whether to be excited or what. It was a hot summer day, and I met an older guy I knew who played in a good rock band. When I told him what I was doing he laughed, told me not to be stupid and dragged me to the bar for a pint. One became two. Two became many. Many became too many. I spent my train ticket money and never got the chance to wear those weird trousers, tartan scarves or be buggered by Tam Paton, their manager.

Thank fuck.

8

EMPEROR SHOWBAND

At last!

I met a guy in the pub, a mad drummer who played in an Irish showband. They were looking for a guitar player and I jumped at the chance. They were all older than me, a couple of them a lot older, and for the first time I was actually being paid to play. I had to learn the songs that were in the charts, plus all sorts of Irish jigs and stuff. The band got good gigs and I made enough money to buy a second hand Fender Stratocaster, my dream guitar, and a battered but decent amp.

The most dangerous place we used to play was an after-hours shebeen, an illegal Irish dance hall in the Gorbals, Glasgow. The police turned a blind eye because it kept the local headcases off the streets until the wee small hours, by which time they'd be too tired and drunk to cause the usual mayhem. They paid us a lot of money, not many bands would play there. We used to do four hours without a break because as soon as the music stopped, fists, heads and boots started flying. Sometimes, the place became a mass of headbutting, punching and kicking; it all merged into one big battle. Two minutes later they'd all be dancing again as if nothing had happened. It was good to watch from the high stage. Some people left with fewer teeth than when they arrived. It was like the Wild West and it had its own Wyatt Earp. He had no mercy.

One night we were into our third hour when some young bampot climbed onto the high stage, lay on his back and amused himself by staring up the skirt of the girl who sang with the band. She nodded to the bouncer who grabbed the guy's feet, yanked hard and launched him into orbit. He hit the floor with a terrible sickening *thunk*. He leapt up, eyes flashing, ready to kill. Then he saw the cold, cruel face of the man who had thrown him, stopped in his tracks, apologized, and backed out the hall. The bouncer at the shebeen took no guff.

Apart from learning a lot of songs in the showband, I also learned to drink when I was playing. It was impossible not to join in – if you wanted to be part of the band you had to get bladdered. Even the guy who drove the van was usually out his head on cheap whisky. I had a great time for a while until we split up. The bandleader had only come to Scotland after money had gone missing from his previous showband in Ireland and they finally caught up with him. The band didn't so much split up as ran like hell to get away from the reprisals.

And so I started a band with a couple of lunatics I knew from the pub. You won't have heard of it, but it was called Powerhouse.

9

POWERHOUSE
Glasgow

There is nothing quite like playing in a rowdy rock band. When you are young, that is. Drunken old geezers marauding around town is just plain sad. I was recently talking to a middle-aged guy who plays with one of the biggest bands in the world. He was bragging about the number of times and 5-star places he'd drunk himself senseless, about the sound checks at massive stadia gigs he'd almost missed, about the first class flights on which he'd knocked himself out with free wine. And I thought, *what a fucking prat*. He was a nice enough guy, incredibly lucky to have landed the jobs he had, but, to many of us less fortunate muzos, it is actually painful to hear someone who gets to play dream gigs yet being so out of it they were barely conscious. What a terrible waste. Maybe we're just jealous.

Ageing rock stars lurching through their lives full of alcohol and drugs really piss me off. They can drink all the fancy bevvy they want, but a grown man permanently drunk on high-class liquor, champagne and wine is as much an alkie as a wee jakey swigging Buckfast wine down a Glasgow lane. There's nothing glamorous about it. Some musicians think it is just fine to work in a near-paralytic state but what would they say if they went to the dentist and found him like that? Or if a drunk plumber turned up to fix their burst pipe? If a wee Glasgow labourer behaved in public the way some rock gods do he'd get a severe and well-deserved doing.

Not long ago, a pal was in a nice restaurant with his family and a drunk rock star at the next table was loudly describing in dripping detail the body parts of girls he'd done on tour. Nobody had the nerve to tell him to shut his mouth, somehow being famous allowed him to behave in a way that would have got a working man thrown onto the street. Maybe he was a big tipper. Besides, he had a hulking minder with a face like a melted welly boot. Grow up for fuck's sake.

But when you are young, now that's different. If you are going to be a rock musician it is your sacred right, indeed it is your duty to create a bit of a stushie before you become respectable, and definitely before you get married and have kids. The gentle Amish people of Pennsylvania have the right idea, a fine tradition that encourages their teenage children to take a year away from the puritan confines of farm life, go to the big city and indulge in every kind of drink, drug and debauchery they fancy. After a year they make an informed choice. What's it to be? A life among the infidels who devote their time to the pleasures of the flesh and the service of Beelzebub, or will they return to the chaste ways of their family, quiet biblical reflection and barn building in the sun? If the young rock bands in that part of the world have any gumption they will be lined up in their bandwagons with tequila and wacky baccy, waiting at the gates of the Amish farms for this year's fair maidens to take their first curious steps into the big world.

I've only ever played with one really rowdy band. Powerhouse. Or *Powerhouse, Glasgow*, as we stencilled in white paint on our amps and other gear, because 'name' bands did that and we thought it looked cool. I've played with lots of drunks and dopers, and with bands that liked to have a good time – who hasn't? But for a little local band, Powerhouse created a whole different level of mayhem.

It was nothing fancy, just me and a couple of pals, Mickey on drums and Alistair playing bass, hell-bent on creating chaos as we roamed the country in a beat-up, barely-legal Ford Transit van that we bought for £100 outside a used-car auction. We loaded it to the roof with our battered old speaker cabs, homemade stage lights and peeling amplifiers. We went through a bewildering succession of singers, male and female, each and every one of them unable or unwilling to keep up with our drinking. One of them became a panto star; back then he was just another big-headed tosser who wanted us to back him on songs such as *Amarillo* and *Ten Guitars*. Another became a TV personality; she demanded a lot of attention and quit when not even our roadie could satisfy her strange and secret lusts.

God knows what would have happened to us if we had ever got off the pub and dance hall circuit. When we were desperate for drink money, which was pretty much always, we even played weddings. We'd give them one waltz – an instrumental of Amazing Grace – then just launch into our usual set, which was loud. We were once escorted off the premises by a hotel owner and his snarling Alsatian dogs.

A word first about our Transit. Nowadays most young bands play at venues where the gear is provided, so all they have to carry is a guitar or perhaps a pair of drumsticks – they can tote that entire bale of hay on an environmentally-friendly bicycle.

If they ever make it onto the next rung of the ladder, if they get signed to a decent record label, they will be provided with a nice little Mercedes tour bus to swan about in. Deep reclining seats, dvd player, Nintendo games and flat screen televisions. They will never have to carry anything heavier than a guitar pick, the label will provide a couple of bi-lingual assistants – they prefer to be called *techs*. These university-educated helpers – some of them even play Sudoku for chrissake

– can speak fluently with local promoters when they gig on the Continent, and will set up their equipment, since a lot of young stars don't know the back of a Marshall stack from the front.

In the 70s, roadies – as they liked to be called – were Neanderthal creatures, squat, hairy and smelly, guys that thought a pen was an ear-cleaning tool, every last one of them carefully selected after passing one test and one test only. Could he carry a brutally heavy Marshall 4 x 12 speaker cabinet up a flight of stairs *by himself?* Language skills were not required; ability to speak at all was entirely optional as long as they could fetch a round of drinks. As far as roadies were concerned, the ability to pack a van with fragile glass-valved amplifiers so that countless dark and potholed loading alleys behind gigs didn't wreck them was all that mattered. Back then – oh don't I sound old? – we had to lug all our equipment from town to town, from the street to the stage, night after night, and the preferred mode of transport was the double wheelbase Ford Transit.

It was brilliant.

Oh, Hilton hotels are fine places of rest, chains of Holiday Inns and more recently Travelodges have all played their part in accommodating bands of wandering minstrels, but I am willing to bet that if you ask any old-timer to tell you about the deepest sleep he ever had his eyes will mist over and he will recall endless nights of perfect slumber on an unspeakably stained mattress piled on top of amplifiers in an old rust-bucket of a Transit as it coasted along the motorway after another wild gig. All the bands had them.

Packing a Transit van was a skill, and not easily acquired. The van had two modes – going to the gig, when the gear had to be packed with seating in mind, and returning, when it had to be arranged in such a way that at least half the band could stretch out and sleep. Transits had three seats at the front and a cavernous space behind. Some bands had old airline seats fixed there, but we reckoned they either had rich parents or were English poofs.

We would lay our largest speaker cabs flat to make a sort of bench behind the front seats and put a single mattress across them. Don't ask where it came from. Or what had been done on it. Another single mattress would be placed against speaker cabinets behind thus forming a simple but effective backrest. Propping all this up would be the cases for the drums – including a large crate that Mickey had acquired from some laundry he briefly worked at – then the amplifiers and, at the top of the pile, the guitars in their tattered plywood cases. We didn't trouble ourselves with seat belts; despite the TV campaign to *Clunk Click Every Trip* we didn't give a shit.

As soon as the gig was finished, the mattresses would serve for whatever bestial purpose we required, then we'd load the van differently, the equipment packed as flat as possible using all the space behind the front seats, so that instead of a backseat there was enough room for three people to stretch out on the mattresses on top of the gear and sleep away the long miles home. It was perfect.

We often played at an American naval base in Dunoon where we had become pals with a lot of guys whose job was cleaning the crap off the hulls of nuclear subs. Known as the Dry Dockers, they were the lowest of the low as far as the US Navy was concerned. At the time, Americans convicted of minor crimes could chose between a couple of years in jail or the same amount of time in the Armed Forces. The Dry Dockers were misfits, outcasts, not what you'd call career seamen.

We weren't allowed to buy alcohol in the base but the Dry Dockers could get Budweiser beer and tequila very cheaply so whenever we played there we would have a huge drinking session before, during and after the gig. This usually meant some of the Dry Dockers would miss the last ferryboat that shuttled them out to their bunk beds in the ship anchored in the Clyde. We couldn't see them stranded – if they had been caught on the streets of Dunoon after midnight they would be arrested by the military police, who would kick the shit out of them. So we smuggled 10 of them into the little guesthouse we were staying in – the owner had stupidly given us the key. This led to a ban from all hotels near the Base and the next time we played we had to leave the gear in the club overnight and doss in the van. One summer night, our Transit accommodated the whole band plus 6 other drunks, 11 people in total, which I think may be a record.

Most bands establish their 'name' and build a reputation based on it. We were exactly the opposite; the more places we played, the better-known our name became and the more often we had to change it to something else if we wanted to get a gig again in the same town. We got banned from a lot of places. Most of the people we played to liked us fine, and some girls were very enthusiastic, and were more than happy to prove it in physical ways. But for some reason we annoyed gig-owners, usually because we would play so loud they'd be in danger of losing their drinks license. Sometimes they would kill the power and eject us; other times they would try to cut our money, which would upset us.

One miserable bastard – English, it hardly needs saying – booked us to play a gig in his large hotel near the grim winter outpost of Fort William. The weather was Arctic yet he refused to let us have one lousy bedroom for the night. What happened to Highland hospitality, we wondered? The road back to Glasgow was closed, we were stranded, yet he wouldn't even allow us to shelter from a howling northern blizzard by sleeping on the stage. Before we headed off to park in a shivering lay-by for the freezing night, we changed the appearance of the backstage area, I'm embarrassed to say. We had got to know a couple of girls who worked at the hotel, as you do, and they told us later that the man had been very fond of the piano we reduced to splinters. More than that, the dull *dong* that the heavy base of a mic stand makes when it crashes repeatedly into a doomed piano carries quite far in the dead of night and several residents complained angrily about the noise. If it hadn't been such a stormy night, when the police had more serious matters to attend to, we would have been arrested.

Being young in a rowdy rock band gives you the opportunity to do all sorts of things that you will look back on from the twilight of your life and recall with a sigh. For me the 70s was that time, the great era of rowdy rock bands. Historians talk about the Pill and the 60s being the peak of the sexual revolution, but I reckon the early 70s was when the party really got going. They were happy times indeed. There were no deadly diseases, at least nothing that couldn't be cured with a few pills. I knew musicians who reckoned the clap was no worse than a mild cold, hardly worth bothering about. But the rock generation didn't invent sex and free love. We thought we did, but all we did was make it cheaper. We did for sex what Ryanair did for air travel. I just said that because I thought it sounded good.

And then there was the band flat.

Instead of hanging out at the pub, a lot of young bands these days spend half their time socialising by text and Facebook, live with their mums until they are 30, never travel anywhere unless it's a cycling holiday in France or trekking in Tibet. They work during the day as web-designers and so have the money to rehearse in air-conditioned studios. They write all their own 'material' and usually they can only play for about half an hour. They never have to do any longer because they only ever perform at unsigned band nights in little bijoux bars around town, sharing the bill with three or four other hopeful groups trying to get spotted by record labels. The crowd is always made up of their pals and, even more awful, their doting relatives. Their *mothers* come to see them *play* for fuck's sake. It is fucking embarrassing. I mean would Iggy Pop or Jim

Morrison ever have become dick-waving legends if they knew their dear old mums were in the front row? I think not.

In the 70s, when you were in a band in Glasgow you went the whole way. You would find some naive landlord that was prepared to rent you a flat – at that time usually a member of the gentle Pakistani community. Hard working, enterprising people quietly building property empires long before all that buy-to–let malarkey; a great many of them were busy buying large, crumbling tenement flats in the west end and renting them out as student bedsits. It may seem incredible now, but in those heady days the State actually paid students to attend university. At the start of every term they would issue a grant cheque. Some musicians enrolled at university just to get their hands on one – the first decent equipment many musicians bought was obtained using a grant cheque. I had a pal with a music shop near Glasgow Uni who would rub his hands at the start of each new term; it was like Christmas. Most apartments near the university were let to students, and were ideal for band flats because in quieter districts the residents would be up in arms in a week.

At first, landlords were blissfully unaware of the havoc that a young rock band could bring to a quiet neighbourhood. For a while, landlords actually preferred renting to musicians. Students only rented for 8 months a year, could be noisy and have drunken parties, and landlords had learned to be wary of them. Some had sworn never to rent to students again, because they abandoned ship at end of term leaving piles of empty beer cans, broken dishes, clogged lavvies and a lot of pissed off neighbours. But when it came to creating chaos, compared to musicians, students were amateurs.

The requirements of a band flat were simple: a telephone so that gigs could contact you, and enough space to set up the amps and the drumkit. There were hardly any rehearsal rooms in Glasgow, and they cost money so no self-respecting rock band would dream of using them. Proper bands rehearsed in their flats; you could walk along Woodlands Road or West End Park Street and hear *All Right Now* and screaming half hour guitar solos any day of the week.

When I had been playing with Greenfly, we had rehearsed in a small flat I was renting. A neighbour was constantly whining to the cops. The old bugger was stone deaf but she was always calling them, shouting that the vibration of the bass was making the ornaments fall off her mantelpiece. It probably was. They got fed up with her yelling at them and would be round as soon as we switched on our amps. Since there occasionally might be the lingering aroma of exotic tobacco in the flat – and in those days the police regarded a wee puff as a capital offence – I felt it was wise to relocate to a different area.

And so Powerhouse began searching for a suitable 'band flat' near Glasgow University. Me, Mickey and Alistair, great pals bound together by the energy and confidence of youth, our love of loud and *who cares if it's in tune* riffs, vast quantities of alcohol before, during and after every gig. Our hair was way down past our shoulders, and we looked fucking degenerate. We were degenerate. Not even the most gullible landlord would be stupid enough to rent to us.

We wanted a ground-floor apartment because loading in and out of it was easier than dragging our equipment up three flights of stairs. Bandwagons were easy targets for Glasgow's teams of thieves – you could break into a Transit van using little more than a banana – so when we got back from gigs in the middle of a winter night our gear had to be unloaded by the foggy glow of freezing streetlamps. When you are drunk and dirty and exhausted this is not an easy task. That alone separated proper working bands like us from the amateurs – big jessies who worked during the day, kept their wanky little amplifiers in the boot of their cars and only played one night a week.

We found the ideal place, a flat that had been rented to a couple of respectable girls we knew; as we gradually moved in they quickly moved out. We used some gig money to give them the deposit they had paid the landlord, they kissed us goodbye and we had it all to ourselves. The landlord lived in a leafy suburb on the other side of Glasgow and had no idea we were staying there. We were supposed to pay the rent into a bank account every month; he was too lazy to come and collect it, which was just as well since we were always late. Sometimes we didn't bother paying anything. Cheap supermarket alcohol hadn't been invented, so we had to make some economies.

In those days bands usually had to play at least three hours every gig, so during the day we would learn new songs from whatever was in the charts at the time. Anything that kids would dance to was fine by us. The neighbours were out at work or attending university classes and so never bothered us. Except one night when we had a drunken jam session with another band at three in the morning. We realised that was a bit much and switched off when we finally heard a posse battering on our door.

At night we'd always be out playing, there were so many places to play. And they all paid. Sometimes not a lot but even vagabonds like us collected a fistful of cash at the end of a thirsty night's work. We were the exact opposite of most bands these days; we had absolutely no interest in finding a record 'deal'. All we wanted to do was play music. Many bands nowadays have no interest in music, they only want to find a record deal. They want to play the life of a musician rather than a life playing music, as we did. God, I'm sounding like an old fart. But it's true.

During the week we'd play pubs in Glasgow and Edinburgh and if there was nothing else, bars in some of the old mining villages like Wishaw – we tended to avoid them because the natives, genetically altered by working deep in the bowels of the earth, were dangerously retarded trolls. Alistair was forever bringing one of them back in the van in a drunken stupor and the next morning we'd have to scrape together the bus fare to send her back to wherever she'd come from, if she knew where that was. I'm joking, but he did bring back some wild women. At weekends we'd be off gigging in pretty little village halls all over the Highlands of Scotland. There were hundreds of these isolated communities, and their teenagers were trapped – kids couldn't afford cars.

These were terrific gigs because the farmers' sons and daughters were very fit from baling hay all week, were full of energy and had absolutely nothing else to do with their time. The usual entertainment in their village halls was a ceilidh that the whole family would go to, which is the last thing a deliriously horny farm boy wants on a Saturday night. So that their kids didn't go entirely mental, these little hamlets regularly brought a rock band up from the big city to keep them amused for a few hours. Most Glasgow bands couldn't be bothered with the 7-hour drive along little single track roads to get there, so there were always more gigs than we could handle.

Of course, centuries of inbreeding and intermingling of red-haired Pictish blood meant these kids were all clinically insane, and as soon as they'd had a few drinks they'd spend the night punching hell out of each other, re-enacting the great Viking battles of the ancient northlands. No one got seriously hurt, it wasn't like in Glasgow council estates where knives and bottles were used even in friendly family tiffs, and they all seemed to enjoy it, like it was a form of retarded rugby. Few of them had a full set of teeth, or an unbroken nose, but that seemed to be the worst injuries. It was great fun to stand on a stage and watch all these crazy kids rolling around in a melee of flying fists and dung-caked farm boots.

The girls were stunning. Toned and tanned, all that fresh air, milking cows, shearing sheep and grooming horses had made them as horny as hell. But they couldn't jump in the hay with the local lads or there would be a queue of them wanting their turn – word of a willing girl spread fast in the villages. So they would choose visiting rock bands, knowing that any tales would be restricted to pubs in the far-off city. Perhaps it was Nature's way of widening a dangerously shallow gene pool. We'd have played for nothing, but the gigs paid enough to keep us in drink for a week. Our Transit van – the Hangover Hotel – was the scene of all our wildest dreams. A steady supply of red-haired Highland Morags and Kirsties kept us happily occupied. We loved it.

Of course, in Glasgow, some gigs weren't fun.

Fights happened a lot in pubs, and anything handy was used as a weapon. One night a guy had his face ripped open right in front of me – it took weeks for the bloodstains to disappear from Mickey's cymbals, I'd never known him to clean them, why bother? Another night someone rushing to the door didn't quite make it and barfed all over the people sitting at the front, which he soon regretted.

Then there was the gig in a Paisley bar when a 6-foot tall cross-dresser appeared. I have no idea where he came from, or what he was doing in this part of town. He must have been crazy, the local headcases were always looking for a reason to start a fight. He was dolled up in a long tight dress, blonde wig, mascara, false eyelashes, high heels, the lot. He was taking his chances. It looked like he'd already been on the receiving end of some trouble, teetering in on crutches. I think we had reached out third song when it all kicked off. A corner of the bar disappeared in tribal war, but the cross dresser was giving better than he got. He braced himself against the wall and was swinging one of his crutches like a ninja warrior. Within seconds, three guys were out on the floor with gaping head wounds. The police stormed in and cleared the place; we never saw the trannie again.

Another night we were playing in a rowdy pub in the East End of Glasgow. We had done our first set and were having a drink when two big guys with scarred faces appeared at our table. They were smiling, and trying to seem friendly. We knew that meant they wanted something.

"Good band. Aye you're a good band, right enough."

"Eh, thanks."

One of them pointed at a skinny guy at the bar.

"See my young brother there? Well, he's doing an audition for Opportunity Knocks this week. He's singing Maggie May. He wants you guys to back him."

"Thanks, but we don't do that. We – "

"No…we're not asking you. We're telling you. You're backing him."

Opportunity Knocks was the top TV talent show, the *X Factor* of the time, and run by an old rogue called Hughie Green. The following Thursday we lined up in the posh Locarno Ballroom in Glasgow with about 20 other acts. The singer's gangster pals were there too, as was a good-looking drag act. I'm sure it was young Lily Savage, and I checked, but there's no mention of him ever auditioning for the show. When he went downstairs to the toilets in full flowing ball gown, one of the gangsters followed but soon came back, looking disappointed.

"Ah offered him a tenner tae dae his bender but he knocked me back."

There was more disappointment when the singer didn't make the final rounds. It wasn't our fault, we played well enough – we were so scared of what they'd do, we probably played it better than the Faces. Hughie Green stared at us, then at the gangsters, then he shook his head, a puzzled look on his face. The gangsters thanked us anyway and gave us £10 each for a drink.

There was an agency in Glasgow that booked all the good bands, and managed Billy Connolly, but after an unfortunate rammy at a gig somewhere in Ayrshire they decided we were a little too crazy even for them. But one of Glasgow's less glamorous agents was happy to find us gigs. Her name was Sweaty Betty.

She was an odd character, was well-known to bands. She had an odour problem, it's true, and she was almost deaf or perhaps it was the wax that always seemed to be clogging her ears. But she loved hanging out with bands, travelling in the bandwagons, even though she seemed very old, although probably only about 38 or so. She had a husband who owned a small engineering company and didn't seem to mind her spending every weekend with young musicians.

She got us some big student dances, including a great gig at Strathclyde University supporting the Kinks. They were terrific... they were about half an hour late going on by which time the crowd were screaming abuse, but the moment Ray Davies bounded on and started singing *Victoria* he had them in the palm of his hand. It was great to see.

Then Betty asked us to back a well-known Scottish country-dance singer at one of those New Year dances in a very posh hotel outside Glasgow. What is known in Scotland as teuchter music. It was very different from the rock music we played, but we couldn't refuse, she'd got us so many good gigs. Besides, they were paying very good money; all we had to do was play his chord sheets quietly, and in time, so that the crowd could skirl about in front of him. They would all be drunk anyway; it would be easy, Betty promised.

The hotel had given us all a large room to change clothes in, as if we had anything to change into, and by the time the gig was over we were paralytic. The gig had gone fine, the crowd were pished out their minds. The star of the show had got out of his Highland dress and buggered off, leaving us alone and helplessly drunk in the room. As these things always did, it had started innocently enough. A favourite game, fruitbowl baseball. We had slightly modified a table lamp and were using it as a bat, taking turns to hurl apples, oranges, and peaches at the batsman, with the best stains on the wall earning extra points. Splat! This escalated to bed-jumping, leaping on them to whack a flying apple while executing a spectacular dive.

There were two single beds in the room, and as I crashed down on one, the damn thing broke in half. I suppose there were a few other damages in the room, the dressing table really shouldn't have looked like that and the drawers, what was left of them, contained the shattered remains of the mirror. The wardrobe door hung slackly on its hinges like a stroke victim. Picture glass crunched beneath our feet like ice crystals and there was a lot of broken wood scattered around.

I lay on the V-shaped remains of the broken bed and we laughed ourselves silly. I'd had a lot to drink and you really would have thought that when I dropped off to sleep a few minutes later my pals would have scooped me up off the shattered bed and got me out the hotel before I got caught. But oh no. They thought it was funnier to leave me there. The next thing I heard was the door being opened by the cleaning ladies in the morning.

"Aye, Jeannie, that's my youngest going off to join the army next month, it's just amazing how time – oh my Goad!"

When they saw the carnage, the two women froze at the door. I had to bribe them £20 – it was a lot at the time – to give me a ten-minute start to get away. The furious hotel manager telephoned Betty but we denied we had demolished the room. We said the Scottish Country singer had thrown an epileptic fit and we had just been trying to hold him down. He was the darling of the Sunday Post and a lot of old dears used to come to the hotel on wee coach trips to hear him sing so they said no more about it. Don't think he ever got a room to change in again, though.

Och, we were young.

10

THE INCREDIBLE STRING BAND 1

Nobody was more surprised than me when I landed a gig with the Incredible String Band. I mean, they were originally an acoustic band, hugely innovative and the first band to play what has become known as 'world music.' If it had a string on it, or it could be banged or blown, it would find its way onto a String Band album. But rock and roll it was not. Although, believe it or not, Led Zeppelin often described their early albums as a major influence. There, that should shift a few dusty copies.

I had bumped into Mike Heron by accident in London; he was chatty with a huge, friendly grin and we shared some jokes over a coffee. I knew he had made a solo album with Jimmy Page and the Who backing him, and I suggested Powerhouse could be just the job for his next one. *We'd be a lot cheaper too, ha ha.* He took my phone number, and I went back to the chaotic gig-circuit I was playing around Scotland. I had pretty much forgotten about meeting him when he called a week or so later. He was planning another album, as it happened, and would I like to come along and play on some demos, see how it sounded?

Absolutely.

We arranged to meet on Sunday morning, not exactly the best time for me since I was playing a wild gig the night before.

From the little I recall, it was a really wild gig. Somehow I managed to get out of bed, grab my Strat, and catch an early bus down to Innerleithen, a village in the Scottish Borders on the banks of the Tweed river, surrounded by gentle, rolling hills. It was very pretty, but my head was pounding. I was angry with myself for getting utterly wasted the night before – I should have been taking this much more seriously.

Mike was living in a remote row of cottages, five miles from the village, which the String Band used as a base when they were in the UK. When I got off the bus I found the local taxi, driven by an ancient old man wearing a chauffeur's hat. He knew exactly where to go.

When I reached the Row, as it was known, Mike was very welcoming, grinning and making strong coffee. Then he switched on his tape recorder, let me hear a song he had just written, and asked me to play along with it. Now this actually suited me very well. I've always found it a struggle to copy other guitarists. Some guys are terrific at that and I envy them; it's a bit like those artists that can make replicas of famous paintings. I had learned to improvise well but that was only because I just didn't have the patience to imitate anyone else. Mike wasn't looking for a guitar player who could churn out the solo to *All Right Now*, and so when I played along with the track and did some interesting wee things he nodded and grinned.

He told me to hang on a minute and went to the cottage next door to get the band's bass player, a tall American guy called Stan who was also very friendly. Then he asked me to play along with another track; it was a rocky kind of thing in a minor key that was right up my street. I decided to really go for it, and blasted out some screaming, wailing guitar parts. I was very pleased when they seemed to like it. We had some more coffee, and then Mike drove me back to the bus stop for Glasgow.

As soon as I got back home I told the guys in Powerhouse that it had gone well with Mike, and that I reckoned there was a good chance we would get some session work. Mike called the next day and asked me to go back down to the Row to do some more demos. When I arrived, he took me to one of the cottages that had been set up as a rehearsal room and studio. He introduced me to a drummer and then Stan came in and plugged his bass into a really cool Fender amp. Mike pointed to a terrific Hiwatt amp and told me to use it, jam for a while, just play anything we wanted, he would record it. Once again I just played all sorts of wild stuff, we were having fun.

After a while Stan and the drummer wandered off and Mike told me he would play some more new tracks; he wanted me to record what I reckoned would make good guitar parts. The songs were difficult, very melodic, based round clever piano parts with lots of chords. I was struggling a bit, didn't have many ideas. I managed to latch onto some of the phrases the piano was playing in the chorus and added some things, being careful not to let on I really hadn't a clue what I was doing. I breathed a sigh of relief when Mike seemed quite pleased: he didn't want guitar all over the songs, he was happy that I had just played some wee touches.

He drove me back to the bus stop, then told me he wasn't planning another solo album, but that the Incredible String Band were due to start a big tour in two weeks. Mike had written a lot of new songs for the tour, much rockier than the band had done in the past. Would I be interested?

I was just 23.

I was very excited: the String Band were huge at the time, playing headline tours all over Europe and America. They were a quirky kind of band with a massive following; they had even played Woodstock, although the least said about that the better. It hadn't been one of their best performances. The band had originally been a duo, Mike with Robin Williamson, but were now a six-piece band that included Stan, the drummer and a multi-instrumentalist singer called Malcolm le Maistre.

We rehearsed at the cottages 12 hours a day for the next 10 days. It was difficult. As well as Mike's new songs, the band would be playing jigs and reels, with Robin on violin and mandolin. These songs had to be played precisely, and were not easy. Robin was a virtuoso musician; I wasn't. I had to play exact harmony lines with what he was doing. When he was on fiddle I could just about keep up, but mandolin was very difficult because of the speed of his playing. I'd rehearse all day and early evening with the band, then practise alone well into the night, playing the parts over and over again; I had never worked so hard at anything. Oh, and I was also to learn to play a song on keyboards. *And hey, you can play some chords on banjo, can't you?* Of course I could. Somehow.

Two weeks later we were doing a warm up tour of France, and I was on stage at the Paris Olympia, one of the biggest gigs in Europe. I was shitting myself. The Stones and the Beatles had stood on this very stage, had been in the same dressing rooms. Our support act was Don MacLean, singing American Pie. I couldn't believe this feeling: I had played that song in the Irish showband. And here I was, my first gig with the String Band, facing a totally sold out crowd.

For the next year or so we were on tour, and I loved it. The band were unlike anybody I'd met before. They were a lot older, never drank, or got wild after gigs. They were all married or in steady relationships, although eventually they all got divorced. I was quite lively and would hang out with the road crew when we were on tour; probably best not to go into details. But I was very professional, never drank a drop before or during a gig. Afterwards though…

One thing I loved about playing with a headline band like the ISB is that you get to meet so many other musicians. You're not a 'fan'; the door is open. There would often be famous people on our guest list that I would never have dreamed of meeting. The guys in the String Band didn't do much socialising, except for Mike, who was very pally with Pete Townshend, Stevie Marriot, Robert Plant and many others. Whenever I got back to Glasgow on a wee break I had to watch I didn't mention names of people I had met – I would probably have had the shit kicked out me. I got to talk to Bruce Springsteen, who we played with in America, Jimmy Page, Kate Bush – she was actually the girlfriend of one of our roadies – Jack Bruce, Ritchie Havens, Steve Stills, Bonnie Rait, and my hero Rory Gallagher, as well as guys from Aerosmith, Free, New York Dolls, Queen, Roxy Music, Lynryd Skynyrd and others. Oh, and Julie Christie. I know she's not a musician but I felt like doing a bit of name-dropping.

After the first two tours I did with the band, the drummer was replaced by John Gilston, a terrific musician who became my best friend. We were to have many adventures together.

11

THE INCREDIBLE STRING BAND 2

And this is one of them…

As soon as the plane touched down in Copenhagen I knew it was going to be a good weekend. It was summer of 1974. We were headlining the Roskilde Festival. As soon as we were through passport control, which in the easy-going way of the Danes was really just a nod and a smile, the band's manager, Susie Watson-Taylor, quietly took drummer John Gilston and me aside. Suze was the best manager I have ever worked with. She was one of those people who could ask you to walk through fire and you would do it. She was very beautiful, had a stunning warm smile, long flowing curly hair and her sensuous, cat-like body had been well noticed by half the executives in the music business. They all lusted after her. The other half, it hardly needs saying, were gay.

She could flirt brilliantly when she wanted to, never messed anyone around and the band owed a lot of its success to her. Promoters all over Europe just couldn't wait to book the band again. For example, headlining Roskilde, Europe's Glastonbury, is not something that is given to many musicians.

"One of the top guys from Island Records is here. He is really into porn films. Do you think you two could take him to some of the shops this afternoon, generally keep him amused? Could you look after him? He wants to buy some movies, you know?" Yes, we most certainly did know. Island was our record label. Anything we could do for the cause.

"No problem, Suze." I grinned.

She looked at me with that wonderful suspicious grin.

"Don't look after him *too* well, Forbesie. Keep out of trouble, ok?"

She smiled her devastating smile. If taking an exec round some seedy porn shops, passing the afternoon gazing at movies of beautiful European girls was what the boss wanted, then it was a small sacrifice to make for the band.

John Gilston was a former public schoolboy, with impeccable manners, always meticulously polite, thoughtful of others, and had a gentle, BBC-type voice. In later life he might have been a newsreader, or one of those guys that read bedtime stories on Radio 4. Everyone loved John. He was a phenomenal drummer, incredibly versatile; he could play any style from subtle, accented soul to full-tilt rock. He is the only white drummer I have heard who could properly play reggie. I have never played with a better drummer; he eventually became a top LA session man working with Michael Jackson, Donna Summer, Rod Stewart; loads of people.

We had heard that John's father was a multi-millionaire living as a tax exile in Switzerland who wasn't happy that John was hitting drums for a living and refused to give him a penny. If John had a few quid, he never made a big deal of it.

As sidemen playing in the String Band, we were hired hands and paid a monthly wage plus, when we were on tour, which we always were, what musicians nowadays call a *per diem*, a posh name for a weekly envelope of cash we knew simply as food money. Some of it we did sometimes spend on food, I suppose, but promoters always laid on a nice pile of grub for us at the venues, so we learned to save our dosh for more important things, like tequila and the sort of girls you'd be ashamed to take home to your mother.

John and I loved being part of a world-famous band. We had been promised royalties on the band's next album, and a share of tour profits. I even had a songwriting credit on one of the albums. The band was doing very well and we had recently played sold out tours in Europe and the UK so we were looking forward to tonight's gig very much. Status Quo had headlined the night before and we were told even more people had turned up at the festival today, Saturday. There would be a seriously big crowd tonight. I was very excited.

We checked into the posh Plaza Hotel in Copenhagen. Mike told us Eric Clapton had recently been a guest who had disgraced himself. The bluesmeister was going through his giving-up-heroin phase and part of his 'cure', Mike said, was drinking huge quantities of alcohol. Mike warned John and me to be on our best behaviour; the hotel would not put up with another night like *that* one. They had almost banned groups altogether. They were watching us.

John and I asked a hotel porter where we could find the best porn shops, then met the Island guy in reception. A quick cab ride and we were in a shop that offered previews of the films it sold. We filed into a private room at the back and were soon watching an impressive black guy humping a gasping blonde wearing a cute little nurse's outfit.

We had recently played in Amsterdam, however, and been to a club there that left no stone unturned in its pursuit of depravity. John quickly became bored with the standard fare, he wanted to see something extreme, really extreme. The Island guy was gaping at the screen, ready to buy the film, but John went out to the front shop and spoke to the owner.

"Pardon me, but would you have anything a bit, well, raunchier?"

The man grinned and changed the film. This one starred three women in school uniforms with a delighted young guy dressed as a boy scout. In a flash they had stripped him and were showing him interesting things to do with a cucumber. The Island guy was sweating as he stared at the screen, delighted. This however was pretty tame stuff compared to the live shows we had seen in Holland. John felt it was his duty to find the hardest core porn possible for the guy. He got up again and went out to the front shop.

"Do you have anything stronger? I mean, would you have anything with animals?"

The shop owner gave John a knowing wink and soon we were settling down to watch Helga's frolics at the farmyard, where an Alsatian dog and a pig were made to feel especially welcome by a very attractive girl I guessed would be barely 20. The Island rep was beside himself; we were sure the label would give our next record a lot of promotion.

What often occurs to me about that particular film is this. Imagine, after her brief acting career, Helga moves back home to Düsseldorf and finds a job, perhaps settling down to less-demanding secretarial work. She meets a nice man we shall call Hans, the manager of the company she works for, rather older than her, but they get along well and eventually they happily marry. One day he goes off on a business trip and, boys being boys, Hans and his companions have a few too many schnapps and stumble to a late night porn club. The room darkens and the silver screen flickers to life. Hans and his pals guffaw as they watch a lovely girl carefully and all-too expertly guiding a grunting pig's dong into her. She looks up at the camera and Hans freezes. It cannot be…but it is…there is no mistaking that cute nose and cheeky smile. His friends stare, scarcely able to believe what they are seeing. *Hans, it is your Helga – you never told us she worked on a farm!*

And so to the festival site.

Backstage at festivals always seems quiet compared to the muddy mayhem that is happening out front. We were assigned a large, comfortable portakabin with a plentiful supply of good eating. Healthy stuff too, the Scandinavians are good at that. Exotic seafood such as langoustines and scallops, fancy rice with glistening green and red peppers, cuts of grinning salmon. The sort of fare that helps Danes keep all their teeth until they are 125.

By comparison, if you played in a British touring band in the 70s, chances are you will be reading this propped up in your bed in the coronary care unit of some hospital. Most UK promoters thought they were being generous when they laid on stiff slices of cheese, cold scraps of curled-up ham and a few scabby lettuce leaves. Bands are usually starving after the show, and we humans are programmed to seek daily hot food. In most towns the only places open after gigs were curry houses. And so the bands of the day quickly developed a taste for Eastern cuisine; daal gosht, chapattis and fat nan bread dripping thick buttery juices, deep fried pakora, and searing-hot vindaloo that needed three pints of ice-cold lager. The overhanging stomachs on many musicians of the 70s tell the sad tale of too many post-gig feasts in the *Shish Mahals* and *Stars of India* of grim and rainy northern towns.

The Roskilde promoter had also provided a nice supply of wine, which John and I carefully stashed for later. Then we went to the stage area and looked out at a sea of people; I had never seen so many in one place. Nowadays festivals are held in every small town and village in the world, there are plenty opportunities to play in the open air. In 1974 it was fairly rare, mainly because promoters hadn't figured out how to stop people getting in free. Fests in the 70s tended to have 20 honest souls who had paid and about 100,000 gatecrashers. Some promoters ended up with a lifetime of debt. Others scarpered with the meagre takings, which is why some bands had the good sense to demand cash in advance.

It was anybody's guess how many people were out front. I remember when we finally walked on the stage I was shaking, especially as I had one of those twiddly bits to play right at the start of the first song. If all went well, and my Vox AC30 amp had survived the long truck ride from London and sounded the way it should, and as long as I didn't fluff a note then I could relax and enjoy the gig; it would usually go well. Fucking up the intro to a song, especially when you are looking out at what seemed to be the entire population of Denmark, was something that could make your spine sweat, like missing a penalty in a cup final. No matter how many times you have played something, it is always possible for nervy fingers to go the wrong way, which explains why many musicians don't want people coming up to them just before they play, asking for autographs or offering chirpy wee comments like *break a leg* or something equally gormless. This is worth remembering.

My biggest worry, especially on a big open stage like this, was that the cool night air mixed with the hot stage lights might have knocked my guitar completely out of tune. Guitar strings expand and contract, it is unavoidable. You know there is a possibility that the carefully-learned guitar intro you need to play might suddenly sound so out of tune that the entire crowd will piss themselves laughing. This was before little electronic tuners were invented; if you watch video of bands playing festivals back in the 70s the tuning is usually all over the place.

These wee tuners have probably made a bigger contribution to the quality of live music than anything else since the first amplifier was built. It's so easy now; roadies can tune the guitar in silence and hand you it when you're ready. Or you can put the tuner on the stage in front of you, plug into it then connect it to your amplifier. You press a bypass switch with your toe and the signal to your amp is cut out. You play each string in turn, you don't need to hear it, when it is in perfectly in tune a wee light comes on – you can *see* when your guitar is in tune, you can even check the tuning in the middle of a song. You hit the bypass switch again and you are ready. Back then you had to hold the guitar up to your ear just before you went on, play a chord and pray the fucking thing was ok. It was nerve wracking.

As it happened the gig went very well. I have often heard football players saying they can't remember a moment of matches they have played in, and headlining a festival is probably much the same, at least for guys like U2 who play them all the time. Big stars get used to playing to huge crowds, anything less than 100,000 people is, to them, an empty gig, but for a wee 23-year-old from Glasgow it was something I will never forget.

I've never been sure if it was a good thing to have experienced. Before I joined the String Band I'd only played Scottish pubs, clubs and dance halls; the biggest crowd I'd been in front of was tiny by comparison. I remember standing under the hot lights on the stage at Roskilde and looking out at that vast crowd and knowing that it was unlikely I would ever experience anything quite like this again. I had a sudden chill, would this be the peak moment of my life? Would it be downhill all the way now? Would the rest of my life be an anticlimax, like an old footballer reminiscing about scoring the winning goal at Wembley? Where would I go from here? It was a high that is impossible to match in regular life; what can you do next? I could understand why some musicians ended up snorting piles of cocaine.

Within an hour of coming off stage we were whisked back to the hotel. John and I were sharing a room on the top floor. After playing a gig like that it takes hours to calm down, sometimes all night. We were bouncing off the walls and glugging the wine we'd brought from the gig. I looked out of the window and realised we were directly above the hotel entrance, six floors below. Mmm.

I quickly filled a waste bin with icy cold water and waited.

John realised what I was about to do and was laughing his head off. A large black car drew up and a lady wearing a mink coat stepped out. As she walked towards the hotel I emptied the entire bucket of water out the window and ducked down so no one could see me. John and I were pissing ourselves. The suspense seemed to last ages, then suddenly there was a howl from the street. We didn't need to look out the window to know I'd scored a direct hit.

By the time we'd started on the second bottle of wine, John decided he was horny. But horny for a hooker, which he'd never had before. It was watching all that porn this afternoon that had got him in the mood. He wanted a professional blowjob. Excuse me – I originally typed that as two words but Microsoft Word immediately flagged that as a spelling error, insisting that the correct word is *blowjob*. I wonder who decided that?

Anyway, John wanted a blowjob and he wanted it now. He said he was just really curious to see how a *professional* went about the task. He had a beautiful girlfriend back in London, but he was in the mood... We had just played to a sea of people... He asked if I would go with him, the red light area was just around the corner. Being a thrifty Scotsman, I didn't fancy spending money on something that was freely available after most gigs, even if String Band female followers tended to be rather coy. We had recently been rehearsing in the same studio that Mott the Hoople used and found some fan mail that described in anatomically precise details what four young ladies of Scunthorpe would gladly do to the band. By comparison the wildest letter we used to get was an invite to drop by some hippy cottage in Puddlewick to sample Vashti's freshly baked bread and macrobiotic rice.

John had the idea that a visit to a hooker would be a valuable educational experience and I couldn't talk him out of it. So, bottle in hand, we walked out of the hotel, stepped over a pool of water at the entrance, and staggered off along the moonlit streets of Copenhagen. Eventually we saw a few girls hanging on a street corner. They looked rough.

"Look at that," said John, grinning. "Filthy looking. Look at that fat one, you can see her arse! They're perfect."

He staggered across the street and spoke to them. They laughed and chatted to him for a minute, before kissing him on the cheek then turning him around, patting his bum and pushing him in my direction.

"So what did you say to them?" I asked.

"I asked them how much they charged for a blowjob," John was laughing. He had the most enthusiastic laugh I have ever heard, full of youthful joy, of life.

"So what did they say?"

"They just laughed at me, and told me not to be ridiculous, they said I was far too young and good looking to be paying for sex. It's the nicest knock-back I've ever had."

12

THE INCREDIBLE STRING BAND 3

I was 24 when I stepped onto the plane at Heathrow with the String Band, bound for New York City. I was so excited I could have flown there myself.

I had played all over Britain and Europe with the band, had done radio and TV shows, festivals, recorded an album with them at Island Records, even been in two movies. I had become used to playing big stages in large venues. We would normally play to around 2000 or 3000 people a night, big crowds. But the thought of playing in America was something else.

I loved touring. There is nothing like travelling to a foreign country to play in a band.

Touring did break up a lot of marriages, many a professional musician came back from traipsing around the world only to find his good lady had buggered off with someone who had more regular hours of employment. Most bands have a simple rule: if anyone wants to take their wife or girlfriend on tour then they pay the cost. So few did. Despite this, all the musicians I knew loved touring. And we laughed at those whining songs about the hardships of being on the road.

I think Paul Simon was one of the first to sing those, with his mournful *Homeward Bound*. I have grown to like that song but at the time thought it was self-pitying nonsense. I guess if you were sitting alone in a railway station with a ticket for your destination and, yes, if you were a poet and a one-man band it could perhaps get lonesome. But if you are young, fit and healthy and touring the world's greatest glittering cities in a rock band, doing whatever and whoever you feel like doing, and playing every night to crazy crowds that love you, how could you possibly complain about being lonely?

I used to hate those whinging songs. The solution is really simple. If you don't like seeing the world, staying in fancy hotels and being cheered every night like extra-terrestrial gods, then fuck off home and start working in a Call Centre, or flipping burgers in MacDonalds, or carrying bricks for a living. I think I can safely promise that once you see how few standing ovations you get in those lines work, and what most people have to do to pay their rent, you'll be back on the tour bus faster than Usain friggin Bolt.

America has always been the land of dreams that musicians long to tour. Some bands that were huge in the UK couldn't get arrested in America. It's still like that, it has always been a different market. The String Band had a really big fan base in LA and New York, could headline even in unexpected cities such as Atlanta, Nashville and Memphis, but would open for much bigger bands in other places.

Nowadays almost everyone has been to America; flights are cheap. I remember how much my ticket cost back then – I'm sure it was about £500, which was a hell of a lot, probably equivalent to about £3000 now. I didn't know anyone, other than musicians, that had been there. None of my friends in Glasgow had even been to Europe. Bands that had toured the States brought back tales of excess beyond our wildest dreams, beautiful girls, fantastic crowds, great food, cold Budweiser beer, tequila and chilli. Whenever I asked Mike Heron if it was true that he and Robin had once shared a Jacuzzi in the Hollywood Hills with Joni Mitchell and others, his eyes just sparkled and he would grin dreamily. I couldn't wait to get there.

There was a Hard Rock Café in London, and that was the nearest I'd been to long legged California girls, juicy burgers and cheesecake. Apart from there, in the UK the only thing you could buy that even looked like a burger was something awful sold by a chain of eateries called Wimpy. It was usually served on a plate with a thing they called a Frankfurter that had little notches cut out of it, perhaps to make it look classy.

As I settled back on the plane, I looked at my passport. There I was, Powerhouse-length hair down to my shoulders. My occupation: musician. And a big red Visa arranged by the band's New York agents. God, it felt good. I was finally on my way.

Many people say they feel very at home in New York, usually because they've seen countless TV programmes filmed there – the buildings and streets are so familiar. When we landed, two limousines were waiting at the airport to drive us to our Midtown hotel, the old Gotham on 55th Street and 5th Avenue. It was a great hotel, with rattling air conditioners in the windows bravely battling the stifling heat. A lot of bands used to stay there; the barman told us he'd served the Stones their first tequila sunrises. While the rest of the band got settled in and did sensible things like having a rest and going for a nice early dinner, John and I went off to wander the streets and check out the bars. We ended up in some country and western place, jamming with the band to *Ring of Fire*. It was summer, and the city was in the middle of a sweltering heat wave; I had never felt anything like it and loved the humidity, even the steam coming out of the subway vents, drifting up like smoke signals. We went into a little shop to buy cigarettes and a girl behind us heard my accent and asked if we played with the String Band. She was a fan, had tickets to one of the gigs we'd be doing. I couldn't believe it.

Next day, the tour got underway. We started with a six-gig run in Philadelphia and soon were travelling all over the place.

We would usually headline, but sometimes opened for other bands. We did a couple of shows with Bruce Springsteen in New Jersey, where he was huge, and a big indoor arena near Cape Cod with the Marshall Tucker Band and Elvin Bishop. By this time, we were playing very little acoustic stuff, and were going down very well, even with crowds that hadn't heard us before. John and I were very excited; things were looking good.

We were booked to play with Three Dog Night at a University campus in the middle of nowhere; unfortunately our tour manager underestimated the distance and we were too late getting there, arriving just as our gear was being pulled off stage. John and I were very pissed off – there were 10,000 lovely female students in the huge hall. Three Dog Night were into special effects, and had rigged a keyboard to 'explode' in the middle of a song. Unfortunately their roadies set the charge wrongly, and the whole damn Hammond organ suddenly blew up halfway through the gig. It was very entertaining, although their keyboard player didn't see the funny side of it.

It was tiring, but the buzz from the crowd always great; if they liked you they really showed it. One night we finished playing a gig in Atlanta, and got back to the hotel about one in the morning. We had to get up four hours later to race off to do a live breakfast TV gig; it felt very strange to play at that time in the morning, I suppose it had been arranged by the local promoter. Things were livened up by the show's chef, who was demonstrating how to cook gumbo or something and set fire to the place. Touring was fun.

New York became our base; if we had a few days off we would head back to the Gotham Hotel, or the Mayflower on Central Park West, another haunt of many touring bands. It's a shame, these places had a great rock and roll history but have been rebuilt as condos. One morning John and I were getting out the lift just as a well-known drummer stepped in with a tall, very attractive black girl wearing tiny hot pants, a little bra, bare midriff, very high heels, but not quite enough make up to disguise that she was actually a man. We looked at the drummer. We looked at the 'girl'. We knew the drummer was married; and he knew we knew. We grinned at him. *Good morning!*

He smiled, pressed the button for the 6th floor, and turned to us.

"I'll deny it to the fucking end."

Then he laughed loudly, and the lift took them up.

If we wanted to see other bands, our tour manager would make a phone call and they would put us on their guest list. One night I was at a place called Max's Kansas City to see the New York Dolls. I was well aware of what some bands got up to and thought I had seen it all, but this was a whole new level of debauchery. Writhing, groaning, gasping bodies everywhere. It was like a porn movie, or one of those Bacchanalian paintings. Backstage was even wilder. They were a great band to see live, especially playing *Give Him A Great Big Kiss*, that old Shangri La's song. They were doing a hell of a lot more than kissing.

Not all was well, though. There was friction between Mike and Robin. Mike was very happy playing rock music, he was writing a lot of great stuff, and the crowds were really enjoying it. Robin had always been a gentler soul, preferring quieter instruments and songs. At the end of the tour, Robin and Mike stayed on in New York to speak to a new label that wanted to sign the band. This seemed a good idea because Warner Bros, who we were with in America, weren't exactly spending a lot of time promoting us.

The new label were very keen to record an album that would be much more commercial than anything the band had done before, and get us to a far bigger audience. We also had tours contracted for America, New Zealand, Australia, Europe and the UK that I was really looking forward to, especially

Australia, but in one hot-tempered afternoon, it all ended. Robin and Mike fell out about the songs the label wanted to record. Harsh words were spoken, doors were slammed forever, and the band crashed to the ground like a burning airship, never to play together again. Hey, that sounds pretty dramatic.

Anyway, it was over.

13

THE HIGHLIGHTS

When the String Band split up, Mike Heron asked John Gilston and me to help form a new band. We went round the clubs in London where we found a great keyboard player and a bass player who had played with all sorts of people, including appearing on the BBC's iconic *Top Of The Pops*. We recorded an album in London, doing the some of songs we'd been playing on the final String Band tour. It was a great band and we toured in the UK and Europe, did the John Peel show and other good radio gigs, but we had signed to an American record label that went bust. Mike spent a fortune keeping it together but it couldn't last.

I came back to Glasgow, as penniless as when I had left. You have to get on with life as it is, not how you'd like it to be. You do, of course, find out who your real friends are. The only time I felt at home was on stage, and travelling to other countries to play in a famous band is an experience that changes you forever. I can understand why so many musicians, after their moment in the spotlight fades, end up in dark rooms with a bottle in their hand. It is almost impossible to go back to normal life. There's not many jobs like that down the local Job Centre.

There's a comedy quiz show in the UK called *Never Mind The Buzzcocks*. Every week they show a clip of some long forgotten drummer, singer, or guitarist in their glory days. Then he joins an identity parade with four other people and the panel have to spot him. Now we have to remember these guys were not stars, or they would be too easy to recognise, often they just played on one of those annoying wee songs that sneaked into the charts. So here's the sad thing: after they have been 'revealed', no matter how old they are now – and some are pensioners – or how crappy the band they played in – and many of them were *really* crappy – the presenter always tells us that they have just finished recording a brand new album and are planning a hopeful comeback tour. I mean, it's great that you're still gigging, pal, but the fucking *Budgie* song yet again is something we can do without. But you see in their eyes they would give anything to turn back the clock, that the days of their youth will haunt them forever. Perhaps it's not our failures we can't get over, it's our successes.

I needed to earn a living. There was nothing for it but to get out playing. I called Mickey and Alistair, the drummer and bass player from my old band Powerhouse, and we rounded up two good female singers – one of them went on to sing arias with Scottish Opera. We called ourselves the Highlights, because that sounded like the sort of name a cabaret band would have, and pretty soon we were playing every night, making a good living – more than I made in the String Band. We weren't at all fussy about where we played as long us there was plenty of cash at the end of the night.

Before the ravages of Thatcher, Blair and all the rest of those professional politicians, there were working men everywhere and they had clubs, so it was possible to find gigs any night of the week. It was almost impossible *not* to find one on a Saturday night. They also – and I know this will come as a stunning surprise to today's army of unsigned bands all clamouring for attention on Twitter and Spazbook – but they also *paid* bands for playing. Some clubs paid a lot.

There were so many of them; the nicest ones ranged from sleepy little golf clubs and minor league football supporters' clubs to glittering palaces that were owned by large manufacturing companies, like Rolls Royce, and were open to employees and their partners only. These places were strictly run. This appealed to many married couples; a working man could take his wife to licensed premises and enjoy a civilized night out secure in the knowledge that trouble was almost unheard of – anyone singing football songs, arguing or shouting about some useless prick that had missed a penalty would be shown the door. If someone started a fight they would find themselves out of a job on Monday. Lone drinkers were rare; the best clubs were a haven for respectable married working people who enjoyed dancing to a good band.

Unfortunately in small towns, especially in former mining communities, many clubs were just crappy drinking dens. There was usually nothing else to do at night, in the windswept streets the local Shell station had the only other bright lights, and that usually shut at eight. And so the people running these joints had no incentive to improve the places, they'd still be packed every weekend.

The clubs sold cheap alcohol. This was long before Asda and the rest jumped on the bevvy bandwagon and started flogging hooch for pennies. Everyone would cram into the miners' welfare club and get utterly pished. You could make a good living as long as you played exactly what the punters wanted, nothing clever, just some country standards and whatever chirpy tunes were in the charts. It wasn't the place to play something by Led Zep, and definitely not a song you might have written yourself. If you could fill the space between tunes with some banter and a few jokes, and didn't play too loud, you could earn a lot of money.

I was also in a band with a clever songwriter that played good original songs. Not a flicker of interest anywhere. It is always disappointing to put a huge amount of energy into a band and nothing happens. Meanwhile, this cabaret band – the Highlights – frankly we didn't give a shit about the songs and ballads that we had to play, it was just a way to make money until something better came along. Yet we were hauling in all sorts of work, even gigs for Radio Clyde, who at that time were a big deal. Some fool even offered us some kind of recording contract, but we reckoned he was just a halfwit.

I remember playing a gig with the band in some village and not being able to get near the load-in door two hours before we were due to play because the car park was packed; the place was full of people who had come to see us. And we really weren't very good. The closest we ever got to actually rehearsing was figuring out some song on the radio in the bandwagon as we drove to the gig. But we were far better than most of the bands that usually played there.

There were songs you had to avoid in some clubs. One night we were playing at a nice little spot on the edge of Glasgow, one of the better places. The job was going well, we'd sold out again, the place was full, a pleasant, family atmosphere. I was enjoying watching happy couples dancing close together. Men wearing suits. Ties. Polished shoes. Smiling happy faces. Easy money.

We eased into what was usually a guaranteed crowd-pleaser, a gentle version of Bridge Over Troubled Water that slid nicely into Danny Boy. The dance floor was full. As soon as our singers started singing *Oh Danny…* the entire crowd halted as if paralysing gas had been released, glared up at us, then marched off the floor. We had forgotten this was a Rangers supporters club; we really shouldn't have played the unofficial anthem of Republican Ireland. It took a wee bit of doing to get them back on our side.

The clubs always had a break halfway through the gig for bingo and we got very good at playing it. Just another wee temporary addiction. Their equipment was usually unsophisticated, a revolving metal drum into which the club 'social convenor' would dip his meaty hand, pull out a numbered ping pong ball, and announce it with some sort of catchy rhyme. The crowd would join in as he called: *on its own, number one,* a phrase that applied to any number below ten. 22 was two little ducks, *unlucky for some* was of course 13, but it could be lucky for someone if that was the final number they needed to win. *Two fat ladies* I think was number 88, while *number 10* was always met with the loud groan, *Downing Street.*

We always played bingo during our break. We would find an empty table, grab a fresh pint of foaming ale, make sure our cigarettes were in easy reach, take the tops off our marker pens, then carefully spread out our bingo cards. We became experts – even Mickey could play six cards at a time, quite a feat for a drunk drummer. The prize money was usually small, but we loved to win because we could yell 'House' and startle anyone sitting near us, which we always found amusing. Our dream was to cause some old dear to have a heart attack. Alistair always got shit-faced before anyone else, was usually too drunk to fill in the cards, and would just scream 'Bingo!' for a laugh, then say sorry, he'd made a mistake. He once yelled 'eat that pussy' when the number 69 was called and nearly got us thrown out.

The more gigs we did, the more we drank. The girls seemed to be sane, except for the fact that they were willing to be seen in public with hooligans like us. It was a low part in my life, not one of which I am proud. It was the drink, you see.

After headlining big venues with the String Band, like the Lincoln Centre in New York and the Rainbow in London, it got a wee bit depressing playing *Right Stoned Cowboy* in East Auchenshoogle Miners Welfare. Even going for a pee in these places was awful – the toilet was a metal wall with a gutter just below waist height. When stocky, drunk ex-miners rush in and start gushing, the spray-back is like an out of control fire hose. Any pop-gods who are feeling sorry for themselves might want to think about that next time they are poncing about the beautifully scented, Artistes-only lavvies backstage at the O2 Arena.

Playing crappy wee clubs every night meant that getting your hands on cheap drink was all too easy. You know the songs so well that you could play them in your sleep. I actually did nod off on stage once. We had played two gigs on Friday night, a pub gig on Saturday afternoon, then a late-finish job on the other side of Scotland, and I was on stage on Sunday morning after four hours drunken kip, backing 'singers' in Clydebank FC supporters club.

You might have assumed that lowly Clydebank would not have a lot of supporters and you would be right. And you also might have thought they would not have good guest 'singers'. They didn't. The club was a magnet for obese council-estate wifies that, after a few Carlsberg Specials, liked to get up on stage and sing a song with the band. I suppose nowadays this would be called live band karaoke, but then it was called a pain in the arse.

If the singers had stuck to simple tunes it would have been easy, we'd have found their key in seconds and played well for them. We were good buskers. But some morons tried to sing big numbers like *My Way* or *Goldfinger*. They hadn't seemed to notice we didn't have the London Philharmonic on stage with us. We knew it was pointless, these would-be Shirley Basseys usually got a few bass notes and a drums-only backing. Which is when I nodded off.

Eventually we had to part company with Alistair, which was very sad. I can't remember why, but I think he got fed up; he just wanted to drink without all the hassle of playing. Alcohol eventually killed him. We replaced him with a very strange, skinny big South African guy who slept in a camper van under a motorway flyover and only ate once every three days, always a huge curry. He was working round Europe and was a good musician but had a pathological hatred of black people, or *kafirs,* as he called them. The puzzling thing was that he was part black. We had to replace him. To be too insane even for us was a frightening thing.

We also often played weddings.

Sooner or later most musicians end up playing them because they pay well. I know a guy who played the Budokan in his glory days but ended up playing weddings for cash. Some are fine, others boring plods. That's the thing about wedding gigs – they go on for hours. You can usually take plenty of breaks though.

Usually.

We were playing a wedding in Glasgow, in a rough and ready hired hall. Trestle tables, beer cans, homemade sandwiches. It was a short-notice wedding and the sort of crowd that you had better make sure you could play their favourite songs; they wanted their money's worth. The girls were doing a good job, getting everyone up, singing well, entertaining the crowd. After about an hour we announced we would be taking a short break. Immediately a wee fat guy charged to the front and shouted at us.

"Aye, that will be fucking right! I had to work 5 hour shifts down the pits before I could take a fucking break and so will you!"

We also played a lot of weddings at a posh hotel in Edinburgh. They usually had one every Friday and Saturday and would give us rooms to stay overnight. As it turned out, this was a mistake. I am still ashamed when I think of what happened.

Scottish weddings are usually very hospitable. I have played ones that ended up in carnage, mainly in districts such as

Larkhall and Coatbridge, but that usually only happened when it was for a mixed marriage, that is, when a Rangers supporter was marrying into a Celtic family. Edinburgh weddings were genteel, dignified and happy affairs. The brides were slim, blushing, and never 7 months pregnant. Princes Anne could have dropped in after attending a rugby match at Murrayfield, as often she did, and would have fitted in perfectly.

The food was always excellent, and the drink – when a thirsty wee band from Glasgow is foolishly offered as much free alcohol as they want then the night can only end one way. Normally, one of us would have to stay sober to drive the van back to Glasgow and it would fall on him to keep the rest of us out of trouble, but since we were all staying overnight...could we really be blamed for what we did?

Our new bass player was a wee guy from Easterhouse, the worst part. He sang well, and knew a lot of country songs but unfortunately he liked to talk to the crowd. Thought it made him seem professional. Glasgow has two accents: understandable with a bit of effort, and totally incomprehensible. Even I had difficulty following what he was saying. Most of the time we communicated with a sort of Glaswegian sign language and phrases such as 'see me', 'eh by the way' and 'nae danger, big/wee man'. If you have grown up in Glasgow this sounds like perfect English. But the wedding guests were citizens of Edinburgh, from places like Morningside. The wee bass player, already half-pished, stepped up to the microphone and in his poshest voice announced to the startled gathering:

"Izvery nice tae see yees aw. Wur gonnae kickaff wi a wee cuntray tune furra furst waltz 'n that."

To them, it sounded like a motorbike revving up. A few glanced around, worried – *has that chap just told us to evacuate the building? Was it a fire warning?*

The wedding went well, as these things go, although

somehow playing a wedding never feels like a gig. No matter how good the band is, you are not the main attraction, which is kind of obvious. You always feel like a human jukebox. They seem to go on for days, and they kept giving us drink. So by the end we were very drunk.

But, it seemed, not drunk enough.

Because we were staying at the hotel, and playing there the next night, we didn't have to pack away our amps. The girls knew from experience it was best if they disappeared to their room. We staggered upstairs to change out of the cheap, cream-coloured suits we used to wear. I think we did over 300 gigs in those suits and only had them cleaned twice. At Christmas the girls sewed on glittery stuff that we were still picking out of the collars at Easter.

The South African bass player had been tall, so when the wee bass player replaced him he was given the suit he'd worn. It fitted him like a tent, and the arse hung so low it looked liked he'd dropped his load. The jacket reached his knees though, so nobody really noticed. We thought we looked great –it was our way of making a bit of an effort for the money they paid us.

As soon as we'd stashed our guitars we hit the Residents' bar. That's when we really started to knock back the drink. As always, it was a sad mistake.

By 1am, I was first to call it a night. I lurched up to the triple bedroom I was sharing with Mickey and the wee bass player. I lay on one of the beds and was just about to pass out. Suddenly the door crashed open. Mickey had the wee bass player in some sort of headlock, yelling at him to calm the fuck down. The wee bass player was raging.

"Wur fucking working here, wur allowed tae huv a bevvy in ra bar!"

Mickey's eyes had a glassy drunken stare, but he somehow explained that the night manager had thrown him and the wee bass player out of the bar, telling them they'd had more than enough. The wee man was not happy.

"Ah'll fuckin banjo the basturt! Naebuddy tells me when ah've hud enough!"

He swayed back and forth, then stared at the mini bar.

"Here – whit's in that?"

Three miniatures disappeared down his throat in a single breath. And a bottle of beer. Then he vomited. When I say he vomited, I mean a tidal wave of half digested food, wedding cake and gallons of beer exploded from his mouth. His jaws sprang open like a wild animal. It was strangely, horribly fascinating to see the sheer power of his gut-wrenching belches, it was as if he was possessed. That wee girl in the Exorcist had nothing on him. He didn't attempt to aim this tsunami of intestinal gunge into the sink; he projected it straight at the wall, and then sat on the bed with his head in his hands, groaning and gulping for air. He wretched again and again, each gut-heaving shudder throwing up another swill of puke on the nice tartan carpet.

Now say what you will, condemn me if you like, but if you have ever seen anyone honking all over a lovely hotel room, you will know it is just so wrong that you are somehow compelled to watch, and – yes – to laugh. Mickey and I started laughing, laughing hysterically.

In a surprisingly short time the wee bass player recovered, ran his hand through his hair, cleared his nose with a short, sharp downward snort, and muttered.

"Jesus fucken Christ. Ah didnae see that coming!" Then he picked up the phone.

"Ahm calling that wee fucking Hitler. Whit kinda hotel's this? There's fucking puke all over the place!"

He rolled his eyes, grinned, then began laughing, tears rolling down his face.

We grabbed the phone and hung it up before anyone could answer it. The room looked awful, but the wee bass player seemed proud of himself, examining sections of his work.

"Fur fuck's sake, ye kin see ma dinner. It wisnae the drink that made me boak, mind, it must have been something I ate."

The three of us were laughing so much we could hardly stand.

"Whit kinda hotel is this, ye cannae get a wee libation when ye finish work? A wee libation. A wee fucking libation."

Then the wee bass player picked up a bedside cabinet and flung it at the mirror.

"And the fucken mirror's broken. That's it, ah want another room."

It is frightening how these things get out of hand so easily, how thin is the veneer of civilization.

Mickey yelled something about Bruce Lee and demolished the dressing table with a hefty few kicks. And the wardrobe. There was a TV set in the room. The wee bass player picked it up and was about to heave it out the window. I realized we were five floors up overlooking Princes Street. If the set hit anyone it would be all over. I pulled it from him and it crashed to the floor.

"If you're going to throw it out the window, do it a bit at a time."

I kicked off the back of the set, booted the inside, then started dragging parts out and heaving them out the window down onto the deserted street. Mickey was still in kung-fu mode and leapt onto one of the beds then kicked a little wall light. It flew to the ceiling. Two bare wires stuck forlornly out of the wall. I grabbed one in each hand.

"I wonder what would happen if I touch these two wires together?"

BANG!

There was an impressive flash, a few sparks, then all was dark. Not just our room, but the entire floor of the hotel. We had blown every fuse in the place. Anyone walking by would have seen the bright lights of the hotel suddenly plunged into darkness.

When Keith Moon, Joe Walsh and the rest destroyed hotel rooms it was expected of them, they were just doing their jobs. And they had accountants to pay for the damages. I am ashamed, it must have been the dumbest bit of hotel-altering ever, especially since we had to play there the next night. I am willing to bet we were the only wedding band ever to wreck a hotel.

Perhaps we should have applied to get into the Guinness Book of Records.

14

WOODY WOODMANSEY BAND

When I was touring with the String Band, I'd got to know Woody Woodmansey, the drummer with the Spiders, David Bowie's band. I liked him, and we had a similar sense of humour. Ok, a taste for the bizarre. He had a habit of frequently clearing his throat with what one music journalist perfectly described as a 'deafening harrumph' or 'a thunderous mucus shift.' He also regularly cleared his nasal cavities in the manner preferred by professional football players. On dry days, the pavement outside his house could quickly look like an artist's palette.

We got along well and he asked me if I would be interested in touring with him in a band he was forming. I couldn't do it because I was heading off to America with the String Band but we kept in touch and always had a good laugh when we met up anywhere. Often with other musicians, you run out of things to say after half an hour, but Woody and I became good pals. After the String Band split up, I was about to head off on a tour with Mike Heron when Woody called and asked if I could do a tour with him. I couldn't let Mike down, so again I had to say no.

Thankfully a next time did come. I was fed up traipsing around Scotland with the Highlights, playing shitty gigs in working men's clubs to wild and vomiting drunks when I got the call. Woody had found himself a manager, a guy who had access to a lot of family money and wanted to put a band together to play Woody's songs, which were actually very good. It is rare that a drummer writes anything worth listening to, in fact there's an old joke: *What did the drummer say just before he got fired? Hey guys, we should do some of my songs...*

Woody had found a great keyboard player who had done a lot of session work, and a terrific bass player, a little guy who had played with some big names. I was desperate to play in a 'name' band again. I dropped everything and headed straight to the train station with my gear. In those times you could pile as much as you wanted into the Guard's van, a separate carriage on the train, and in went my guitars, Marshall cab, Fender amp, old Vox AC30, all sorts of stuff that today would have been worth a fortune on eBay had I not been stupid enough to lend them to the teenage sons of friends who were starting bands and who I have never seen since.

Woody and his new manager met me at Euston Station to collect it all. They had brought along a roadie, and on the drive to Sussex where Woody lived, the roadie kept us entertained with tales about women he had boffed. For some reason, the roadie could only get turned on by shagging married women, and he spent all his spare time pursuing them. He'd travelled the world and when he was on tour with some famous band or other he had limitless opportunity to have young, long limbed and utterly accommodating 20-year-old groupies. But in them he wasn't interested. No sir. They had to be married, *preferably with stretch marks.*

Woody had managed, somehow, to talk a building society into giving him a mortgage, despite the fact that any money he had made from touring with David Bowie was long gone. He didn't have a coin. Sensing that property could only increase in value, he had bought a big house, only a short walk from the nearest pub, where he'd first met the gullible buffoon that became his manager.

It was the middle of a freezing cold winter, late and dark when we arrived and as soon as we'd dropped off my stuff we hurried to the warm and welcoming lights of the pub. And got guttered, as I did in those times. Too often and too thoroughly. When we staggered back, Woody pointed me to my room and apologised – all the lights were out. A little misunderstanding with the electricity company that the manager would take care of next day. I fell into bed in the dark room and passed out, as I usually did in those healthy-prostate days.

In the early morning I woke, freezing like nothing I had ever experienced before. It was even colder than sleeping in a brutally cold Transit van after winter gigs in the Highlands of Scotland. I was shivering and looked at my breath misting up as the pale dawn light gradually clawed through the icy windows. *The wall. Jesus Christ. Look at the wall.* It was completely covered with blue and black mould. The room stank of decay and dampness. I was so cold I thought I had been embalmed.

I pulled on my clothes, went downstairs and met Woody in the kitchen. He looked rough. There was no heating in the house, and he'd been terrified the water tank would freeze then burst and flood the place. He'd managed to find a power outlet on his neighbour's wall and run an extension cable all the way to the attic where he'd sat up all night with a hairdryer, blasting the pipes to keep them from turning to solid ice. The other guys in the band appeared and I knew this was going to be fun; we were all laughing and joking, we couldn't care less about our long frozen night. When the power came back on we had a fry up and then piled in the van and drove up to a nearby rugby club that the manager had hired for us to rehearse in.

The band sounded great, terrific players. I was going to enjoy this. I had recorded some demos with Woody over the previous couple of years and so I knew some of his songs. He had learned a hell of a lot by touring and making albums with David Bowie, as you would. Woody was a great rock drummer, and sat up very high when he played. He was almost standing. He told me that Bowie had ordered him to play that way so the crowd would see him. The keyboard player really knew his way around, not flash, playing just the right amount – many keyboard players, used to playing alone in posh cocktail lounges, do far too much with their left hands. The bass player was brilliant. He was an odd wee guy, had some sort of mental problems. Many musicians do, but the nature of the job is such that they can usually play just fine even when suffering a thousand inner torments and hearing wailing voices in their tortured minds.

Even with the power restored the only heating in my room was a single light bulb and the dampness on the wall was so bad I'd end up with TB in a week, so Woody suggested that I share a room with the bass player in the manager's house. We each had a nice comfy single bed; it was warm and cosy. The bass player would mutter to himself in the dark– long, twitching, jerking conversations with unseen musicians he had played with and who had slighted him in any number of ways. In the middle of the night I'd hear him opening a can of beer and lighting a cigarette. He never smoked during the day or went to the pub; 2am drinking and smoking seemed to be part of one of his other personalities. He also had a nightly ritual of examining his dong in meticulous detail, whether anyone else was in the room or not. I believe he ended up in a mental hospital, but he was a harmless, likeable soul.

The manager was always dropping in on rehearsals. He was an affable big moron, always blindly enthusiastic and eager to tell us what he'd been up to. He would start off by proudly telling us he'd just been on the phone to Peter Grant, Bad Company's manager, about us doing a 50-date tour with

them in America. *Fantastic! That's great news! Well done!*
The big eejit would then say that unfortunately they already
had someone else. But we had been *this* close... Then he'd
called Queen's management and – I soon realised the dunce
hadn't the faintest clue about managing a band. He did have
more money than sense though. Local car dealers would break
out the champagne whenever he walked into their showrooms.

One day at the rugby club we were having a break when
the keyboard player mentioned that Yamaha had just brought
out a revolutionary electric grand piano. It was supposed to be
fantastic, sounded exactly like a Bechstein but was built for
touring. Which Bechsteins weren't. Apparently there was only
one in the UK. It was just idle chat, but next morning a Fedex
truck appeared at the door. Our manager marched in with a
huge grin.

"Elton John has the only other one, except for you guys!
Enjoy!"

The Yamaha had cost about the same as a new car, I'd never
seen anyone spend money like this. The band exchanged
knowing smiles. Neither had they.

One morning he told us he had arranged a showcase gig
for us at a big venue in London. He'd spent a fortune hiring the
place, had taken out big ads in the papers, all the music press
would be there, record companies, everyone who was anyone
would come to see us. He promised we'd have our pick
of record labels. A recording contract would be in the bag.
Going over the set in the rugby club had been fine to get us
started but now it was time to move somewhere far better.
There was only one place good enough: Pinewood Film
Studios, where Clapton rehearsed.

I was worried, and quietly suggested to the buffoon that
we should do some warm up gigs, even in small pubs, anywhere
to get the band sorted out. On rehearsals you really only learn
the tunes and the twiddly bits; it's live gigs that pull it all

together. But Our Leader smiled at me as if he possessed great knowledge and gently told me that he had a *purpose*. He said Pinewood would be perfect for us. He'd hired the huge sound stage there for 24 hours a day for a full week. We'd take mattresses and sleeping bags and sleep right there on the studio floor. Wouldn't it be great? If we had a song idea at two in the morning, why, we could work on it right then. How perfect would that be?

Pinewood was fun, because we were able to wander around the place – once you were past the security guards at the gates nobody bothered you. So we messed about the huge indoor pool where they shot the underwater scenes for James Bond movies, and wandered onto the top secret, closed set of Superman when they were filming him flying (they stuck a rocket up his arse). I even managed to whip a copy of the *Daily Planet* for my young brother, who loved movie memorabilia. We ate in the staff canteen and played spot the movie star.

Everyone in the canteen was staring at us, all these seen-it-all film set workers wondering who the hell we were – Abba had rehearsed in the same studio the previous week. Did we play with them? *Where's the lovely dark haired girl today? And the blonde one with the cute arse and pointy little nose? The one that likes choccy biscuits with her tea? She'll have trouble keeping that bum if she doesn't cut back on them.*

The studio was a huge aircraft hanger with a full size stage. Very impressive. Old gaffer tape stuck on the stage with *Eric – Fender Amp* written on it. We rehearsed the songs until we could do them backwards. At night we lay on the floor and stared up at the huge metal roof high above – I don't know where our manager had got the mattresses but judging by the exotic stains they had clearly seen a lot of frantic nocturnal activity. To get to sleep, I'd 'play' my parts in my head. You could have sung any two notes and we'd instantly know what song it was from. But we had never played a gig anywhere.

I asked the manager again to set up some warm-up shows, but he seemed incapable of making a couple of simple calls to local pubs. He got a tad irritable with me, suggested I was somehow opposing him and his management strategy. He said I was being *counter-intentioned*. I told him I was just worried about the amount of money he had spent and how much was going to be riding on the first ever gig we'd played together. Surely a few warm-ups would be wise? He wouldn't listen, and told me the whole point of rehearsing was to get tight. We should just make it happen, *make it go right!* Then, instead of finding a nice sweaty little rock bar to play in, he hired some ridiculous London venue to do a final run through behind closed doors. I think it was the Hammersmith Odeon, for fuck's sake. I couldn't help feeling uncomfortable; this was madness.

Despite my worries, the feeling in the band was great; we were having a terrific time. Musicians can become very close, there's a sort of comradeship in many bands that I imagine is almost impossible to find in most jobs, except perhaps cup winning football teams or something. Once they are successful, of course, it all changes as they bicker over royalties and all the other shit. But when a band is on the verge of breaking through there is an excitement that is hard to find anywhere else. It's like you against the world. You become very sensitive to the atmosphere in the band, what everyone is thinking. And so I became very sensitive to a change in atmosphere on the train to London for our showcase gig.

When a band has had a wee secret meeting without you, you can see in their eyes. There is guilt, they avoid looking at you. You just *know*. The bass player, who couldn't keep his mouth shut about anything, shuffled away every time I came near him. He was even lighting cigarettes during the day. The keyboard player, a Cockney geezer who was always playfully taking the piss out of everyone, suddenly became very quiet and gently friendly, as if I had some terminal disease. If you play with a football team, you know there's always the chance you'll be dropped, but that it's nothing personal, you'll play again. It's just tactics. But bands don't have substitute benches. You are either in or you are out.

We played the gig and it went fine. We sounded exactly what an over-rehearsed and under-gigged band sounds like; tense, self-conscious and stiff. We all knew that if one person made the slightest mistake it would throw everyone out – we'd become far too used to playing the set perfectly. And of course someone always makes a mistake and the band becomes like one of those oil tankers that takes forever to turn. Mistakes were made. Somehow we got through it; we weren't great but good enough.

I'd been away from Glasgow for quite a while and went back for a wee break after the gig. We had been rehearsing night and day for about 6 weeks. I needed to earn some money, because the one thing the manager wouldn't spend a penny on was a few quid in expenses for the band members. I was broke or, as we say in Glasgow, *skint*. The manager told me he'd telephone within a few days to let me know when signing a record deal, rehearsals and touring would start, so off I went, pleased that we had put a band together that was going places.

After a week I suddenly realised that I hadn't heard from Woody, which was unusual. He used to call a lot, was always full of enthusiasm and great ideas. I dialled his number, but his phone was cut off. I thought, of course, it would be, he was always short of cash. I called the manager and knew something was wrong as soon as I heard his voice.

"Well, Graham, it's like this. I was approached by a guy who is a songwriter. And he told me that he has a recording contract but no band. And I told him that's funny, I have a band but no recording contract. So, well, the thing is, we have decided to join forces. "

"That sounds great! So when do you want me back for rehearsals?"

"Eh, well, that's the thing. He plays guitar and he says he doesn't want two guitar players."

They didn't last long. I haven't seen Woody since, which is a shame.

It was great fun while it lasted though.

15

THE SWINGTONES

After the disappointment of Woody's band I realised it was time to concentrate on earning a proper living.

I was living in Glasgow, had got married and had children who needed financially responsible parenting. This meant that playing in bands would be a hobby for the foreseeable future. Playing as a friggin' hobby had always been a horrible thought, but the moment you hold your newly-born sons and see the trust in their eyes everything changes for the better. Life makes sense. I had taken up hillwalking, stopped drinking altogether and of course quit smoking cigarettes. I had never been fitter. I had started a business – nothing glamorous, just a moving and storage company.

At the beginning my old drummer pal Mickey and I did all the carrying and we loved it. We had learned how to pack vans really well when we played in Powerhouse, and a lot of antique dealers hired us to move expensive stuff from Christies and other posh auction houses. They paid more for that than we could earn for a whole band playing a club gig. I found it much easier than trying to make a living as a musician and often having to work with deranged people, many of whom would let you down in a heartbeat if a better gig came along. I built it up very quickly to being a proper company employing lots of people who wore smart uniforms and all that sort of thing.

After a short while, Mickey moved to New Zealand and settled down with a nice girl he'd met hitchhiking round Scotland when we were gigging with Powerhouse.

I missed him, and also missed playing the occasional gig with him. A pal who owned a music shop would recommend me to bands needing a stand-in guitarist or bass player. So for fun on Saturday nights, I played with anyone who telephoned, as long as they didn't want me to rehearse; I was too busy and, besides, I preferred spending any free time with my young sons.

It was usually club bands that called, and I knew I could busk my way through most gigs. Most of them had one thing in common; all they were interested in was how much money they could get paid. For me, doing a gig was, and still is, a thing of joy even if it could be a pain getting to the job and dragging a heavy amplifier, especially on freezing Scottish nights when you had to wade through icy snowdrifts. Winter was even worse.

Of the club bands I sat in with, the ones that earned the most were not necessarily any good, in fact sometimes they were awful. But they had one thing in common: the guy who arranged the gigs usually had a well paid job during the week and hated leaving his house on a Saturday night to play somewhere unless there was good money in it. And so he would charge so much that only places desperate for someone at short notice would hire them. Bandleaders like that loved wringing money out of people. The best, or worst, was a grumpy singer/guitar player who often called me to play somewhere at the last minute.

"Hi big fella. We've got a gig tonight, can you do it? They've been let down by another band. Paying good money."

Then I'd hear an evil chuckle, like a pantomime villain.

Whatever a club was offering he would scoff and demand more. Only when he got the price high enough would he agree to play the gig. Despite the money he extorted from club owners, we never rehearsed, not even once, and he would never tell you what key a tune was in; he'd just start playing and he expected you to know what it was as soon as he hit the first chord. He would time the set to the second, and I am convinced he would even end a song early if he thought we were going to play a few minutes longer than the agreed time.

At the back of the stage was a wee drummer who was an unfortunate shape, with some sort of large lump between his shoulders. I don't think it is allowed these days to call him a hunchback, but he was. His hump made him hang over his kit and he would look up from it like someone just rescued from drowning. I don't think I was ever told his name. I am certain it wasn't Quasimodo, but the only time the guitar player mentioned him, this was the name he'd use.

"Hey big fella, could you run Quasimodo to the job? He says his car's off the road but I bet he's just too miserable to pay the petrol. Or maybe he's been done for drunk driving, the stupid bastard. He only ever drinks two fucking pints. But you know what that does to him."

I don't recall anyone ever speaking to Quasimodo, and the guitar player ignored him, but he always turned up and played well. He did the two most important things that so many drummers can't. He could tune his drums so when he hit the snare it sound nice and crisp, and he kept time well. He could also cue song endings, which was important in an unrehearsed band. He was a painfully shy wee character, never spoke, avoided eye contact at all costs. If you offered him a cheery hello and how was your week, he'd twist his head away and shuffle off as if he were being asked to donate money to the Jehovah's Witnesses. I always imagined he lived in a dark cupboard somewhere.

The band did have one saving grace, and she was special. The guitar player only hired the minimum number of people needed to make a band, so there were just the four of us. The fourth person was his wife. And there was the mystery. The guitar player was not a handsome man; at some time in the past someone had flattened his nose. And I mean really flattened. I'd hate to have seen the fist that did that, it must have been huge, like a leg of lamb. Where the guitar player should have had a bridge, there was nothing, just a thin column leading to a wee bulbous bit that had reddened with the years. It was no longer a nose; it was a breathing tube. The punch that did it must have been brutal. It couldn't have been his looks that had attracted such a beautiful woman as his wife.

He was by far the most irritable, bad tempered little man I've ever met, so it was hard to imagine it was his personality that had kept them married for 20 years He also smoked an endless stream of cigarettes, and she didn't. It wasn't just because I was an ex smoker that I hated the thick stench of old tobacco from him; it was because he always had at least one, and often two, full strength Marlboros on the go. He always seemed to have one hanging from his mouth and if he had to sing a song he would stick it in the strings at the top of his guitar. He would have another burning in an ashtray on top of his amp, just in case the first one went out. He would always grab a few drags at some point in whatever song we were playing, although that usually meant a sudden gap filled only by bass and drums. As far as he was concerned that was just fine, that was what the fuck he was paying Quasimodo and me for.

His wife wasn't a sexy woman in an obvious way; she didn't wear the cheap sort of crap that many female singers were hanging out of, like Dundee lap dancers. She dressed in simple, tasteful things, but you could see every man in the crowd gawp at her. There was just something about her, perhaps the look in her eyes, or maybe the innocent way she grinned; she seemed to have no idea of the effect she had on men. She was the guitar player's opposite; always smiling and laughing. She'd chat with you, and joke, and her laugh was like music. He would mutter and curse all night, he could never string a sentence together that didn't feature the word *fucking*. To her, life was wonderful, and she transmitted warmth to everyone who was near her. She was also a really good singer, and when the wee guitar player did the main vocal she would sing beautiful harmonies. She was the only reason I played in the band.

Quasimodo was besotted by her; I swear if she'd thrown a ball in the air he would have leapt up and grabbed it in his mouth. He used to stare at her back the whole gig, and every so often she would turn around and give him a smile that would make his eyes roll.

One night we were playing at a golf club dinner dance. It was a very nice clubhouse, surrounded by perfect green lawns and with a spectacular view up a sparkling river to distant summer hills. It was a warm night, and the organisers were unusually pleasant. Many gigs were run by beefy power-crazed guys and their main aim in life seemed to be to find some excuse for cutting the band's money, pocketing as much of it as they could. The guy running this dance couldn't have been friendlier. He welcomed us, showed us where to set up our gear, asked if we would care for anything to eat, there was plenty food. Despite this the wee guitarist just grunted, lit another cigarette from the glowing ember of the one he had just about finished, stuck out his hand and grunted.

"Money."

The organiser looked slightly surprised, then apologised.

"Oh of course, would you like me to pay you now?"

"Aye, I told you that on the phone, we always get paid when we arrive. That's the rule."

The man handed the wee guitarist a fat envelope. He opened it and counted, leafing through the bundle, his face a mask of suspicion. Satisfied, he rammed the notes in his pocket, took a deep drag on his cigarette and brushed past the organiser to get his amplifier from his car.

The gig followed the usual pattern, for some reason the wee guitar player liked to do slow songs for the first hour, one after the other. After we'd played about six, the organiser came up to him.

"I wonder…could you play something fast? They'd like to dance the *Slosh*…"

The wee guitarist barely glanced at the man.

"We'll do the *Slosh* and other fast ones soon."

Then he started another slow tune.

After five more slow country dirges it was obvious the happy throng wanted some songs they could leap about to, something that wasn't about divorce, illness and dead dogs. They were a genial crowd, despite the dreary stuff we were playing, but I had the feeling they were getting restless.

The organiser sidled up to the wee guitarist again.

"Look, I hate to bother you but could you please play something fast? They really want to – "

"Away you and take a shite! We'll play what I fucking decide! We'll play fast songs when we're good and fucking ready!"

I quickly moved as far back as I could, expecting to see blood and teeth flying. Everyone in the crowd heard the wee guitarist yelling, and I waited for the man to throw us out the building. I wouldn't have blamed him. The guitar player's wife immediately began singing something fast. Quasimodo and I joined in, the guitarist glared at her then reluctantly played along.

At the break, I suggested to him that he'd perhaps been a bit rash.

"You got to watch these people. I used to be nice to them but it didn't work. I learned my lesson."

He briefly touched his nose, and a dark look flashed across his eyes.

I had already decided that I wouldn't play with them again; the people at the golf club had been great and his attitude to them was fucking embarrassing. A couple of days later he called me.

"My work has just told me I've to move to Bournemouth, so that's the last gig. Thanks, big fella, it was good playing with you. Try and find a band for Quasimodo will you? He's a good drummer but most people go by appearances, you know?"

16

JOHN GILSTON

When I had moved back to Glasgow after Mike Heron's band broke up, John Gilston moved to LA. We spoke on the telephone every week, we were like brothers. He had found it difficult at first because the standard of playing there was so high, but eventually he got noticed and became a top session player, working on Thriller, Flashdance, and with all sorts of big names.

So when he called and asked if I'd like to play with him in a band there with some other British musicians I couldn't get on the plane fast enough. I enjoyed playing bass with him and he reckoned we could easily pick up tours, which would be a lot of fun. Besides, I thought my sons would love growing up in sunny California, away from the rain of Glasgow, enjoying skateboarding and surfing rather than Rangers and Celtic wars.

It was a warm February evening when John picked me up at LAX and we grabbed some pizza on the way back to his lovely duplex apartment in Santa Monica. He was doing well, had loads of sessions to play. The next night we went to a rehearsal studio and I met the rest of the band. I can't remember who the singer or the guitarist were, although they were terrific. But it was the keyboard player – Nicky Hopkins – who really stood out. He had played with everyone, including the Rolling Stones. He's the piano player on *Imagine*.

I felt a bit out my depth; actually it was scary playing with session players this good. So I just concentrated on playing the bass parts nice and simple. I reckoned there were flash bass players on every street corner; these guys would have heard it all before.

John and I worked well together, and the rest of the band could hear that. When we'd played with the String Band we'd often spent hours at sound checks and after rehearsals jamming together and we always knew exactly what the other would do, we had all these wee accents and breaks and things up our sleeves. I loved Santa Monica, the relaxed feel of the place, the sunshine, the beach and the pier with the big sign on it. I'd had enough of running a removal business. It was time to get back to being a full time musician.

After a week I flew back to Glasgow and was about to tell my son he'd soon be starting a new school when I got the call.

John had drowned in Malibu.

17

THUNDERSOUP

And then there are corporate gigs.

Everyone does them, there's a lot of money in corporate gigs, even big stars like Rod Stewart and Elton John are not above sticking their snouts in that deep trough. If you have won the lottery, or are a banker, and you have several million quid to spare and would like Rod to do a wee private show in the comfort of your own home, just call his agent. If you can pay, I am sure he will play.

When the billionaire chairman of Ryanair, David Bonderman, was having a party, he thought nothing of giving the Stones $6 million to play for him and his pals at the Hard Rock Hotel in Vegas. For his 70th birthday party he booked Paul McCartney.

There was a famous Glaswegian couple, nouveux riche, as I believe the polite term has it, that even attempted to hire Frank Sinatra for their daughter's wedding. Of course, some of these little soirées take place at out-of-the-way locations, often the walled estates of rich geezers holed up in Marbella or Dubai. Guys whose wealth came easily and that have money to burn, if you get my drift.

A member of one famous band told me they were doing a gig for some well-tanned blokes in Spain, all of them lavishly tattooed, some with distinguished facial scars. The host informed them that his girlfriend, a barely-pubescent waif called Tracy or Cherisse or something, would be joining them to sing their biggest hit, her favourite song. They reckoned it best not to quibble.

Most corporate gigs are usually just staff parties, charity events, Christmas knees-up sort of things. As long as they don't want you to play for hours on end, they can be good fun. When the economy is good and businesses are making money, there are rich pickings to be had playing in Hiltons, Marriots and other large hotels at weekends. You have to play exactly what the punters want, wear a suit and tie, smile and move about the stage enthusiastically so you get them all up onto the floor, and keep the volume turned down. That last bit is really important. No one wants to dance to screaming, wailing, feedback-laden guitar playing or battering drum solos.

It's best to stick with things they all know, like *500 Miles* and that catchy tune by the Fratellis. *Brown Sugar* and *Rockin All Over the World* always go down well and no one ever seems to get tired of *Brown Eyed Girl*, except the band of course. It's not hard work. You also get to eat good grub at corporate gigs, especially desserts. These high-flying female execs didn't manage to squeeze into their little black dresses by wolfing down large helpings of gateaux and cream so there's usually plenty leftovers to scoff as long as you can beat the Polish waiters to it.

My sons were growing up fast, and the business was taking up more and more time. I had stopped playing stand-in gigs, there were too many unpredictable characters, but I was missing playing – if you are a musician, Saturday night just feels empty if you are not on a stage somewhere. I would have liked to put a band together, play some interesting stuff, but I just didn't have the time or patience. Semi pro bands take a huge amount of organising.

I wanted to play in a soul band, something with a good

brass section. This was not an easy task. Good horn players, as they are known, are usually in such demand that they are very sniffy about rehearsing. They want paid just to open their cases. And too many trumpet and sax players get upset when you ask them to stick to only the four or five notes that make up the brass parts in most of the great soul songs.

If you listen to Otis Redding, Sam and Dave, Wilson Pickett or any of these great artistes you may notice that the horn sections are playing very simple phrases, usually just little accents and patterns of a few notes – *the adjectives*. An awful lot of brass players don't seem to be able to hear this and insist on trying to tootle out free form jazz solos, which is a pain in the arse. Nobody, no matter how drunk, not even the most liquored-up double-glazing salesman can dance to that shit. Getting a couple of these jazz freaks to just play the solo from *My Girl* requires the tact of a bereavement councillor. Some of them think they are Miles bloody Davis.

Then you have to get gigs, not too many or the players just won't turn up, their wives will be bitching at them to spend Saturday night at home for a change, showing off their Ikea furniture to the neighbours over wine with cold cuts and canapés. Too few gigs, and the band forget each other's names and just drift apart. You also have to put in some rehearsal time and most musicians enjoy that as much as footballers like pre season training. You have to know you will be doing enough gigs to merit the time spent learning cues and chord changes and being oh so careful not to upset temperamental players' self esteem when they try to rearrange *Hold On I'm Coming* into some sort of jazz fusion nonsense.

On the other hand, you can't rehearse too often, everyone has day jobs and it is simply too much hassle to meet your weekly sales targets. After yet another gut-churning day of trying to outflank the competition it is so easy to slump in front of Sky Sports or play around on your laptop; you just don't feel like trailing off to a yet another rehearsal room. But corporate gigs pay well and you have to be reasonably well rehearsed – at least enough to make sure you are all playing in the same key.

I was missing playing regular gigs though, and thankfully someone came along and asked me to play bass with a corporate band that was picking up good jobs around town. It was an interesting band that had been formed by a charismatic property developer; a big guy who had played in the minor but tough rugby leagues. This combined with working on his building sites had given him hands like boxing gloves – he looked like he could have crushed bowling balls. He loved playing and he was good at organisation, happily doing the hard work of picking up gigs and all the tedious crap that goes with running a 12-piece band. He also had terrific contacts in top companies all over the place.

Most of the band were like him, rich kids from the exclusive suburbs. The other guitarist owned a large doss house, an old hotel filled with derelicts and meths drinkers. He stormed off after the singer asked him to play in the same key as everyone else – he wasn't used to being told what to do. The drummer was a nice guy, but always seemed to be keeping an eye out for debt collectors. Carol Smillie, who was a well known TV personality, sang with us. She was really nice and good fun.

We would rehearse once a week in the stone-floored barn of the builder's country mansion on the windswept edge of a bleak and lonely moor. His long driveway was always strewn with Jags, Mercs and Range Rovers. He often had houseguests who were well-known sports or television people. The band would nail down a few chord changes then he'd grin and tell us he was expecting company. While we drove back home across the dark moorland, he would slip into his large Jacuzzi with his famous friends and pop open the champagne. He knew how to enjoy life.

In winter his barn was the coldest place in the world.

I would play with gloves and a coat on. When anyone looked about to slip into a hypothermic state, he would fire up his industrial space heater. Within five minutes we would all be toasty but on the point of asphyxiation – the burner would consume all oxygen within a hundred yards.

Most bands have a real character in them, or they are pretty boring. This lot's shining star was Big Rory McCann. He was a good front man, who loved stage diving, even if there was a strong chance that the crowd would part like the Red Sea – the sight of six foot six, 17 stone Rory flying through the air was pretty daunting.

He would do absolutely anything for a laugh, was always getting into scrapes. He once tried cutting down trees for a living but had to leave town fast after chain sawing every second tree at a nice house called Beech Tree Cottage. He had misunderstood the owner's instructions to cut down every *other* tree, the ones which weren't beech. So the place was now just called Tree Cottage.

His big goal in life was to be a Hollywood star, and, specifically, the next James Bond. He was prepared to starve to make it in the movie business, and often did. He was picking up as much acting work as he could find, including a few television commercials. Then he graduated to a couple of TV soap-type series before hitting gold with Oliver Stone and a speaking part in the movie *Alexander*. He would spend the day filming battle scenes in the desert.

"It was terrifying. The place was full of bloody great elephants charging all around us. People would get hyped up with adrenaline and fear of these animals. A lot of the extras were headcases, guys who loved to fight, there were real battles every day".

Every night Rory would drink expensive booze with the cast until five in the morning, grab a few hours shut-eye, and get back to it. At the end of the shoot, the stars went back to their mansions but Rory was penniless – he'd blown all his pay for the movie on drink and other stimulants. He ended up in Glencoe, living rough, surviving on nothing. Then he heard there was work in Iceland, so he went there and lived in a tent scavenged from a campsite – "most people just abandoned their gear at the end of their holiday".

He managed to pick up enough equipment to survive an Icelandic winter's blizzards and sub zero temperatures. This is one of the things I love about playing in bands – you don't get to meet guys like Rory working in a Call Centre.

One night we were playing a very posh gig on the west coast of Scotland, some sort of sailing regatta. The crowd were all rich folk, our bandleader knew a lot of these people. For some reason, one of them seemed to have taken a dislike to Rory and kept taunting him throughout our set. Maybe he had seen him chat up his girlfriend or perhaps it was something to do with the Scott's Porage TV advert Rory had done. The guy was big, looked like he might have broken bones for a living. I avoided eye contact with him, played through the set, knowing there was unlikely to be a happy ending.

The drunk kept shouting at Rory, yelling in the middle of songs, tossing plastic bottles at him. He was a real pain, and the crowd was starting to get pissed off. He wouldn't shut up, standing right in front of the stage, stuffed into white sailing trousers and white silk shirt, like some sort of hulking mutant. Rory kept his cool, biding his time. Near the end of the set, the guy lurched off to one of the portaloos off to the side of the stage. As soon as he'd closed the door, Rory leapt off the stage, ran to the portaloo, waited a moment, and then pushed it over.

There was a godawful scream from inside.

Howling like a banshee, the guy crawled out of the portaloo, his eyes blazing. Every turd that had been dropped in that toilet had spilled on him and dirty ribbons of tissue paper were plastered all over his nice white clothes. He was covered in shit. His hair had piss dripping from it. He ran around in circles, apoplectic, screaming that he would kill whoever had done it. Rory was innocently back onstage singing *Mustang Sally* as if nothing had happened.

We played a lot of good gigs together before breaking up, acrimoniously as always. Bands always fall out sooner or later, it is one of the axioms of the music business. One of the last times we played was an end of term gig at Jordanhill College in Glasgow. I told this story in another book but I like it so I'm telling it again. I had been working all week, rushing around like a scalded cat, and had already done a corporate gig with the band at a hotel in the town. After playing for three solid hours we finished at about midnight. As soon as we had loaded our gear, we raced to the marquee set up in the grounds of the college. It was two in the morning before we went on and I was knackered.

It was sauna hot, the place dripping with sweat. It was a wild night; the students were seriously up for it, every one of them pissed out their heads on Red Bull and vodka. A fat girl was standing just below me at the front of the stage and when we blasted into the last song of the night, *Sweet Home Chicago*, she went crazy, lifting her dress up and swaying her arse like a stripper. Then she tore her bra off, jumped onstage and started to dance right next to me. She shouted something at me but with all the noise – there were twelve musicians belting it out – I only caught one word – *bed*.

Fuck's sake, I laughed, *she wants to go to bed. This is just like the old days.* I felt like I was twenty again. At last we finished the song and above all the yelling and cheering I asked her what she had said.

With the sort of sympathetic look she might give her weary old father, she patted my arm and said, "You look like you should be home in your bed."

18

KIM BEACON BAND

Can I wander down this wee side street for a minute?
It has always fascinated me that so many great musicians wrote their best stuff when they were teenagers, or not much older. Glenn Frey began composing *Desperado* before he was 20 and finished it with Don Henley a few years later. Living in sunny California, surrounded by blonde and beautiful, gloriously-tanned long-limbed girls, where did they get the insight to write: *Your prison is walking through this world all alone* ?

Or Mick and Keith, who must have been having the time of their lives, lapping up all that the swinging 60s had to offer yet somehow understood how it felt to *watch the girls go by dressed in their summer clothes*, having to *turn my head until my darkness goes.*

And way back in 1966, how was smiling, thumbs-up Paul able to create *Eleanor Rigby*? What could he possibly have known about loneliness? It says in a few haunting moments as much as a thousand-page book; it will still be played in a hundred years. It is almost as if these guys get some kind of advance insight from their later lives, as if flashes of all the knowledge they will ever possess is somehow given to them when they are young.

I've known successful businessmen like that who had an

unshakable conviction that they knew exactly the path to follow at a very early age, as if they knew the numbers to play on the lottery, and never wavered in their careers, no matter how much advice they got to the contrary. On the other hand, I've known a lot that had the same self-belief and failed spectacularly, like a warbling *X Factor* contender.

Journalists who take music very seriously have remarked that only a few bands do anything worth listening to after the members reach about 25 or so, probably the age most musicians start to wise up and get a grip on themselves, that sobering moment when you realise the hellish hangovers last far longer than the sparkling highs. Many musicians have wondered if their creativity dried up *because* they stopped behaving like cavemen, and some try to recapture the glorious confidence of their youth by retracing their steps to white powder and tequila. It's always a mistake. When your body has had enough of that lifestyle, it tells you very clearly. Only a fool doesn't take heed. But where do these great rock songs come from?

Quite a few songwriters believe the songs somehow already exist and they are just channelling them from somewhere else. Keith Richards said that he didn't reckon anyone actually composes great songs. He seemed to be saying that some people can "put up an antenna", perhaps like spiritualists. Joe Walsh and other musicians reckon that old guitars have songs in them, especially if they belonged to guys like Buddy Holly. When Bob Dylan heard Van Morrison sing *Tupelo Honey,* he remarked the song had always been there and that Van was merely the earthly vehicle for it.

Many young musicians think that drugs are an essential part of the life of an international rock star. It has been pointed out that probably almost all great rock songs were written while under the influence of hash or heroin, cocaine or alcohol. Who knows? Perhaps they were. Maybe if all our greedy politicians and bankers had just said yes when they were young and inhaled some herb we would be living in a happier world.

So perhaps drugs, especially those that are just natural plant life, are Nature's wee way of helping composers tune into the cosmos. Perhaps future generations will wonder why we passed laws that created a brutal criminal world, and will use drugs much like we use Starbucks. When athletes use clever substances, sports records can be easily broken, they can sprint like scalded cats. It would be very interesting to see a Drugs-R-Us Olympics, just to see how fast some of these people could run.

But if drugs do help the composers, why do so few musicians write anything worth listening to by the time they are only halfway through their 20s? Why don't they get better as they get older? Many of them keep taking dope all their lives. I have seen members of a well-known American band spark up a joint at a friend's house in front of his kids. These guys were over 50, but they were so used to smoking wacky baccy that it never even occurred to them that not everyone wants his 8-year-old breathing in clouds of Acapulco Gold. Maybe they wrote their best songs when they were young *in spite* of drugs and not because of them. Perhaps it's like saying the reason Tiger Woods was a great golfer was because he was shagging loads of women.

I'm sure anyone who can play a few chords can come up with some sort of song, but writing really good ones, the kind that you feel you instantly know, is a gift not given to many. Then again, some songs that are really popular might just be using 'golden' note combinations. For example, songs written for films often use octaves to create a feeling of drama, like the Star Wars theme and the music from Titanic. For centuries, classical composers have known about the mystical Circle of Fifths. But if it were as easy as that everyone would be writing them.

One guy I played with who definitely had the gift was Kim

Beacon. I saw an ad in the List magazine, a popular Central Scotland what's-on paper aimed at bright young professionals who would have money to spend on fancy meals in back-alley restaurants and enjoy watching subtitled French films, ones without car chases and big explosions. I used to like reading the lonely-hearts column because it was funny. *Woman seeks man, any old bloke will do. Good-looking fireman, well built, loves cooking, cleaning and ironing, seeks woman who doesn't mind a man who lies a little. Woman, 40, outgoing and bubbly – yes that does mean I'm fat, but if I wasn't I wouldn't need to do this.* I think some of the ads were posted just for a laugh, maybe even by the staff at the mag. *Woman, 82, very optimistic, seeks guy for long-term relationship.* A lot of the ads said that the lonely seeker did not drink. Eh, perhaps that's why you're all alone. Get down the pub!

I noticed an ad in the Musicians Wanted column: *Bass player for rock/soul band playing original material.* I was onto it like a shot. I had been working daft hours, building my wee company, was finding it hard going, and wanted to get out playing, give me something to think about other than people screaming about the packing materials for their removal not being delivered at precisely 8.30am. And playing original songs would be great, not the same old covers of chart hits and Tamla classics. As long as the songs were good. Fingers crossed.

The guy who answered the phone was called Maurice, and he invited me to hear what the band would be doing. He was living with his son Kim in a shabby rented flat in a district of Glasgow packed with people who knew they were just passing through and so didn't worry about the hazards of tossing rubbish out of the window. I picked my way through generously filled disposable nappies and abandoned mattresses in the street, recognised the unmistakeable aroma of *eau de piss* in the hallway of the crumbling tenement, and climbed the worn, dark stairs to Maurice's door.

Kim was about 40, a wiry sort of guy, shaved head, spoke with a strong London accent, and had restless, suspicious eyes, like an ex-convict. When he was young he'd played football, almost making it as a pro, before quitting to concentrate on music. He played me some of the songs he'd written and my spine tingled. He had a great voice, very soulful, with just the right amount of harsh edge to it. The songs were in different keys, so he had a good range – some singers can only sing in one or two keys.

His songs were terrific. If you listen to the usual stuff that would-be song writers come up with and then play a well known rock song right after it, the difference is so obvious that all but the most deluded realise they should stick to their day job. You could play many of the Stones or Little Feat tracks beside Kim's songs and his would stand up just fine. What was this guy doing here? I couldn't believe he hadn't made the big time.

Ah, well, he had. When he was young he'd toured with a band that had been signed to Chrysalis, then when Peter Gabriel had left Genesis he'd been asked to sing with them – his voice was something else. Kim should have been living in a mansion in Surrey by now, spending his days wheeching round a track in racing cars and attending vintage wine auctions, but he'd blown his career by chasing the dragon.

When he was young, living in London and on the verge of becoming a rock star, a lot of musicians used to smoke heroin. It was easy to do, much safer than injecting but just as addictive. Kim had clambered down onto that endless underground train, and his youth had vanished in pursuit of the unattainable high. Many junkies will tell you that their first high was the best they ever had, and all they were doing afterwards was trying to recapture that first moment. Which is why it was called chasing the dragon – they could never catch it.

Kim said he was writing songs much more easily now he

was 'clean'. When he was hooked on heroin all he had wanted was the next fix; now he was spending all his time on music. His Dad was managing his band, and wanted to do everything he could to help him. I loved the songs and arranged to rehearse with the band. Kim gave me a tape of the songs we'd be playing and I went off to learn them.

I turned up at the rehearsal room a few days later and immediately realised that Kim's way of staying off heroin was staying on alcohol. He lurched into the room, eyes glazed, breath stinking, fag hanging from his mouth, barely able to stay on his feet. The rest of the band seemed used to it. I looked at him and wondered what the hell I'd got myself into; I had a difficult enough time quitting alcohol and cigarettes myself.

Kim picked up a battered old Telecaster he'd borrowed from a pal, somehow plugged it into an amp, fiddled around with the controls as he swayed above it. He staggered up to a microphone, holding the stand for balance. *Eh guys, I was standing at the bus stop and I've come up with this idea.* And then he played the most sensual, most dirty, most swampy rock I'd ever heard close up.

This used to happen almost every rehearsal. The whole band would just stare then we'd all jump on it, excitedly finding parts we could play. It was a great thing to see songs born like that. You couldn't help loving the guy. I really enjoyed the gigs we played together. But time and life ran out for him; he never made the gold album he was so capable of making. Some time later he was found dead.

Rock music has always had this image of stoned and drunk musicians – Keith Richards was once described as being 'the world's most elegantly wasted human being.' But he's probably the best rhythm guitar player that ever lived and it's hard to imagine how he could pull that off night after night if he was out of it.

Most pro musicians I've met live disciplined lives; when

they are on tour it just isn't possible to get rat arsed every night any more than it would be for an office worker – and touring is far more demanding. The crowd might be high, but only that one night, they don't have to travel 500 miles to the next town and do it all again tomorrow.

It's such a shame that Kim, and so many talented people like him, didn't figure that out.

19

DARKWATER

I had often been asked to manage bands, but wasn't interested. The only reason I offered to manage Darkwater was because my son played bass in the band and co-wrote all their songs. He was putting all his time and energy into it but without breaking free of the pay-to-play pub circuit. It seemed to me that since I had plenty of business experience, as well as playing in bands for most of my life, that I could help, especially since I had no thought of making any money out of them.

My son was very reluctant to let me get involved, and I could completely understand why. Go to any unsigned band night at those half-empty pubs all over the country and there is no sadder sight that the parents of the band members cheering on their offspring. Rock music used to be about parents and sons ditching each other, dads yelling down the street at their departing sons to get an education. Watching these doting parents idolizing their kids is, frankly, fucking embarrassing. But if a band is going to have any chance of making it, they need to use every possible asset they have. So it was agreed I would manage his band until someone else came along who could take over. I would get them as far as I could then I'd be happy to step aside.

If you are ever asked to manage a band you must expect

two things: you will work harder than you have ever done in your life, and it will cost you a fortune. It is like being chained to a roulette wheel; it might be wise just to give them about half of your worldly goods and walk away. It will be cheaper. You may have guessed that already. But it is so worth it, every last penny. It is the most exciting thing you will ever do, especially if the band *almost* makes it. It will probably cost about the same as it would to climb Mount Everest, but is much more fun – I mean when you've climbed one mountain…

As part of managing the band, one of the jobs you will happily do, and probably the most exhausting one of your life, is tour managing. Most tours would grind to a halt within a few gigs without a tour manager. He (or she) is responsible for making sure the band gets from one gig to another on time, that no-one gets lost along the way, that expenses are paid and any payments that might be due (ha!) are collected. The tour manager must make sure the stars are eating properly, and generally keep the show on the road. It is usually a thankless task and many tour managers become cynical, bitter and twisted long before their time. If you ever see some guy in a worn leather jacket having a lonely drink in a hotel bar while he sits hunched over a laptop and a pile of soggy receipts, muttering and swearing under his breath, then you'll know what he does for a living.

Young aspiring rock stars are usually full of energy, or something that gives them energy, and can never sleep in the 6 hours following a gig. When they should be resting, getting ready for the 200-mile drive in the morning to the next gig, they gather in their hotel rooms, eat pizza, drink, and some even smoke little cigarettes, on at least one occasion setting off all the hotel's fire alarms, forcing over 100 startled and shivering guests to be evacuated to the freezing car park at 3am. Sometimes when they do fall asleep, they forget they have left the bath running; it overflows and drenches the room below and they wonder why Travelodge do not see the funny side of it.

And of course part of the tour manager's job is to blag guest passes to any gig that the band want to see, and you really would think that certain people would remember that a certain tour manager arranged for him to meet his hero, a certain guitar player called Slash. Yes, you would think so.

After a while you will be so tense with nervous energy yet so tired you will have trouble remembering your name. This does not apply to the band. Since the only thing the band members have to do after a gig is to relax, have a good night's sleep and be refreshed and ready in their hotel rooms waiting for the tour manager's cheery knock, you really would think they would make your life easy. But oh no.

Sometimes, as in the case of some singers, they are unable to manage 24 hours on tour without arranging to meet yet another Facebook 'friend' and disappear into the night, let's say for example, in the bloody Midlands. Next morning you are going nuts trying to track them down because the band has a really important gig booked at a festival and if they do well it could mean all sorts of good things but if they don't turn up all the weeks you spent pleading, begging and grovelling to scaffy wee fat promoters to get them the fucking spot on the fest will be wasted and worse – they will likely be banned from all such future gigs, because word gets around really fast especially among scaffy wee fat promoters, and nobody cares how cute the singer's little friend was that night or how the singer was horny to the point it became a medical necessity to get laid. And why the hell didn't the singer just call to say where they were? That was why the good Lord invented mobile phones, but they are not much bloody use if you don't switch them on, are they? And when the singer finally did call, you have to drive an extra 40 miles to collect them, with all the pressure that comes with racing across the country like an escaping maniac and barging through miles of traffic to reach the festival site in time for the band's slot– *and just get changed into your fucking gig clothes in the fucking van will you and don't you DARE light that cos at the speed I'm going I'm a cert to get pulled by the cops.* Is it a big surprise that sometimes you, the tour manager, get just a teensy weensie bit stressed?

And you wonder why the hell you are doing it, and then they play a set that is just stunning, the crowd goes nuts and you know why.

It's not all stress, there are exceptionally happy days when the road-gods smile on you. Sometimes it works out better than you could ever have hoped, like when by a sheer fluke the very cheap hotel you have booked for the band near the Shepherds Bush Empire, for example, had rented its basement to a porn film company to shoot lesbian love and the place was full of half-naked nymphets waiting for their cues. And they didn't mind in the least the band hanging around watching them. So of course you take full credit for arranging that little breakfast treat. That kind of thing makes the tour manager very popular, for a day or so at least.

So I was tour-managing Darkwater and they were playing at the O2 Academy in Newcastle. The singer was a Geordie so there was a big home crowd. Things were going awfully well. The band finished their set, the crowd roared for more, they played another couple of songs and headed back to the dressing room, very pleased with their night's work. I was manning the merch stand, selling their tee shirts, cds, all the goodies that would provide the ready cash to chow down a massive *Empire Breakfast* at the Happy Eater next day. A very nice woman came up to me with her 12-year-old son. She smiled at me.

"It's his first ever gig."

I remembered the first gig I went to. I told her. It was the Rolling Stones. You never forget your first gig. We grinned at one another; her first had been Roxy Music. How the time has flown.

The young lad seemed very shy. I smiled at him, gave him

a couple of guitar picks with the band's name on them.

His mother said, "He'd like to buy a souvenir. Something to remember the gig by."

I still had my Stones programme. In a cupboard, somewhere, but I knew I had it. He was looking at one of Darkwater's cds. I handed him it.

He looked up at me as though I was Santa. I had been exactly like that when I was his age, so excited to see a real live band.

"What's your name?"

"David."

"Ok, David, would you like me to get it signed for you?"

He turned to his mother, his eyes sparkling. I thought for a moment. What could I do that would be really special for the wee guy? And then I knew, I could let him meet not only Darkwater, but the headline band, Hayseed Dixie. That would really give him something to tell his pals at school.

As soon as I saw the look on his mother's face I knew I had said the wrong thing.

"David, would you like to come backstage with me?"

20

THE REZILLOS

Motorbikes and rock music go together. Where would motorbikes be without Elvis, Easy Rider, Bruce Springsteen and even the very talented Shangri La's? They were one of the first girl-groups, when the Spice Girls were just the sperm girls, and had a hit called *Leader of the Pack,* a cheery little tune about a young lassie who falls for the devil-may-care, rugged good looks of a biker lad. Unfortunately their romance was not to be; his speeding motorcycle crashed in the sunset. Great pop music, none of that *Puppy Love* shit.

Personally I hate motorbikes, they give me the heebie jeebies. I've been on one, a helpless and defenceless passenger hurtling along an early-morning city road at just below a hundred miles an hour, knowing with absolute terrified clarity that if the front wheel hit as much as a pebble there would be absolutely no chance; they would have to use a hose to get what was left of me off the pavement. There's a point where a motorbike becomes a guided missile. Ever since, the nearest I've been to one is listening to *Born to Run* while skiing in the Alps. I reckon even if I soared off a cliff by mistake I'd still have a better chance of surviving.

Maybe I'm just a big jessie – many musicians love these contraptions. In the 80s, one of the most successful of the punky, new wavey sort of bands was a group called the Rezillos.

The founder, who played under the name Eugene, loves motorbikes, as I was soon to discover.

I was having a great time managing Darkwater and working longer hours than I had ever put into anything in my life, even when I employed an army of desperadoes in the moving business. I would climb into bed late every night after another long session of phone calls and e mails and couldn't wait for the alarm to go off early next morning so I could start again. I spent endless hours badgering agents, promoters and band managers to give them a support slot – I would check all the upcoming tours and start dialling. I had already managed to talk Darkwater onto two tours playing Carling Academies all over the country and noticed the Rezillos were about to do a reunion tour, playing the same venues. They were old enough to be the parents of the crowds we were aiming for, but I figured it would be a good tour for Darkwater. They would hopefully be able to pull in a lot of the people they had played to on the previous tours and this would impress the local promoters, exactly the people we needed to get to.

When bands do tours, they are usually organised by an agent who farms out the gigs to local promoters. These guys are one of the magical keys to getting a band signed by a record label. If a band is creating a buzz, the promoters are often the first people to tip off the labels. And so I added the Rezillos to my target list and tracked them down. Eugene, real name Alan, was still playing in the band and managing it. After speaking to him a few times he invited me to his home on the outskirts of Edinburgh to meet him and the band's energetic singer, Fay Fife.

It was a cold winter night and it took me a wee while to find Alan's home, a very secluded building down a dark country lane, probably a former farmhouse or something. He was very friendly, and took me into a converted barn in which he repaired old motorcycles. He excitedly showed me a row of

Indian bikes in various stages of being dismantled and reassembled. Indian Bikes are an iconic name and were manufactured in Springfield, Massachusetts until about 1953. They are metal horses, the sort of roaring machine used by Steve McQueen to jump over fences and things. To many bike nuts, they have far more charisma – *mojo* – than any other brand, even Harleys.

Alan is one of the world's top Indian restorers, and when he talked of trawling the internet to find any for sale his eyes sparkled. He had just returned from a trip to the frozen far north of Denmark where he had bought a bike from some old farmer. He had travelled there by plane, train and bus with his toolkit. The bike was a mess, but he had been able to get it going and ridden it all the way down to Copenhagen before shipping it to Edinburgh.

I have no liking for oily old engines, and ran a trucking company for enough years never, ever again to want to see a crankshaft or a bearing again, whatever they might be, but I am fascinated by people like Alan, guys that spend their lives doing something completely different than most people. He loved these bikes, and he was not alone; he mentioned that Tom Cruise had ordered one from him.

Fay arrived, and we went upstairs to Alan's office. Fay is also a character. As YouTube clips from *Top of The Pops* in the 80s will show, she was a star, no doubt about it. Alan told me that there was a lot of interest in the band but he had too much on his plate to be running it. They needed a manager. He had been impressed with my enthusiasm for Darkwater, and the gigs and tours I'd got them. Would I be interested in managing the Rezillos?

I was flattered but told them I doubted I could do much for them. I told them that although I was happy managing Darkwater it was really only a temporary thing. As soon as a record label or manager came along I would hand over to them.

"Well if you are prepared to manage us, we'll take Darkwater on the road as our support band."

I told them I would get back to them; that I was really a musician and wanted to get back to playing. I hadn't really planned on being involved in band management for any length of time.

"What do you play?"

"Bass and guitar. Either. I'm ambidextrous," I grinned.

Alan and Fay looked at each other.

"Interesting. We're having trouble with our bass player. We're going to have to replace him. Would you be interested?"

Definitely.

A week later we had another meeting with the other founder member of the band, Jo Callis, at his flat in Edinburgh. Jo had co-written the Human League's song, *Don't You Want Me Baby,* and since it had been picked up by an ad on television it was enjoying a surge in sales, the benefits of which were being spent on the classy interior decoration work being done in Jo's apartment. It was very nice to see someone making a few quid out of music for a change. We had coffee and the band told me about their history, how way back in 1978 they had been signed to the same label as Talking Heads and the Ramones; it had all been going wonderfully well with huge sales for their debut album and a world tour set up.

The thing about strong personalities is that clashes are inevitable, especially in the white-hot heat of touring. When bands sense they are on that launch pad to greatness, emotions run high, they know that they could be only days or weeks from the big time and all the glittering prizes that go with it. And so, six gigs into the tour, ambition, anger, frustration and differing ideas collided in one awful moment, the band imploded and that was more or less that.

Since then, Fay and Alan had gigged together many times in differing line-ups; Jo had toured with Human League.

And now here they were back together. I was excited that I could be a part of this. They were planning a new album, and let me hear what they had recorded so far. It was very good, but I asked if they would be doing their hit songs when they toured.

"Well, we want to do new material. We think we can appeal to a whole new young audience. Kurt Cobain is quoted as saying we were an influence, and..."

I began to feel uncomfortable. There are many bands from the 70s and 80s that are still great to watch, but the last thing most crowds want to hear is new songs. And – how could I put this? Eh, without being unkind, although Fay is still a very attractive woman with boundless charisma and energy, how many 16-year-olds are going to have, eh, bedtime fantasies about a woman almost old enough to be their granny?

I suggested that it might be wise to include the big hits in the tour, which was due to start soon with a warm up gig in a small venue in Perth. I also asked them about the new songs they were recording – did they have a label that would release them?

They had some sort of arrangement with a record company, but someone needed to contact them and sort out exactly what it was. They also had an agent, but the record label seemed to be involved in that too. The bass player was saying he was going to quit, he had a business to run and had very little spare time, but it seemed like he would do the tour. To me it all sounded very complicated, but worth the effort it would take to sort out. They said they would like me to play bass with them, but the tour was so close they wanted to keep the line up as it was for these gigs. I agreed that seemed sensible.

A week later, Darkwater opened for them in Perth. When the Rezillos came on I could see right away why they had been so successful. They played a great mix of glam-rock and punk in a very over-the-top theatrical way. It was great, they were very exciting. Fay was one of the best performers I've ever seen. Perhaps teenagers would have fantasies about her after all. Suddenly I was very excited about the idea of managing them.

And so the tour got underway. I spent a lot of time working Darkwater's merch stand, doing everything I could to help them, and agreed to start managing the Rezillos as soon as the tour was finished.

I started the following month, January. Alan gave me a list of their contacts. They did not have a band email address, and their website needed a lot of work. My son designed a new one for them, and I set up a Rezillos email account and started firing off messages. It soon became clear that there was a lot of good feeling towards the band, although this was mixed with caution: they were known to have a low flash point. But it was fascinating to see the difference between helping to re-establish a well-known band and attempting to break an unsigned one. In the case of Darkwater, even trying to speak to an agent or promoter took weeks and a huge amount of persistence, but within days of my sending out e mails, the Rezillos were being offered tours of America, Australia, Japan, the UK... they still had a big following. For a moment I thought that perhaps this might be a lot easier than I had imagined.

Each member of the band had careers in other things, and the drummer lived in Germany where he was a successful architect. Before I could confirm any dates I had to email each member of the band for their approval on the date, the venue, whether the band would be headlining, and other things, like how much money they'd be paid – they said if they were going to take time off work to do gigs it needed to be worth it. Sometimes four members would agree and one would be unavailable so a new date would be suggested and I'd fire off another bunch of emails. These would then meet with different responses; sometimes a member would be annoyed that another one was refusing to play on a particular date and they would start digging in their heels. Very quickly it began to get tricky. I could see there was the real danger of a big fall out; I would have to be very patient.

I spent hours on the telephone. Days. Weeks. But I enjoyed it. After a month or so, things were shaping up. A UK tour later in the year, an American tour coming together, some gigs in Japan, the record label and the agent agreeing who would do what, release date set for a new album, we were making progress. The one thing any band manager needs to keep in mind is that most musicians like to be kept informed, preferably on a daily basis, of exactly what you are doing to further their careers. I was well aware of this. Musicians' careers are their lives, and are all most of them think about. If you ask a musician how he is doing he'll never tell you if he is well, he'll immediately start talking about a tour he is about to play, or an album he is going to record. It makes a change from people moaning about their sore backs or what they'd like to do to their boss. So I made sure I sent progress reports to each person.

The bass player was still hanging in there. When a band member just doesn't want to be in a band any longer it's time to move on, it's not like staying in a boring desk job for the pension at the end. The band had told me that he kept threatening to quit; there was a lot of tension. It seemed to me that they were spending far too much time bitching about this. Every band has been through a situation where one member falls out with the rest and it becomes a 'them and us' situation, it's always difficult.

The bass player's brother was also involved in the group, as their soundman and recording engineer, and was working really hard for them. He'd done a good job on the new album. I was keen to play bass with them but I wasn't going to push it; I told Alan that I would only do it if the bass player quit.

I carried on working for the band, putting in a lot of time.

They had no money to pay a manager, or they might have hired someone with more experience than me. But I was happy to do it. I love skiing, so after a couple of months decided to go to Italy for five days.

I had just finished the first run when Alan called.

"The bass player has quit. We had a big row and he says he's never playing with us again. We're having a full rehearsal on Saturday. The drummer is flying in from Germany. He wants to hear you play the songs."

I should, of course, have learned all the songs long before now, especially since the bass playing on Rezillos songs is not easy – it is precise and very fast. On songs that have been chart hits you need to play the exact parts on the record, you can't just busk along or make up new parts. I had been so busy with management work that I hadn't got around to it. But I was 8,000 feet up an Italian mountain. I kicked myself; I should have learned the damn songs long before now!

I got back from the ski trip late on the night before the rehearsal, and grabbed the band's cd. I listened carefully to the bass parts and began figuring them out. Some musicians are great at doing this; I'm not, it takes me a while. So I had a choice. I could do the professional thing, which was to start by nailing the hardest song note for note, or I could learn as many of their songs as possible and do the really tough one or two when I had more time. And when I wasn't completely knackered after skiing my brains out all week.

Next morning I turned up at the rehearsal room, a little place near Edinburgh, at the edge of a frozen field. We played through most of the band's songs and it went well. Alan asked me to play one of the more difficult ones, and I felt stupid saying I hadn't quite learned it yet. But the rehearsal was good, and it was great to play with them. Even in the little room, Fay put in a huge amount of energy, leaping about, getting right in there. She's good.

After the rehearsal we headed for a pub dinner. They told me they'd fallen out with the bass player and would definitely not work with him again, his business was taking up too much time, so yes, I would be playing on the next gigs which would be the UK tour. I was very pleased, especially since this was their decision and I had not done anything to force it.

Every day I set aside time to practise the bass parts. I made sure I had them perfectly and continued doing management work. There was a lot to be done, I reckoned the band could do really well if it actually got out and played, especially in America and Japan. The offers of tours were coming in thick and fast, but it was difficult to find dates that the whole band would agree to do. My telephone bill was frightening, but I figured it would be worth it in the end. I was so looking forward to playing with a pro headline band again.

We also had a few gigs arranged in Brazil, where the band seemed to have a following, and a couple of good contacts. Then Alan called and told me the bass player had changed his mind; he wanted to play these dates, wanted to go to São Paulo. Alan asked if I'd be ok about that, and promised that I would start playing bass on the very next tour. Definitely.

I decided to call the bass player and had a long, friendly chat with him. He knew that the band had spoken to me about taking over on bass, and he was happy about that. He told me that he enjoyed playing with them, but he had a business to run and needed to focus on that. He said that after the Brazil gigs he would call it a day. I had fancied playing these with the band, because I've never been there, but fair enough, I didn't mind.

After more weeks of working 14-hour days, I decided to take a day off and went to climb a Scottish mountain, as often I do. Near the top, my phone rang. It was Fay. She wanted a meeting in Edinburgh that night. Was it about anything in particular? She would tell me when I got there.

This sounded ominous. We were due to start the UK tour in just over a month. We hadn't been able to rehearse, everyone was too busy with their jobs. Were they having second thoughts? Were they going to blow out the tour? That would be bad. Climbing mountains is kind of tiring but I raced back to Glasgow, jumped in the shower, and charged through to meet her and Alan. They both smiled and thanked me for coming at such short notice.

Fay spoke. "We wanted to meet for a progress report."

I was puzzled.

"Everything's coming together well, I e-mailed you all yesterday."

"Yes, but I don't always get my emails. I wanted us to talk over things."

I was tired, and felt a rush of annoyance at being summoned like this, especially when I had sent everything to them. But I went over all that I had done, the agreements I had reached with the agent and record label, the tours that were confirmed, the ones about which I was still in negotiations.

They were very pleased.

"Now there's just one thing. The tour we're starting in a couple of weeks, well, the drummer called to say he can't do it. We have to get someone else to cover for him. Now we know you are supposed to be playing bass on the tour, but we can't have two new people starting at the same time, it's too difficult, so we've asked the old bass player to do it. But don't worry, you will definitely play on the tours later this year."

I felt like an idiot. I knew I was very tired from climbing, so should keep calm, not say what I felt like saying. We had a coffee and a friendly chat. I went back to Glasgow. I'd been really looking forward to touring again with a well-known band, but quit next day.

And that was that.

21

MARSHA HUNT 1

August in Scotland can be miserably wet but often it is sun-baked – I'm not kidding, sometimes we have fabulous weather. I've known summer days when I only needed to wear two fleeces. But always, rain or shine, it has the Edinburgh Fringe Festival, the biggest and best entertainment show in the world. Every kind of comedian, play, and music imaginable; they all start here and some go on to achieve greatness.

I love wandering around the beautiful architecture of the old town, going from one show to another, many of them held in fascinating little venues that lie dusty and dark the rest of the year. Edinburgh is a genteel, cup and saucer sort of place, but in August it really lets its hair down and opens doors to places you would normally never see.

I always go to as many different shows as possible. Most of them last exactly one hour so even a bad one doesn't take up too much of your life. Some venues, such as the old Assembly Rooms on George Street, can usually be relied upon to have a high standard; Charles Dickens and Sir Walter Scott did gigs there, so it has quite some history. Even if the show is disappointing the carved wood staircases and corniced ceilings are nice to look at – I enjoy staring at them and wondering how many people over the centuries have passed time in the building, staring at the same woodwork, perhaps wondering if people in the future like me will...yeah, some shows can be boring.

I was at a chat show given by an ex-roadie of the Animals, a guy who had toured with them way back in the 60s during the British invasion of America. It must have been a fantastic experience for working class English boys to be treated like royalty in the land of dreams, and he certainly talked nostalgically about it; I got the feeling his life after the 60s had been an anti climax, perhaps back to the building sites or working as a plumber. He was yapping about how he used to round up willing girls for the band – *goin' fishing, like,* as he called it.

He was bragging about how it was actually him who had played that great guitar part on House of The Rising Sun, about the various Hollywood stars that had invited him to play golf, and, in the case of one famous actress, to join her for indoor athletics. It was all a bit sad. I've known a lot of wee fat roadies and all rock bands depend on their skills, but I doubt that Dean Martin really would have invited a sweaty Geordie with a chain of keys and screwdrivers hanging from his belt to join him for a round of golf at California's finest courses. I suppose it is faintly possible that there might have been a glamorous diva who wanted his body for a bit of rough but in my experience roadies usually got the girls even the drummers didn't want, which is a frightening picture. The stars he claimed to have been great pals with were all dead, so I guess he was on safe ground. Until he started on about Jimi Hendrix.

He announced that Jimi had been murdered by his manager. The wee roadie spoke quietly, confidentially. It had been done to collect a huge insurance payout. He said that the manager had told him the whole story at the time but he had been too afraid to say anything until tonight, 40 years later, when the villain was also safely dead.

Aye, right.

I looked around. Many of the audience seemed to be swallowing this tale, possibly the same willing souls who believe Elvis is still alive – the sort of cheery folk that timeshare salesmen dream about walking into their offices. The hall was hushed, the crowd listening politely. All of a sudden there was a commotion at the back of the room, and a small, frail black woman stood up. She spoke loud and clear. Everyone turned to stare at her.

"I can't listen to this rubbish any longer. This man...this man is lying."

Fringe shows are known for their unpredictability, and audience 'plants' are common, but for once this didn't seem to be part of the act. She was almost lost in the darkness at the back of the room and looked tiny, not much taller when she was standing than the people sitting in front of her. But her voice was powerful.

"My name is Marsha Hunt. I knew Jimi Hendrix and what this man is saying about him just isn't true. Don't believe a word of it."

There's an old Glaswegian word – *sherrackin*. It means to be publicly harangued, given a showing up, have your misdeeds mercilessly exposed to all. Traditionally it might have happened when a fair Gorbals maiden had been impregnated by some smooth-talking Romeo in the back close of a dark tenement building and she would seek the support of the community in condemning him. If he didn't stand by the girl he'd get a 'right doin'.

Of course, Edinburgh is far too refined for such undignified behaviour, but Marsha certainly ruined whatever the guy had planned for a finale. The show pretty much drooped to a close as the amused crowd wandered out, leaving him with a pile of unsold books. It was great entertainment, typical of the Fringe.

On the way out of the building I turned a corner and there

was Marsha in front of me.

"Hey Marsha, how are you? That took nerve."

She took my arm. She was shaking.

"Oh hello…eh, could you walk me along the road a bit?" She looked over her shoulder as if a posse of angry wee fat roadies might be after her.

We went out into the bright sunshine of George Street and along the busy pavement. She was hurrying – she seemed afraid.

I had never met Marsha before, but remembered her from the 60s when I was a schoolboy. She had been the 'face' of the rock musical Hair, a slim black girl with a huge Afro hairstyle, and the naked posters of her at the time show she was extremely beautiful, a fact that was not missed by Mick Jagger who got her up the duff fairly quickly. They had a daughter, and are still close friends and doting grandparents. I remembered her appearing on *Top of the Pops* wearing, for the time, an incredibly sexy top. I mentioned that I saw her on that show.

"Yeah, yeah… and you jerked off to it," she laughed. "I've been told that by so many guys."

We were walking down Hanover Street and a light rain started to fall – the weather here can change very fast.

"Thanks for walking along with me, I was worried that guy would come after me."

"Oh, you're welcome. You certainly livened up the show. "

"Did you believe any of his stories?"

"No. And certainly not the bit about Dean Martin asking him to play golf."

"I'm going into this bar for a drink, steady my nerves. Can I buy you one?"

"Thanks Marsha, but I have a ticket for a show. It starts in 15 minutes."

"Where are you from?"

"Glasgow."

"I was there the other day. At the U2 gig. My best friend manages them."

I froze. I was still managing Darkwater and desperately trying to find them a record label. And she knew U2's manager.

"Marsha, I can go to a show any time. What are you having?"

That was how I got to know her. We ordered a glass of wine and a coffee for me. She told me she was writing the definitive book on Jimi Hendrix. She had heard about the wee fat roadie's claims that Jimi was murdered and had driven all the way from France to the Fringe to see for herself. She had arranged to do her own show at the Assembly Rooms and would set the record straight. She was really pissed off at the guy. She mentioned that she had only a couple of days to get organised for her show, and needed to hire a movie projector, a laptop and screen. I told her I had these very things, and would be happy to lend them to her. She thanked me; that would be a huge help.

After I'd known Marsha for a short time, I began calling her 'Hurricane Hunt'. Her energy was impressive, especially bearing in mind she'd been through breast cancer. She must have been fearsome in her 20s, back in London in the swinging sixties driving all the young men crazy. Before I knew what was happening, I'd agreed to run the audio-visual gear at her show. I arranged to meet her the following morning at the flat where she was staying with a couple of friends.

They were nice Edinburgh New Town guys, had a very tidy, tastefully decorated apartment with nicely scented candles and made great coffee. While we were chatting, I casually picked up a guitar that was sitting in a corner and noodled about on it. Marsha suddenly stopped mid-sentence.

"That's it! That's what I need in the show tomorrow. The set will be like a Greenwich Village apartment in the 60s, people hanging out, you know? Could you sit on the stage just playing guitar? Those blues riffs you just did? That sort of thing?"

"I don't know, Marsha, I've never really done theatre work before..."

"It'll be great. I'll also have naked girls on stage. Models."

"I'll be there."

Next morning we met at the Assembly Rooms for a quick tech-check, as theatrical chaps call it. Marsha had given me a flash-drive with a film she wanted running as a backdrop, and I'd brought my projector, screen, and laptop. I also had a little amplifier and my nice old Fender Strat of the right year to be suitably authentic. Marsha had told me that because there were other shows on at the same time at the Assembly Rooms I needed to bring the smallest, quietest amplifier possible; the only thing I could lay my hands on at short notice was a tiny little Japanese thing that had belonged to my son when he was at primary school. But I reckoned it would sound fine for a wee bit of quiet background guitar.

Marsha is used to taking charge, and began efficiently and professionally giving the tech crew their instructions. Then she "dressed" the set in black, as I believe the term has it, and told me where to sit onstage.

"Right Graham, I'll be talking during the whole show but every so often I'll ask you to play some riffs from Jimi's songs. *Purple Haze*, *Hey Joe*, you'll know them all..."

Gulp.

Part of Jimi Hendrix's sound was due to the fact that, unlike me, he wasn't playing through a toy amplifier. The other part was that he was a friggin' genius. I suddenly realised what I'd let myself in for. I'm used to playing in bands, where there's always someone else playing beside you and you can easily get away with making the odd mistake. I'd be sitting here alone, trying to reproduce parts of great rock anthems, songs everyone knew exactly how they were supposed to sound. A sudden cold chill ran through me. I'd make a complete idiot of myself. We'd had no time to rehearse. Marsha told me she'd just give me a cue every so often when it seemed right. She didn't know when that would be.

Oh fuck.

Half an hour to go. We gulped nervous coffee in the artistes' bar. Marsha is highly thought of in show biz circles and some interesting people had dropped by to see her show: theatre directors and actors, Ray Coleman, one of the top music journalists in the UK, the lady who was head of the Edinburgh Festival... every other person seemed to be a major celebrity or mover and shaker. Then Britt Ekland came up to Marsha and they greeted each other like sisters.

"Graham, this is Britt. She's catching a plane back to Sweden after the show. Will you be passing the airport on your way to Glasgow? Could you possibly drop her off?"

I thought I could just about manage that.

I still didn't know what songs Marsha might ask me to play, it was impossible to talk to her alone for a minute. I never usually get nervous before a gig, so the terror I was now experiencing was not fun. My nerves were jangling, perhaps I shouldn't have had two double espressos. *I'm about to make a complete fool of myself in front of the whole of bloody Edinburgh.*

It was time.

We trooped through to the backstage area. Another show was just finishing. As soon as the house lights went up and the room emptied, Marsha had everyone organised, including two girls and two guys who would be sitting naked at our feet, to give the set the feel of a 60s 'happening'. I think that was the idea.

The crowd trooped in. Then I noticed Antonio Forcione in the front row. He is one of the finest guitar players in the world; he's often called the Jimi Hendrix of acoustic guitar.

Another friend of Marsha. Great. That was all I needed. My hands were trembling. *Aw bugger it, I can only play what I can play*.

I sat at the side of the performance area right in front of the audience and quietly played some blues riffs, trying not to take too much notice of the models. I couldn't help thinking they should have brought a couple of cushions; sitting on their bare arses on a wooden floor for an hour must be uncomfortable. They were art school models, though, I guess they're trained for that. How do you train your bahooky to be comfortable on a wooden – *concentrate*! As usual my mind was wandering. If I didn't concentrate I'd miss my cues. Oh shit.

The show began. Marsha talked eloquently and interestingly about Jimi and his life. At least I think she did. The crowd certainly enjoyed it. All I remember was sitting in front of all those celebs with nervous sweat pouring down my face as I waited for Marsha to tell me to play.

I heard her say something about *Hey Joe*, and dutifully played the intro as well as I could. The wee amp bravely farted it out. Even it seemed terrified, knowing it was way out of its league. As I looked up at Marsha a big dollop of stinging sweat rolled into my eye. I tried to blink it away, but it must have seemed like I was winking at her. She gave me a curious glance and carried on. I sat frozen. *What if she asks me to play something I don't know? Christ...*

Marsha was talking about the Animals and House of The Rising Sun. *Oh shit...that was a cue, she wants me to play the chords*. Everyone knows them. I used to teach kids to play them. I hadn't played the song for years, but who could forget them? Me, that's who. For a horrible endless eternity of about 5 seconds I had a complete mental blank, like meeting an old friend and forgetting his name. I sat frozen in the spotlight. I heard her say *House of the Rising Sun* again, slightly louder this time. My fingers took on a life of their own and I heard the song crunch out the wee amp. Clearly there is a God.

Another half hour, a few more cues, a few more terror-stricken moments, a few more riffs and it was over. *Thank fuck*. Huge applause. House lights on. Crowd filing out. During the Fringe, one show follows immediately after another and the next performers were impatiently barging us out the way so they could set up. A loud American comedian I'd seen on TV many times charged on, glanced appreciatively at the naked girls as they hurried backstage to get dressed, then glared at my little amplifier.

"Get this piece of shit out of here! *We're* on now."

22

MARSHA HUNT 2

In October the weather in Florida is beautiful. Hot and sunny, turquoise ocean, white sand, low humidity, gently sighing palm trees – Sarasota in Autumn is a dream. Much hotter than Scotland in July. I think Scotland is the most beautiful country in the world but when the winds are howling in the Highlands I love escaping to Sarasota. I love getting up early in the morning, going for a long walk on the beach then coming back to look at webcams to see the wet and windy weather back home. Sorry, I better shut up.

I hadn't heard from Marsha for a while but when I checked my e mail there was a very nice note from her, thanking me for my help in Edinburgh and asking if I fancied doing six shows with her in a small theatre in Dublin in November. There was no money in it. Maybe some expenses if all went well, which of course meant no, there would be no money.

Dublin in November is one of the dreichest places on earth. No wonder they spend so much time drinking Guinness. I bet the inventor of Prozac could pay his rent on what he sells there in one day. Weather-wise it's even more miserable than Glasgow; damp, wet, cold, dark, and windy –the opposite of sunny Florida, where I'd been swimming in the warm waters of the Gulf. This, and my terror playing in the show in Edinburgh might lead you to expect me to turn down Marsha's invite in a heartbeat. So I said yes, of course I'd love to do it, even if I would be paying my plane fare. It would be a laugh. Besides, I was still spending hours every day calling record labels and agents, desperately trying to get Darkwater signed. Her best pal was U2's manager and he lives in Dublin...I had to go.

And so a few weeks later I was back in Scotland getting ready to catch a flight to Dublin.

My phone rang. It was Marsha.

"Hey Graham, I need a couple of flags for the stage. It will look great. I've got an American one, but can't seem to buy a Union Jack anywhere."

"Yeah, well that's because you're in Dublin, Marsha."

"Can you get me one in Glasgow?"

"Possibly, but why do you want one?"

"Because Jimi was American but he made it first in the UK, so I want the two flags on the stage as part of the backdrop."

"In Dublin? You want a British flag draped across the stage in Dublin? You remember all the trouble they used to have with the IRA? Are you sure about this, Marsha?"

"Look, can you get one or not?"

"Ok, leave it with me." I've learned that it is best not to question the artistic vision of the person whose name is on the tickets. If Marsha wanted a Union Jack then I'd get her one.

It was Sunday morning, the shops were closed, my flight was due to leave in a couple of hours, so I looked on eBay and found the nearest supplier. I called him. Yes, he could sell me one today, but his shop was miles away. If I drove there I'd never have time to get back for my flight. I asked him if there was any possibility of meeting at Glasgow Airport. He agreed as long as I paid cash for the flag and a wee bit extra for his petrol. I gave him my mobile phone number and asked him to call me when he got there. Then I headed to the airport and checked in.

The guy cut it fine, but called just in time.

"I've got your flag. Can you meet me in the drop-off zone inside the parking building at the main entrance?"

"No problem. What are you driving?"

"A silver Mercedes."

I hurried out to the car park and saw his car pull in and screech to a halt. Glasgow Airport was the target of a terrorist attack a few years ago and they are still very jittery. They have rebuilt the approach to the airport with all sorts of barriers and huge lumps of concrete to stop you getting anywhere near the building. They are also alert for drug dealers, and Mercedes sports cars with private number plates are, I am told, a favourite brand of such guys. As soon as the flag supplier's car pulled in I felt sure I could see all the security cameras whirring round, recording every move. Then he stepped out of his car. Now how do I say this? The guys who attempted to bomb the airport had been of – uh – of Indian subcontinent appearance. As was the man in dark sunglasses who was now holding a brown parcel in his hand for me.

He stuck his hand out and I gave him the cash. I took the parcel.

I headed for the security check at departures convinced that I was about to be spreadeagled over a metal examination table. I quickly checked the package to make sure the guy had only given me a flag. Nobody looks more guilty than an innocent man, and I could feel sweat run down my back as I went through the various checkpoints. But none of the machine-gun toting cops gave me a second glance and soon I was on the green and white plane to Ireland. And very nice it was too.

Marsha had told me to meet her at the theatre so I caught the airport bus to the town centre, then jumped in a cab and headed there. It was a nice wee place near the river, in a busy, touristy, stag night part of town, just across the street from a fine hotel that Bono and the Edge apparently own. *Fecksake,* said the cab driver, *that could describe almost any feckin number of buildings in Dublin.*

Actually, I'm not telling the truth. He didn't say it in an Irish accent. He was from Poland. When Eire joined the EEC they cashed in brilliantly for a number of glorious years and raked in all sorts of grants. But they'd always been so busy kicking out the English that they never thought to keep a wary eye on who was coming into the country. And so Polish is now the country's second language. Of the three million people living in Dublin, the cab driver told me, only five hundred thousand are Irish; most of the rest are from Eastern Europe. *But,* as one Irishman said to me, *at least they're not feckin Rangers supporters.*

I finally reached the gig and wandered in. Marsha was doing another of those tech-check things, going over lighting cues, covering everything on the stage with black cloth and hanging up the Union Jack she gratefully accepted from me. Oh, and she was standing on a big aluminium ladder. She intended to do her talk about Jimi perched halfway up a ladder. I never found out why, but it did set her apart from the other people on the stage, which would be me and four nude models she'd hired for the event.

I'd been playing a wee gig the night before with some friends in Glasgow and was tired, so I was glad when, after only five hours or so tech-checking, Marsha called a halt and drove me to the apartment she'd arranged for me to stay in. It was a lovely place belonging to one of her friends; very comfortable with cable TV and some nice food Marsha had bought me. I was happy at the thought of spending a week there, even if the weather was horrible.

Marsha told me she was staying at the house of her friend Paul, the manager of U2. I eagerly felt in my bag and touched the dvd I'd brought of Darkwater. Should I ask her to give it to him now? No, best to wait until later in the week when Marsha would be elated at the success of the show. Apparently he was on a stadia tour of America so he wouldn't be around right now anyway. Marsha told me he works very hard for the band, goes to every gig U2 plays, as I would too, if only I could get Darkwater signed.

Next morning, Marsha collected me bright and early and drove me to the theatre. She told me she'd been up since four. Early that morning she'd driven all the way to the other side of Dublin to the flat of one of the stagehands to collect a little amplifier I'd be playing through, then she'd given him a lift to the theatre. That done, she'd gone off somewhere to collect a prop or something, then she had... It was still only ten in the morning; I've never met anyone who was such a ball of nervous energy.

I didn't know why we were going to the theatre so early because the show wasn't due to start until eight. The kind of guys I usually play with turn up for gigs about five minutes before showtime. But apparently there were more tech-checks to run through. I assumed this attention to the tiny details of lighting and sound was usual for theatre shows so I kept my mouth shut. Best not to show my ignorance.

The gig was at the New Theatre, a very nice kind of socialist-cooperative, community sort of place. A coffee shop/bookshop at the front mainly selling political and environmental sort of stuff, even the *Thoughts of Chairman Mao* – what *would* he think about China these days? And a cosy theatre at the back, perhaps 80 seats. It was brilliant, a lot classier than many of the sweaty pubs I'd been playing recently. The backstage cludge even had a proper seat *and* a choice of toilet paper: tissue or, for old troopers with arses like leather, the *Sun*. Or perhaps that was just for reading.

The only theatre work I had done before was many years ago when I managed to talk myself into a job as a stagehand at the Palace Theatre in London in the Danny La Rue Show, an extravagant cross-dressing spectacular. It had been good fun once I got the hang of it. The stagehands were an old bunch of seen-it-all Cockneys and they had the times of their cues down cold. They would swiftly change the set then, while Danny was on doing his Golden Age of Hollywood routine, they'd dart out the stage door to the pub on the corner where the barman kept their usual drinks poured and waiting.

I soon got into this habit. The only problem was that I was only 19 and could never keep up with them, so as the night wore on I would get more and more blootered. There was one other stagehand my age and he could handle even less alcohol, although he bravely tried to keep pace with the crew.

Every night we had one very fast set change; the curtain would drop and immediately the crew would shove a large trolley across the back of the stage. The hands all enjoyed this because they used to see how fast they could get it moving and, for extra points, crash it into one of the crew. One night it was my turn to attempt to break the land speed record and so I aimed at the other young stagehand. He'd drunk more drink than he needed and had forgotten about the guided missile that was now hurtling at him. He didn't even see it until it threw him in the air. He crashed to the deck. The crowd heard the thump of him falling as well as his unkind scream that I was a fucking Scottish bastard. This got the best laugh of the night. Danny was not amused.

I was finally sacked when I screwed up a very simple job after my fourth rushed pint of the night. The grand finale of the show was when Danny appeared through a doorway at the top of a large staircase, then walked regally down to the stage. I was hidden at the side, holding a piece of black string that I would use to pull the door closed after Danny had made his grand entrance. I let the string slip. For some reason I reached out to get it, the audience saw me and began pointing and laughing. I really shouldn't have grinned at them and waved.

Marsha's tech-check at the theatre went on from eleven in the morning until six at night. I was impressed by her patience and attention to detail, getting the computer-driven lights just right, covering my little amplifier and anything else that wasn't black with polythene bin liners. When she unfurled the Union Jack, the lighting guy and stage manager looked surprised and glanced uneasily at one another. Marsha spent some time hanging the flags perfectly level, and I couldn't help thinking it looked like a Rangers banner inside a Celtic supporters club. Oh, and the ladder, she spent a fair amount of time getting that in the just the right position.

I kept out of the way, took the white Stratocaster I'd brought for the show out of its case – very authentic I felt – and very quietly practised as many Jimi Hendrix riffs as I could think of, still worried Marsha would suddenly ask me to play something I didn't know.

By the end of the day Marsha was looking very tired, and I suggested she have a wee snooze. Before and after any show, there are always things to be done. I know how time consuming and mentally draining these things can be. I told Marsha I wanted to help her any way I could, and to let me do any little jobs to save her energy for the show. She told me that she had to go out to buy wine and cake for friends coming tonight. I offered to do this – I don't drink but all Glaswegians know how to buy a bottle of wine. Marsha refused, she wanted to attend to it herself, make sure she got exactly the right one. She told me to go and eat.

I went across the street to Bono and the Edge's hotel and bought the cheapest dinner on the menu, sausage and mash costing eleven quid. I noticed that the room rates went up to over a thousand euros a night. For that kind of money I'd be expecting Bono to sing me to sleep. I was glad Marsha had provided me with a free apartment, even if it was a long way from the theatre.

At last it was time. The Irish Times had done a great preview. Show pretty much sold out. Room buzzing and very busy. The four nude models didn't arrive until just before the start which didn't amuse Marsha, although they did get their kit off in seconds. They looked like they'd done this type of work before.

The show started with a black guy Marsha had hired walking onstage and smashing an old guitar while I played the riff from Purple Haze, all very dramatic. It grabbed the crowd's attention almost as much as the swinging dick of one of the models – it was festooned with metal chains and piercings. Marsha was standing halfway up the ladder, gazing thoughtfully into the air, creating a bit of theatrical ambience. When she noticed his decorated dong her eyes widened, and she looked like she was about to burst out laughing. For a second I thought she was going to fall off the ladder, but she quickly regained her composure and began her monologue about the life and times of Jim Hendrix.

Every so often without warning she would throw me a cue to play something. It was as nerve wracking as the gig in Edinburgh. I couldn't relax at all and was wondering if I was crazy putting myself through this for six nights. Then I thought of the people in the crowd, perhaps one of them could help get Darkwater a record deal. The wife of U2's manager was there, as were the former head of MTV Europe and various other famous friends of Marsha. Yeah it was worth it. But I had a horrible feeling she would suddenly ask me to play something I didn't know and sat tensely throughout the show, listening carefully to every word.

Marsha seemed to be talking off the cuff, I could see she was tired and it lacked the sparkle of the Edinburgh show, but the crowd gave her a warm reception. After the show she hosted a little wine and cake party in the bookshop and some of Ireland's top arts people were there. Their chat was bright and breezy. Most rock bands do meet and greets after their gigs these days, but the level of conversation tends to be fairly basic, mainly enthusiastic grunts and highly imaginative swearing about how good the gig was. Marsha's guests were educated, erudite and very witty. I had no idea what I was doing there.

I had just packed up my guitar when Marsha offered to run me back to the apartment. I knew she was staying close to the theatre and she'd been on the go for at least 18 hours so I thanked her and told her I'd get a cab.

"Not at all. You've come from America to do this. I'll give you a lift."

"Thanks Marsha, I really appreciate it, but it's fine. I'm quite happy to get a cab"

"I'm driving you, now don't you argue."

"But, Marsha, really I don't want to take you out your…"

"Don't argue…"

So I didn't.

On the final night, Marsha collected me at the apartment and I couldn't help noticing her car was rapidly filling with discarded bags, boxes, pieces of paper and other debris. And that there was a new and impressive dent on the back bumper. We battled through the heavy traffic and finally found somewhere to park that seemed further from the theatre than where we had started out. While Marsha went over some tech stuff with the lighting guys, I went off for a cheap meal in a pub down a side street not far from the theatre – I had eaten every night at Bono's hotel and my credit card was melting.

Alas, I soon realised that it had been a false economy. By the time I reached the gig I could feel that all was not well. I swallowed some anti-acid tablets and hoped for the best. As I sat at my spot on the stage I could feel my stomach begin to churn.

During her show Marsha was speaking skilfully from her perch on the ladder, knowing how to hold the attention of her audience, at times lowering her voice for effect, as do all good and trained actresses of the National Theatre and Royal Shakespeare Company, as she is. She knows her craft.

I, on the other hand, know my bowels.

I was painfully aware that something spectacular and unwelcome was happening. I knew I shouldn't have eaten at the slop shop I'd gone to. Too late, I realised, feeling another deep and ominous rumbling, like an approaching thunderstorm. If I wasn't very careful this was all going to go terribly wrong.

I looked around, hoping no one had heard. The four nudes on the stage seemed unaware of my intestinal trauma. The two girls lolled around, as if reading Ginsberg poetry at a 60s 'be-in', whatever that might have entailed. The guy with the metalwork attached to his tadger was sitting at the corner of the stage a comfortable distance to the left of me, and one of the girls pleasingly close to my right. There was another low growl from my guts. I prayed Marsha wouldn't hear. She would not be amused. Not at all.

She threw me a cue and I played the intro to *Purple Haze*, using the noise of the guitar to cover up a gratefully released burst of trapped gas. I knew instantly there was a lot more where that had come from, and worse, much worse. The beautiful naked girl sitting near me glanced up from her book with a surprised expression, then smirked and carried on pretending to read.

The show wore on. I stared up at Marsha on her ladder, and made it look as if I was listening intently. I knew from my limited knowledge of theatre that this would have the effect of helping direct the audience's attention to her, lest it had strayed to the naked breasts of the girls or the curious sight of metal-dong-man, who seemed unable to sit still for more than a few minutes – perhaps his bum was cold. I wondered if I could set up a wee electric current at the spot where he sat on the stage, nothing dangerous, maybe just some tin foil and a couple of batteries, just something that might make him twitch – it would be hilarious to see his balls spark. I quickly dismissed the idea. Marsha wouldn't stand for such capers. Not for a moment.

Again my stomach shifted with near-cataclysmic consequences and I glanced at the naked girl beside me. She was staring at me with an amused expression. Oh God, did the crowd hear that? My guts were growling and groaning. If it got any louder the people at the front would definitely hear; I was sure a couple of them were looking at me suspiciously.

And then the inevitable happened. A fart of biblical proportions, released entirely against my will. Oh, I tried to stifle it, I did, honestly I did. I squeezed my cheeks tight, as you do, but nothing could prevent its rush for freedom. Marsha shot a glare at me, then cued me to play the chords of House of the Rising Sun, which I did, perhaps a little too loudly. But needs must. This allowed me the blessed relief of letting some more painfully turbulent wind to burst forth without, I prayed, the all too near front row being let in on my shameful secret.

At last the show was over and I quickly headed backstage to collect my jacket and escape. The beautiful naked girl who had been sitting near me grabbed my arm, grinned and spoke in a thick Dublin accent.

"Jaysus thank fook that's over. Oi t'ought you was going to shoite all over me."

23

VELVET HAMMER BAND

After Darkwater fell out and split up, as bands always do, I was very disappointed and went off to Florida for a while. I'm very lucky I can do that. I know a lot of musicians in the Sarasota area, especially blues players. Like Beth. I've jammed with her many times in bands around town. She's a softly spoken woman, thoughtful, cares deeply about politics.

She stirs her coffee, milk no cream, *thanks*, medium-black, pauses for a second, gathering her memories.

She has a lot.

It has been a long and winding road with many potholes and rough uphill turns to get here, this busy breakfast and lunch café on sunny Main Street. She glances at the diners, mainly retired folk, some twisted and bent, others lean and slow moving with skin stretched tight over liver-spotted hands, gnarled knuckles, arthritic pain that no pills will ever cure, hands that have worked all their days and been careful with a dollar.

Some of them are not much older than she is, but Beth knows how to look good. She is glad to have her health. Life hasn't quite worked out as she planned, but she has no complaints. She's never been one to dwell on what might have been, or what she once had. She didn't always have to read the prices on menus, didn't always have to check the blackboard for the lunch specials. There were times – good times– when things were oh so different. But that was back then and now is now.

Beth is a bass guitarist.

She was born into a musical family in the Midwest, and pretty early on discovered she had perfect pitch. It never occurred to her that this was unusual, that she could have studied piano or perhaps something with strings like cello or violin. She could have passed her life easily and gently in an orchestra, or perhaps with one of those TV house bands, reading the dots, playing whatever the visiting guests needed.

When she had been in college she had loved working student radio; she had the soft easy-flowing voice for it. A local cable TV station was looking for a weather girl, and they liked her. Soon Beth was telling nervous commuters if tornados were heading for their towns, which tropical storms she was watching in case they exploded into hurricanes and how the northwest mountains were shivering in blizzards. It was easy work, and fun.

Then the news anchor was feeling far more depressed than anyone suspected and committed suicide on air.

The call came within an hour. Could she do the late news that night?

She could, and did.

Soon she was a personality. She was a success, so much so that other stations began calling, offering big salaries and expense account lunches. She was quite settled at the local station, but she'd always liked a challenge. Despite a nagging doubt, she accepted one that seemed too good to turn down. They promised that she would head the news team, make the big decisions, it was her dream job. She had always been passionate about politics and hated that many things were only reported in a way that would keep the station's advertisers happy. And she hated that many things that should make the evening news didn't because it might upset them. She could make a real difference. She would piss off her current employers by taking the job, would definitely be burning her bridges. She took the leap. It lasted a month, then the station was sold to someone who didn't appreciate her frank views. She was out. The door was closed.

Beth had an eye for antiques and had the kind of memory that any dealer needs, the ability to remember prices and obscure hallmarks. She could glance at rows of tat and junk in any English auction room and spot anything that would fetch four times as much when she brought it back to America. For years she flew back and forward to London, driving hundreds of miles round provincial sales, gathering jewellery and little items small enough to pack in her suitcases to bring back to satisfy her growing list of clients. Then came 9/11 and it all ended.

"It was like someone turned off a light. Suddenly no one wanted to spend money. Everything crashed. I was out of business overnight."

In the UK, we think all Americans have piles of money. The tiny percentage that hold the power, the super-rich, have always been expert at convincing hard-working citizens that they are living the dream, that they have endless opportunities. Americans work far longer hours than Europeans – according to one report a third have no paid holidays. Everything has to be paid for in America and these days nothing is cheap. Walmart recently ran a TV ad to convince people that owning their own toothbrush was not a luxury. I think we can agree that such a nation has a way to go. The average working American, as Beth puts it, is "two paychecks from bankruptcy". Beth found this to be true. The bank called her mortgage, she lost everything.

She moved back to Sarasota, picked up some work in a local radio station and began playing bass guitar. But not any bass guitar. She has small hands, not an advantage for a bass player, and finds it tricky to move up and down the fretboard. Beth discovered a guy who would build her a 7-string bass so that she can stay within the same four frets and play across the fretboard instead. I've never seen anyone do this before, and the bass is heavy, but Beth loves it, wouldn't play anything else.

Beth plays with a lot of people around town and, sadly, these days too many gigs are benefit concerts to raise money for musicians who are ill and facing large medical bills. Not many musicians have pension plans. If they are lucky, they made some money when the going was good and they managed to buy the roof over their head, but that's about it. You can usually spot a musician by the beat up station wagon they are driving. Sarasota has a lot of excellent blues players – it is cheaper to live here where it is warm than in freezing Chicago – and many of them are getting on in years. Health is always a worry.

Beth's main band features a black bluesman from Tampa, Johnny 'Guitar' Scrivens. He's around 60 now and has been playing all over Florida since he was a kid. The band was doing well around town, getting noticed, picking up some nice work, but one day the pain came. It was so bad he couldn't eat or sleep. The first diagnosis was pancreatic cancer, the kind that kills suddenly and often with no prior symptoms. Johnny lost a lot of weight, and had to undergo a lot of tests, some of which were covered by his disability allowance. But Johnny doesn't drive and had to rely on public transport to get across Tampa to hospital. Anytime I've been in buses in America I've noticed how hard the seats are, it's like a Republican thing, *yeah, we'll give public transport to the poor, but don't expect it to be comfortable...* Florida has better public transport than many places, but the pain must have been awful.

It looks like Johnny is clear of cancer, although they are not sure what is wrong, and he is determined to keep playing, despite the pain – *what else am I gonna do?* Beth has been offered a good gig at the Ritz Calton, the classiest hotel in the area. Hell, it's one of the classiest hotels in America, and some seriously rich people live there most of the year, escaping to the Hamptons when the humid summer heat comes. The band usually has a slide guitar player, but he is out of town this weekend. Beth has asked if I can cover the gig. I'm very excited. I'm getting the chance to play with a black blues band from Tampa. Damn right I can cover it.

I know Johnny will be dressed immaculately; he always is. Tonight he is wearing a gold three-piece suit with long tails, gold watch chain and gleaming black wingtip shoes. Doesn't matter if he is playing in a downtown saloon bar or the fanciest hotel; Johnny believes that dressing well shows respect for the audience. So I've borrowed a jacket from my next door neighbour. He's a banker and I'm kind of hoping he might have left a wee wad of money in it. I also nipped up to an Outlet Mall and bought a respectable shirt and a tie. Got to look the part.

The Ritz is very posh, so posh that the musicians must use the service entrance at the back to bring in the gear. The main entrance leads straight into the very grand room we'll be playing in and it would take less than a minute to carry in my amp and guitar from my car, but there's no chance of using the front door. To get to the room I have to drive round the corner and up the street to the rear entrance, carry my gear up the loading dock, give my driver's license to the security guard, get a pass from him, go down a corridor for about 50 yards, then turn left and walk 100 yards to the service elevator. There are all sorts of chirpy motivational posters on the wall: 'At the Ritz I can succeed.' 'I respect my co-workers in the Ritz family.' And my favourite: 'I only occasionally think about finding another job.'

Suitably inspired, I squeeze into the elevator beside the trolleys of dirty sheets and trays of discarded room-service items and take it to the ground floor. Then turn right out of the elevator, walk to a double fire door, turn right out of it and walk through the basement to another elevator in a corridor piled high with spare tables, mattresses and all sorts of hotel stuff. There is the muted sound of hidden machinery humming. It is very hot down here and I'm dripping with sweat already, my new shirt is sticking to my back. This elevator takes me upstairs to the kitchens and I shoogle past the blazing stoves, yelling chefs, and harassed waiters to get to the back of the room we'll be playing in.

One of the waitresses is very attractive and a grinning Mexican waiter is chatting her up, clearly eager to give her some Latin love. From the kitchens it's only about a half-mile walk to where the band is set up. The Ritz is a big place. I like finding my way around buildings; the only one that has ever defeated me was the 02 Academy at Islington, London, which was obviously designed by an architect with a very strange sense of humour.

The rest of the band are there with Beth and the quietly spoken drummer who has the excellent name of Bob Laflamme. His lovely oriental wife is with him, and he tells me that we get a complimentary dinner from the Ritz, but we have to pay for any drinks. I like gigs that have free grub, especially when it's not served in cardboard. The band's mysterious keyboard player, known only as Skofield, is a black Florida bluesman, mild mannered and also dressed in all his finery. He played trombone in the swaying brass sections of soul bands for many years until, I think, his teeth fell out. It's not the sort of question you ask someone.

Knowing all about the 2-mile walk to get from the loading bay to the room, Beth had come in the afternoon and set up her bass gear and the PA. She has perfected some sort of trolley system, has wheels on everything, piles all the stuff together and rolls it along the corridors. We've set up chairs in front of our amps, the Ritz is the kind of gig you can sit down – we'll be playing from 9pm until 1am, and none of us are getting any younger. Beth has her usual high stool; her bass is so heavy that standing is a guaranteed route to a slipped disc.

The Ritz is famed for its fine cuisine. As hired hands, we have a choice of a burger or a Grouper sandwich. It is a tasty Grouper sandwich. It is especially tasty since it didn't cost me the $20 menu price. And the $7 fries were good too.

At last it's show time, as they say. It feels a bit weird playing blues songs here, the place is dazzling bright and we're surrounded by opulence: glittering chandeliers, gleaming leather sofas, marble floors with hand-woven rugs so thick you need to step up onto them. There's a balcony that has a breathtaking view of Sarasota Bay and a shining grand piano that's just sitting there doing nothing. The headwaiter was not amused when I tapped out *Chopsticks* on it during our break – hey, lighten up, pal, the place only *looks* like Buckingham Palace.

Johnny sings very soulful blues songs and improvises a lot. Some songs last about 20 minutes but that's the short ones. The crowd – you can't really call them a crowd – the *guests* look at us in a puzzled kind of way, and I can see in their eyes we're not really what they expect at the Ritz, there's no chance of us playing a selection of their favourite Barry Manilow tunes. These people look rich. Seriously rich. They smell it. Any of the wristwatches in here would cover Johnny's medical bills for a year. But they are very polite, always clap in a dignified sort of way when we finish a song, and get up to dance in that wonderfully enthusiastic, jerky, arm-flailing, leg-twitching gawky grinning way that wealthy white folks do once they've had a couple of single malts or glasses of chardonnay. It's all terribly civilized.

We're playing an extended version of *Stand By Me* and Johnny puts his guitar down, gets up from his chair and wanders around the room with his radio mic, stopping at random tables and singing to the ladies, assuring them he will be there forever at their side, *baby, you know I will*. One elderly lady wearing the Koh i Noor diamonds has a startled look, but most are enjoying themselves. Johnny sings to her, then speaks earnestly into the mic, kneeling and gazing up at her: *You know babee ahh'll always be right here fur you. You know yoo just have to call and I'll be standing here by you.* She has a look of mild panic in her eyes and glances toward her escort, a younger man wearing a million dollar suit. As Johnny stands up a bead of sweat drops onto her table and I think she is going to faint. He slowly walks back to his chair and we end with long guitar and keyboard solos – we're a wee bit short of songs. Perhaps two hours short.

Some old bag with a face like a nippy sweet comes up to us and demands that we turn down the volume, but we just ignore her and she pisses off. There's always someone who likes to bitch. She wasn't too happy, looks like she is not used to being ignored. But we couldn't play much quieter, Beth has super-sensitive hearing and warned us all before we started; she has the PA amp at her side and knows how to work it.

By the time it gets to midnight I am seriously flagging, and I can't imagine how Johnny must feel. But he sings and plays on with great style and dignity. He's got more tests to endure next week, more buses to catch. He plays every gig like it might be his last. I guess one day it will be.

24

PUPPET

Some gigs in Sarasota, like the Ritz Carlton, are very posh. Some aren't, especially the biker bars in the lower-rent part of town, or up in Bradenton – *Bradentucky,* as it's becoming known. There are lot of rednecks in Bradentucky, guys that like to put fat tyres and gunracks on their trucks, and love the roar of their motorcycles.

Puppet is a wee pal who lives there. We get on well together, perhaps because we've both got screws holding our spines together and we know what fun that is, or maybe it's our interest in ancient civilizations. We get irritated with archaeologists who claim that everything they dig up, whether it's a small cross or something as big as Stonehenge, must have some religious significance.

I first met her when her drummer, Andy La Croix, invited me along to play guitar with the band she sang in. Sometimes you just hit it off musically with someone and the gig went really well. After that I sat in with Puppet whenever I had the chance.

When she writes songs, they "just come spilling out of my brain. I have no control of what they are about or how they sound, it just happens. Words will spin in my head and get louder and louder until they are screaming."

She says: "I can't sleep or eat while writing. I went 7 days without sleep because of the screaming in my head. It's almost a madness but it's not me, it's the music coming through me."

It isn't easy making a living by singing songs, and isn't easy being gay even in Sarasota, a place that is much more understanding than Arkansas, where she grew up. Her mother kicked her out when she was 18, because "being a lesbian meant that I was possessed by Satan."

She escaped to the army, and served in the desert as a *petroleum supply specialist,* although she preferred to call herself a jet fuel pumper. After a serious back injury, she was bedridden for almost three years, and eventually found her way to Florida. Since then she's been gigging all over the State, following in her ancestors' footsteps: a distant grandfather was bandmaster in Napoleon's Imperial Guard; another was Michael Gabriel D'Esposito, a well known mandolin player and composer in Italy.

At the start, she didn't find it easy getting gigs: "I've had hassles because I'm tattooed and pierced and look like a boy. I've had places not hire me because of the way I look. A lot of people think I do drugs. Hell, I don't even drink. I've walked in and heard everything from *fuckin dyke* to *what the fuck* is *that* but after I sing they want me to come over for dinner. Some guys buy me a shot and ask if I'll have sex with their wives while they watch.

"I've had ladies try to kick me out of the women's bathroom, until I showed them my titties to prove I'm not a guy. I've been beat up cause I'm gay, all kinds of shit especially comin' out in the early 90s in the heart of the bible belt. I've always lived in a type of war zone."

She prefers playing in bikers' bars; they might be rough places but they show her some respect. I've played with her and the band in a few of them. Harleys outside. Jail pumped muscles tattooed with snakes and women's names and the flames of hell, leather jackets, denim, chains, pool cues, black tee shirts, fat bellies.

Everyone seems to smoke – *who's gonna stop us?* Apart from that, I loved it. If you put a bit of sweat into your playing, these guys really appreciate it, they come up and shake your hand with their big oily paws, talk to you like a long-lost pal. *Hey, buddy, what can I buy you to drink?* It feels great when a 250-pound biker says they love your playing.

Puppet met her partner in one of these bars and says things just got a whole lot better: "I have true love from an amazing woman and her son. I finally have a family, which I was always told I would never have because I'm gay. I have a family now in the biker community here and I'm starting to write happy songs that are actually about my life".

It's only a few miles from the Ritz, but a long way just the same.

25

LEO FENDER

Without amplifiers, there would, of course, be no rock music.

In the famous scene in *Spinal Tap* where the guitar player turned up his amp to '11', he little dreamed of the massive, nay, cataclysmic forces of the universe with which he was tampering. Amplifiers, how they work, and why a few sound so good, is one of the greatest mysteries of the cosmos, and to some extent every thoughtful guitar player is but a disciple.

There are many people who lay claim to being the founders of rock and roll, but the title really belongs to a wee electrician called Leo Fender. Way back in the 1940s he worked in a radio shop during the day. By night, when everyone around him was enjoying the glittering postwar prosperity of America, he was locked in his little workshop, summoning the dark forces of Beelzebub, taking radios apart and reassembling them as guitar amplifiers. He had tasked himself with finding the perfect combination of valves, resistors, capacitors and speakers to create the future guitar sound of Muddy Waters, Buddy Holly, the Stones, the Beatles and everyone who came after.

If AC/DC, Stones and Zep are the juggernauts of rock, then Leo Fender is the freeway that made it all possible. He is the M1, the autobahn, the Route 66. Without him, Springsteen and Hendrix and all the rest would forever have been strumming acoustic guitars, trundling along little back roads in the countryside. Jesus, I just read that last wee bit. I don't half talk a load of pish sometimes. But it really was Leo Fender who provided the tools that rock music needed.

Although fascinated with repairing radios since he was a young lad, Leo Fender had no formal training as an electrician. He was actually an accountant and had worked for the California Highway Department before getting his jotters in government cutbacks. Then he worked as a bookkeeper with a tyre company, but was made redundant after only 6 months. Times were hard.

He was obsessed with electronics. I guess the California girls at parties couldn't wait for the specky wee guy to come and chat them up. And his name was a tad geeky: *Clarence Leonidas Fender*. Perhaps if they'd known that in a few short years he'd be able to get them backstage passes to ANY gig in the world...

Out of work, he managed to borrow $600, a hefty sum in 1938, and started his own radio repair shop in Fullerton, California. He got chatting to local dance band leaders, discovered there was a shortage of good PA systems and began building them. At the time, guitarists had to strum ferociously to make themselves heard above all the brass players and he began working on ways to design high quality guitar amplifiers. The aim was to build a portable amp loud enough to be heard, but that didn't distort – the popular songs of the day, ballads like *Begin the Beguine* and *Alexander's Ragtime Band*, weren't exactly written with wailing guitar parts.

By the end of the War, big bands had lost their popularity and been replaced with small and much cheaper to hire groups playing rhythm and blues, boogie woogie, and country music. Guitar bands made sense; it was far easier to travel from gig to gig with a few guitars and amps that could fit in a station wagon, than with a whole brass section and a piano, especially the damn piano.

The war had played a big part in the advances made in electronics. From the start of WWII, it was obvious that electric circuits had to be rugged to withstand the rigors of military use. You couldn't have a pilot on a bombing mission fiddling around with a crystal radio set. Leo realized that amplifiers should be just as tough to handle the abuse they would receive from the new breed of travelling bands. Musicians beat a path to his door and by 1946 he decided that building and selling musical instruments and amplifiers would be much more interesting than repairing old wireless sets. It was a wise, and for the world, a fortunate decision. He got out of bed one glorious morning, the sun bathed him in golden light, and he changed the name of his shop to the 'Fender Electric Instrument Company.' The ball was rolling.

Leo's amps became more and more powerful, making it possible for guitar players to take their first steps to playing behind their heads, setting fire to their guitars and battering them off their speaker cabinets. The guitar quickly moved up from being a backing instrument to the main event but still had a way to go. Guitarists in these small bands used the only guitars available – dance band-style acoustics with big magnetic pickups clamped onto them. These guitars howled with uncontrollable feedback any time the player got too close to his amplifier, which, in little bars and cramped dance halls, was all the time. A brand new design was needed.

And so in early 1950 when he released the Fender Esquire, the first commercially available, mass produced, solid bodied electric guitar, it was then the party really started. After some modifications he renamed it the Fender Telecaster. It is one of the most instantly recognisable shapes of the century, and has scarcely changed. Keith Richards, Bruce Springsteen, Jimmy Page, Jeff Beck, Rory Gallagher… countless guitar players have used them and still do.

One of the first people to play a Telecaster was a Chicago-based bluesman. An old guy once told me how he'd been walking down a side street in Chicago in the early 1950s and heard this huge sound coming from a basement bar. It was Muddy Waters, playing a Tele through a stack of little amps all piled on top of each other. Imagine that moment, seeing this awesome, sweat-dripping black man growling *ah jes wann make luv t'yoo* and blasting out this incredible wailing guitar sound. Most people never even knew there was such a thing as an electric guitar, what must it have been like to be there at the start of it all and hearing one at ten times the volume of anything that had been heard before?

Leo then turned his attention to building a bass guitar and in 1951 brought out the Precision Bass. Up until then bass players had been stuck with double basses, cool for rockabilly music, jazz and orchestras, and really good for climbing on if you happened to land a gig with Bill Halley. *Hey boy, you sure can slap that bass fiddle, but how good are you at climbing up on it?* But it wasn't much good for Honky Tonk Women. Apart from anything else, it was a lot taller than wee Bill Wyman. It also needed a car all to itself, or a really good roof rack.

The Precision bass was not much bigger than a guitar and was so called because, unlike a double bass, it had frets, so the notes could be played precisely, provided the bass player had practised his scales. Just one slight problem – it needed a more powerful amplifier than anything that was available. If you plugged a bass into the small amps of the time, they just made a horrible farting noise. Since Death Metal hadn't been invented yet, not many bass players fancied that sound.

I'm always fascinated that what seems intuitive is often the opposite of what actually works. The existing amplifiers were made with 12-inch diameter speakers. That's about 30cm, although I've never heard anyone anywhere ever use the metric system when talking about speakers, probably because it's French and as everyone knows the French haven't a clue about rock music. Anyway...because bass guitars produced lower frequencies it would seem logical to suppose that the solution would be bigger speakers. But no. Leo discovered that four 10-inch diameter speakers working together produced the most responsive sound. It was all about how much 'air' the speakers moved. And so bass players were, in a word, sorted.

The equipment needed to play *Hey Joe*, *Purple Haze* and *Leyla* was almost ready. Almost, but not quite. Many guitar players found the Telecaster guitar a bit too 'twangy', and although it became instantly recognisable for all time as the 'sound' of country music, there was a need for something more versatile. Guitar players also complained that the flat, hard edges of the Tele made it uncomfortable to play long gigs standing on cramped bar stages. Leo listened, and in 1954 gave the world the Fender Stratocaster, a work of art equal, if I may say, to anything DaVinci did.

Some say it was inspired by the shape of a desert cactus. It looked, and still looks, beautiful, had three pickups, sounded wonderful, came in a glorious Sunburst colour like the setting sun, and had a smooth contoured back, shaped to fit comfortably against the guitar player's stomach, if he had one. What would Jimi, Eric, Stevie Ray, Jeff, Rory, and all the others have played if Leo hadn't come up with the Stratocaster?

Sometime in the 50s, guitar players discovered that Leo's Bassman amplifier was even better for guitar than bass. All over America and the UK, early 'r 'n' b' and 'beat' groups were belting it out to soon-to-be screaming crowds – and sparking a huge demand for amplifiers. British companies began manufacturing their versions of the Fender Bassman – I didn't say electronic copies, although I don't think Jim Marshall would have denied his first amps were.

Leo's business boomed. Suits in penthouse offices noticed. In 1965 the giant CBS Corporation offered him 13 million dollars, which he gratefully took, as you would, especially as he hadn't been in the best of health. Of course, one of the first things CBS did was to set up mass-production assembly lines, changing the very thing that had made Fender guitars so successful. This cut costs but did not improve quality. In 1969, Leo's main rival, Gibson, who had developed the Les Paul, another iconic guitar, was taken over by a South American brewing company with plenty of dosh. Sadly, the golden age of beautifully made American guitars and 'hand wired' amplifiers was over. It was only a matter of time before they were being assembled in Japan, Mexico, China and even Korea. Any Fender guitar or amp made before the CBS takeover is now worth serious money to collectors.

They were so well made that many of Leo's tweed-covered amplifiers purchased in guitar shops over half a century ago are still on the road today, and it is no secret that early Fender guitars can fetch staggering sums on eBay. This is not something that inexperienced investors should consider as a way of building a wee pension plan. The guitars that fetch really big money have to be complete in every detail, right down to the little screws that hold on the plastic scratch plates. There are collectors that have bewildering knowledge of such things.

I have been playing since the 60s and I am never sure when looking at an old guitar what bits are original and what aren't. I can tell a good guitar the minute I hold it, and the really old 'vintage' ones usually have a distinctive 'feel'. But thankfully I'm only interested in how the guitar plays and sounds; in fact my favourite guitar was built in the 70s, a period that is usually regarded as a low point in factory-produced Strats. Mind you, I've had a few things done to it, thereby greatly reducing its value to anoraks. But it sounds fearsome.

With big money being involved, there are of course countless fakes kicking around, and now there are factory-made 'roadworn' models of Strats and Teles designed to look exactly like beat-up vintage ones. It must be the only brand new product in the world that someone will buy because it looks old and damaged. Even Rory Gallagher's beautiful peeling old Strat has been duplicated exactly by Fender for sale to keen fans. God knows what next century's Antiques Roadshow will make of it all.

Professional guitarists in 1948 were looking for 'clean' sounds, but by the time Cream and Jimi Hendrix came along rock guitar players wanted natural distortion, that is to say, the kind of pure, warm overdriven sound that can only come from an amplifier that is being pushed to its limits. In the 1970s, many guitar players began using huge Marshall amplifiers that needed to be turned all the way up to distort, and gigs became deafening but some guitarists, such as Rory Gallagher, Eric Clapton, Neil Young, Don Felder of the Eagles and Billy Gibbons of ZZ Top used small 1950s Tweed-covered Fender amps such as the Deluxe and the Bassman. Keith Richards reckons the 1957 Tweed Twin is the best amp ever made. I know if you go to rock gigs the stage might have a wall of Marshall stacks on it, but often this is just because they look cool, the guitar player's sound is actually coming from a mic'd-up little Fender amp.

One of Leo's amps, the Tweed Deluxe, was first made in 1948, and was originally intended as a small practise amp because it distorted when turned up. Many rock guitar players including Slash have discovered that these ancient amps are perfect for studio use because they could produce a huge sound and for some mysterious reason recorded beautifully. The Tweed Deluxe is also exceptionally touch-sensitive, it responds very well to the guitar player's hands, much better than modern digital amps that are big on noise and low on quality. Searching for the perfect guitar sound is an obsession.

And so Leo's early amplifiers have been copied and reissued by Fender and, interestingly, also by many little workshop-based amp makers, building them lovingly in wee places not unlike Leo's original radio store. These amps are not cheap, but they are handmade and do not have any of the printed circuit board and transistors nonsense that large production lines use.

In the UK, two of the most highly respected makers are brothers Stevie and Chris Flynn, working in their little basement workshop, which is packed to the ceiling with the repair work they do to modern amps. Whenever they get a spare minute they are building amplifiers. They are obsessed with detail, and work feverishly to make exact replicas of 1950s amps. Sometimes they even add a few wee 'mods' – modifications – that can make a huge difference to what is old technology.

This is a very unusual situation, because the improvements made in electronics and engineering has rendered most 50s stuff obsolete. I mean, nobody in their right mind would choose to watch a black and white TV, or drive along the motorway in a truck built in the 1950s with a crash gearbox and no power steering. The rock music industry has always been at the cutting edge of technology. I had a pal who was the sound engineer with Manfred Mann, one of the first bands to use portable lasers. On wet afternoons he used to set up the laser in his flat and project a spot onto the pavement below to bewilder anyone passing by.

In an industry that embraces new things very quickly, it is very odd that amplifiers using circuitry over half a century old are still the first choice of so many professionals. In theory all an amplifier is designed to do is increase the sound coming from the guitar. Modern components should sound far better than glass valves that were designed in the early part of the 20th Century. But they don't. They just don't.

I have one of these amps in Florida. I love them. I was playing at an open-air gig at the height of the steamy season. The heat and humidity were unbelievable. When the humidity reaches about 90% the air is so heavy and damp that sweat can't evaporate from your body and you feel as if you're being cooked.

The little amp powered on bravely, even though it seemed like the speaker was underwater. As soon as the gig was finished, I jumped in my car and headed for the nearest shop to buy a few bottles of water. I must have looked rough, my clothes were drenched in sweat. I handed the guy behind the counter a few crumpled dollars. As soon as he felt how wet they were he glared at me like I was a tramp. I knew what he was thinking: *you've peed in your pants, you bum.* Actually, I might have.

Anyway, I'm just off to the Flynns' workshop to blow a grand on yet another hand-wired Tweed Deluxe. I know, I said never again, but this is the last time. I promise. Just one more. It's time someone started Amplifiers Anonymous.

26

BIG SCOTT'S BAND

If you have ever been successfully lured to a band's merch table and forked out a quickly-regretted £30 for a £2 tee shirt that shrinks to a rag the first time you wash it, you will be familiar with those garments that list the towns and cities of the tour. They make impressive reading: London, Paris, Stockholm, Rome, Berlin. Copenhagen, Oslo... all those powerful names, each city as sparkling and exciting as a bottle of fine champagne. How cool it is to travel with a big-time rock band!

I'm willing to bet the town of Airdrie has never appeared, or is ever likely to appear, on any shirt other than the local football team which is usually found holding up the lower Scottish divisions, playing to a couple of hundred on a big day. It rose from the ashes of the old and much loved Airdrie Football Club, which in 2002 like so many other businesses in the area, went down the pan.

Airdrie is twinned with Salzburg, a tad ambitiously some cynics might sneer. Salzburg gave the world Mozart; Airdrie was the hallowed home of the also-dead Fran and Anna, those loveable mini-kilted singists. In Airdrie there are no von Trapp families warbling about the hills being alive, but there are plenty who do sing at Rangers and Celtic games, although their songs are a lot less dreamy. It's not a romantic town. The two towns do have one thing in common: in winter they are both bloody freezing.

Airdrie is not classy and its nearest neighbour, Coatbridge, is even worse, but at least gives Airdrieonians someone to look down on. Coatbridge's local team is called Albion Rovers; as if they are too embarrassed to admit the name of their hometown. If a Coatbridge girl moves into a council flat with a lad from Airdrie, the whole family celebrates her moving up in the world; if she goes off to live in Glasgow they say she has emigrated. Airdrie and Coatbridge also have their own dialect which even Glaswegians have trouble understanding. It sounds like some sort of growling, but with the words *so ah did* or *so ah will* at the end of every sentence.

I played some gigs with an excellent guitar player who lived here. Any parents pushing their offspring into musical careers in the belief that a glittering life awaits might benefit from meeting him. He has played with some of the best-known bands to come out of Scotland, toured the world, is always kept busy on one music session or another, yet he lives in Coatbridge in a tower block that he calls Methadone Heights. He reckons that the only residents not on the heroin substitute are alcoholics. He keeps his guitars locked up in a studio in Glasgow, and avoids the neighbours' regular cheese and wine parties. Averaged out what he earns in a year, if he ever reaches State pension age it will be a pay rise.

I have another pal who plays in the area most weekends. Scott Wallace is a great singer, a big guy with a terrific rock voice. He might have made the big time if he had concentrated on singing, perhaps moved to London, or put a band together when he was younger and trucked up and down the toilet circuit of pubs and seedy backstreet clubs. It's what all rock bands have to do to build their all-important fan base. Scott always made earning a living his priority, never quite had the courage to risk everything when he was young. Once you get beyond 25, living on bags of chips and dossing night after night in the back of a freezing Transit van in the lane behind yet another small-town pub gig becomes too tough on the bones, too draining on the soul. And if you have an infant child to take care of, pretty much impossible.

Or maybe he was just unlucky, perhaps he was never in the right place when the right band was looking for someone. I'm always keeping my ears open for a gig that might be up his street – if Brian Johnson ever quits AC/DC then Scott's the ideal man for the job. There are a lot of very successful singers who don't have half as good a voice as Scott, but the dice rolls and lands the way it lands.

Scott was playing with two other guys in a pub in Airdrie. I hadn't done a gig for a couple of weeks and was going stir crazy. I still find it almost impossible to sit at home on a Saturday night, I get all agitated. I'll play in a bus shelter rather than watch weekend TV. I have a damaged spine, it's held together with screws and stuff – years of hanging guitars from my shoulders, lugging heavy amplifiers, rock climbing and all the dumb things I did have wrecked my neck. Every time I play, the next morning I wake up feeling as if I have been hit by a truck. If I were sensible I would call it a day, but if I were sensible I wouldn't have taken up guitar in the first place. And besides, I was dying to play through the new amp I'd bought from the Flynn brothers. So off I went in torrential rain to sit in with Scott's wee band.

I eventually found the pub Scott was playing in by asking a cab driver. I had sat nav, but the woman on it was far too posh to give directions around Coatbridge. Before the days of GPS, an old roadie trick to find a venue in a foreign town was to hire a cab to drive to it and just follow him in the truck. But I was confident I could understand the local language so I thought I'd just ask directions. I found a minicab sitting outside a pub in some dark street I'd blundered into. I pulled up beside it and asked the driver if he knew the bar I was looking for.

"Aye, jist haud oan. Ah'll be right wi ye, so ah will."

I knew this meant I should wait.

He was busy collecting a fare from someone he seemed to have locked in the back of his cab pending settlement of his bill. Grudged money changed hands, the muttering passenger exited and headed into the pub. The driver leaned out of his window.

"Right, yegoes doon err up yon hull an' right dooon at ra toap an' yeel see a wee choo sign at ra chinky jist go left err and right an' hits right err oana right. Ye cannae mus ut soyecannae."

"Eh..thanks...."

"Aye, up an' right an' doon an left at ra chinky an' roon an' right. So it is."

"Thanks..."

I never did see the wee choo sign but I drove up an' right and doon an' left at ra chinky an' roon an' right and it wis ther right enough, so it was.

When I first started going to pubs many of the places were spit and sawdust bars, with wood floors polished smooth by the working boots of countless shipyard and factory workers. The sort of timber floors that West End folk now put in the best rooms of their houses even though they can afford carpets. At some point big brewers bought the pubs and turned them into formica palaces complete with plastic chairs and tables, recorded music and clattering gaming machines. These soon lost their appeal and the brewers reverted to the old formula, with dark walls, oak tables and chairs, and imitation wood floors polished smooth by the hands of countless eastern European factory workers. The gaming machines were still there though, like miniature light shows.

There was a free–hire function room upstairs in which somebody called Maggie was having a hen night. I thought this was where Scott would be playing and went up to it. Airdrie lasses don't feel the cold, they've developed a resistance to the bitterly fierce north winds – most of them were half naked, proudly showing off their bare and bulging mid sections, like signs of fertility. I think it's called the muffin-top look. They were singing along to a karaoke machine and having a terrific time.

Scott's band is not really a band – to me a band is only a band if it has a drummer, unless it's a folk group or something, but they don't count. It's just Scott with a guitar player and bass player. They have a huge repertoire, as it used to be known, hundreds of songs they can play – they invite the crowd to request anything they want, and there's a good chance they'll know it. They use a drum machine and backing tracks though, and I have no idea why. Maybe it's a generation thing.

I suppose that compared to bands nowadays, old-school rock music is very uncluttered, very simple. I recently watched an old film of the Eagles playing *Hotel California* live and, compared with modern music, it's amazing how sparse it sounds. But brilliant.

Scott and his mates are good enough players to get by easily without pre-recorded tracks. I'd rather see them get rid of these and hire a good drummer; there is nothing like the crack of a snare drum, it's the spine of a band. I always think backing tracks just make noise. I suppose using them does mean they can do some chart stuff that has brass and keyboards and synths and all that stuff, but I'd prefer to hear them with nothing added. Yeah yeah, I know, I'm getting old.

I'd never played alongside backing tracks before. It is kinda weird playing exactly on time from the start of every song to the end, I quite like the way a lot drummers speed up a wee bit; adds a bit of feeling. We did *Sweet Home Alabama*, and I am sure whoever provided the tracks had the timing absolutely spot on, but to me it felt like a funeral march. I tell you though,

Scott has some set of pipes, no matter where he is playing he gets stuck right in there. The locals like him: *goanyersel big man, gie it laldy.*

Of course, many people use backing tracks, a lot of top singers these days would be lost without them, especially the ones that put on big stage shows. Much of the time they're miming. There is a simple rule; it is pretty much impossible to do a dance routine and sing at the same time. It's not just teenage pop idols that use tracks, many well-known rock bands do it to add in all those layered guitar parts they have on their records. There is a good clue: bands that are using backing tracks have to play exactly in time to them so the drummer often wears headphones and plays along to an electronic metronome – a 'click' track.

Backing tracks are not new. A pal that worked for the Who told me about a rehearsal where they were using a tape for the first time. The notion of perfect timing was a wee bit lost on Keith Moon. He's one of the top five rock drummers of all time, actually he's probably the best. My mate watched all day as Pete Townshend went over and over the intro with Keith until he would play it in time with the tape. Keith felt, not unreasonably, that the tape should follow him.

Sometimes the locals can get a wee bit boisterous, especially when they are pished, and definitely when the outcome of a Rangers – Celtic match has been decided by a last minute goal. So the bars of Airdrie and Coatbridge have bouncers. Big ones.

Bouncers in the old days were local hard men who would give hooligans one quiet warning. If this was ignored the lights would go out. They did not mess around. Of course, many bouncers were just cynical thugs who liked knocking out teeth and flattening some good-looking kid's nose just for a laugh. Some would go out their way to antagonise you. I once went to a bar with a well-known musician, but the bouncer wouldn't let him in because he was wearing Nikes. Another time a guy I know nipped out of a long queue outside a club to have a pee. When he got back, the bouncer wouldn't let him rejoin his pals and made him go to the very back of the line. When he finally reached the door the bouncer put his hand up and smirked at him. *Not tonight, sir*. Then told him to fuck off. My pal is a physicist working on nano technology.

The bouncers tonight are all smartly dressed in the black modern-day uniform of professional door staff, as I think they prefer to be called. One of them is so big I can't imagine anyone taking him on. He is quietly walking around the room, collecting glasses, everyone knows he is there. There's another one at the door, alert, evenly balanced on both feet. He's watching the street, keeping an wary eye on smokers coming out for a cigarette, this area is his territory. If a fight breaks out or someone tries it on he'll sort it fast before it becomes a street battle.

He looks as hard as nails; these guys must have had to prove themselves to the local nutters time and again. I guess he is a former boxer, maybe ex-army, or perhaps he was always good with his fists. Kids growing up in Coatbridge learn very young and very quickly if they can handle themselves in a fight.

The bouncer has to keep in shape, maybe he spends a lot of time sparring in gyms or martial arts clubs. Most drunks who get into fights have no chance against a pro like this guy. Sure, they'll lunge in with a head butt, swing a few punches and they might land a lucky one, but a skilled fighter knows that he only has to push his attacker off for a moment then wait calmly and watch him try to catch his breath. As soon as the drunk's adrenaline rush leaves him he will be shaking with exhaustion. One solid punch and the guy goes down. Two and he is hopitalized. It's simple but effective.

I've decided to leave after the first set, I don't really fancy being here later when the place will be packed with drunks. The hen party upstairs will attract jealous boyfriends, that's for sure, and fights have a way of spreading. I've enjoyed playing a few tunes with Scott and I'm carrying my amp out the front door to my car. The windswept pavement is cold and dark, streetlights weakly glinting in rain puddles, shop fronts with closed metal shutters, dark alleys disappearing into silent blackness. There is a huge dog shit on the pavement. I sure as hell wouldn't like to meet the animal that squeezed out that thing; it must be the size of a small horse.

I edge by the bouncer, careful not to step on his foot. He is solid, his huge fists clasped behind his back, like lethal weapons that must be kept hidden. For a moment our eyes lock. His are dark, I feel as though I can see in them generations of street combat, hardship and political betrayals, unemployment, closed factories, and lifelong grinding poverty.

He looks at me, then speaks. His voice is soft, gentle.

"Good night sir. God Bless."

27

GARY INNES

In a previous book I mentioned that some rock music comes from old Scottish folk songs that had been played at ceilidhs then transported to America during the Highland Clearances when so many Scots were forced off their crofts by fat bastard English landowners. Silly me, I don't think I'm allowed to call them that. In the book I wrote a short but detailed history of how Scots found work on farms and cotton plantations in the southern States. There was no TV then so they played the old songs at their weekend barn dances. Some songs evolved into bluegrass then country music, and some to blues.

I'm not an academic, I didn't even go to university, but a couple of people were annoyed, they thought I was being dreadfully serious. You know the kind of guys, they write bitter 'reviews' on any little bed and breakfast place they stay at, post scathing comments on Amazon about every product they buy; happy chappies. Just to annoy them further, I will make this musical observation based on irrefutable scientific research.

In fact, ALL rock and blues, country and soul music comes from old Scottish folk songs.

In music, 4 is a magical, indeed mystical number. Blues is almost entirely based on a repeating 12-bar sequence. Ceilidh music is based on either a 4-bar repeating sequence, or an 8-bar sequence. Is it any coincidence that 8 and 4 added together make 12? I think not.

Now I have cleared that up, I might as well offend a few more people.

The great James Brown was deservedly called the father of soul, partly because he was credited with discovering what he called the 'one'. He would emphasise the first beat in the bar, thus creating the rhythm of soul music. But was this really his discovery? I'm afraid not. For centuries, Scottish pipers knew all about the power of the first beat in the bar when they played marches for big Highlanders striding into the face of white-hot bullets. They'd whip the troops into a frenzy of blood lust and the quaking enemy into a shitting rabble.

In peacetime, in barns and crofts and wee village halls all over the Scottish Highlands, ceilidh bands played these same songs on the long winter nights of the north to keep everyone warm. Everyone loved dancing to them. Soul music is all about dancing. Could the link be any more obvious?

You can see why I didn't get to uni.

I did, however, get to play bass and guitar on many fine tunes with the great Gary Innes, one of the world's best accordionists, at the BBC and a couple of cool places including the Jamhouse in Edinburgh.

It wasn't rock and roll but I liked it.

28

RORY GALLAGHER TRIBUTE BAND

There are really only two types of gigs. One is where the band is playing 'covers' of hit songs in a bar, or at a wedding, or a dance, or as background music in restaurants. Almost all musicians will spend their musical lives playing these kinds of gigs.

The other type of gig is where the crowd are there to hear the artiste play their own material. This usually means that they have been signed to an enthusiastic record label that went out its way to get them known and heard, something of a rarity these days. Am I sounding cynical? Just a tad? If you are a musician you will understand only too well. But of course, there are many well-known bands that have achieved that level of success. Nobody goes to hear U2 playing Chuck Berry numbers. But then, if Chuck played U2 songs his fans would probably be mighty pissed off. So most working musicians can only play famous artistes' material, while famous artistes can only play their own.

It is heart-warming how many well-known bands from the 60s and 70s are finally raking it in on world tours these days, especially since a lot of them never got the royalties they should have when they were young and naive. In a way most of them have become their own tribute bands. I know a few guys in bands like that. It is weird; when they were young they got fed up playing their hits; now they are old they dread the day fans will get fed up hearing them. They wish to hell they could write something new, spend years trying, putting everything into it, and pray it will sound half as good as the great tunes they quickly scribbled on the back of a motorway café menu way back in the day, the songs that are still being played on all the classic rock stations.

But sadly it very rarely comes to pass. Most radio stations have rigid playlists chosen by advertising revenue, and there is no room for new material, even by superstars. Someone told me recently that even Stevie Wonder couldn't get a new song played on most American stations. There are rock gods approaching their 70s that cannot enjoy what should be contented memories of a wonderful life because they are bitter that they have been unable to come up with a number one song for over 40 years. Guitar players often feel the same: I've been told that Jeff Beck refuses to play his old solo from *Hi Ho Silver Lining*. But has he ever played better? I suggest not. It is absolute perfection.

Most musicians realise the joy of playing their own compositions to an appreciative crowd is only a dream, and they head off to play their local venues week in week out, providing terrific live entertainment, often for very little money. In most of these gigs the musicians are interchangeable, the crowd are just there to dance, drink or eat, they don't really care who is making the music. As long as the band plays familiar songs at a reasonable volume everyone is happy.

Sometimes a band is so good that it attracts a following, but even then it is likely that they will be playing 'covers' of the hits of today and yesteryear. Good 'covers' bands can be excellent entertainment, far more interesting than listening to records – do people still call them that? – played by some surly dj slouched over a couple of decks in the corner. Wouldn't it be awful if there were no live bands?

I am willing to bet that *Brown Eyed Girl* is the most popular 'cover' song of all time – I've played it with countless bands, never even close to as well as Van does it, but it still gets the dancers on the floor in double quick time. Eh, here's a hint to songwriters: forget all those complicated chord changes, just concentrate on writing a simple melody that 'cover' bands can easily play. If a cover band does your song, you know you have a gold disc on your hands.

Playing covers can be a kind of hollow satisfaction, especially if you are doing exact copies of the originals. Some bands are absolutely slavish in this, I think more so in America. I know bands there that write out the parts note for note: *if y'all heard it on the record then we play it*. Of course, the original bands have to play their hits just like they were recorded too, it's what the fans want and expect, like signing your name.

A good guitar player told me when he went to see Stevie Ray Vaughan he was devastated because he 'just regurgitated the songs on his album with each solo note for note'. It's the price of fame. Little Feat are different; they love to improvise and probably haven't played any song the same way twice. Bob Dylan often plays bizarre new versions of his old songs and to hell with what anyone thinks, but that's Him. But most stick exactly to what sold millions of albums. I was at a Bruce Springsteen gig once and some lunatic kept yelling *Born To Run*. Eventually Bruce had to shut the guy up. *Do you really think there's any chance I* won't *play that?*

It is very interesting to watch YouTube and see bands playing their songs in different venues. *X-Factor* type acts of course always do exact dance routines when they're miming their hits – they'd look pretty stupid otherwise – but some proper bands even use the same well-rehearsed moves on every gig, the exact same facial expressions in the screaming guitar solos. If you have a working formula, why change it?

When you are playing 'covers' you know you are basking in the reflected glory of the original band. The crowd are not there to hear *you*, they are there to hear you play someone's else's work. Some musicians find this hard to accept. Probably the worst gig of all is playing background music in some crappy airport-hotel restaurant that likes to believe that smothering each and every bit of food with some posh-sounding swill makes it classier than Pizza Hut. It's a pain being constantly told to turn down because you are making it difficult for the waitresses to yell out the dinner specials. It is hard to put your heart into playing to some bloated oaf whose only interest is wolfing down a steaming plate of linguine and clam sauce before rushing off to catch a plane. But if you want to earn a living from your instrument it will probably be necessary to do it sooner or later. It comes to most of us.

If you are playing a gig like that, I think it is important to do the best you can, you are getting paid after all. But some musicians seem to think they can get away with using the captive audience to try out their own material – in a bar the customer can always toss back his beer and go next door, but no hungry traveller is going to leave his grub untouched because he doesn't like a song. Some musicians are incredibly insensitive about this. I was in a restaurant in America the other night where the guitarist must had been given a birthday gift of a book showing all the obscure jazz chords – *what's the difference between a rock guitarist and a jazz guitarist? The rock guitarist plays three chords to thousands of people and the jazz guitarist plays...*

And so, like countless other would-be songwriters, he'd turned them into 'original' songs that he and his wife were warbling while the rest of us tried to eat our burgers. You know the kind of thing, no tune but scores of fancy meandering chords. Demented sixths and mental flattened ninths. If there is one thing worse than listening to *Moondance* played badly it's listening to some dirge called 'I Will Never Leave You, My Soul, My Love, My Life' – *available now folks right here on our very own cd*.

I once sat in with a husband and wife band like that. Not only did they write awful songs that were almost impossible to busk along on, but they managed to include religion in them; they were real God-sters. American bands always have hopeful 'Tip' jars at the front of the stage and the lovers had a brief but bitter misunderstanding over the cash. Despite their simpering love songs, she walked out, and just to really tie his ulcers in a knot, was shacked up with a martial arts trainer she'd met on the beach. It's always the most devoted soulmates that have the most entertaining break-ups.

Man and wife duos are very common musical acts in restaurants, where space is at a premium. Every inch given to the 'band' is another inch that could be used to feed a hungry and paying customer. I've seen some very entertaining restaurant duos, sometimes for the wrong reasons. The funniest was in an Austrian ski resort, a father and daughter playing Beatles tunes. She'd grown up breathing deeply of the mountain air, was attractive in a buxom way, and happily favoured the traditional plunging neckline of the Bavarian Alps. Their English was not exactly authentic and the well-known songs were butchered in a Germanic way that made even *Yesterday* sound like a threat of invasion.

The place was full of super-fit young lads, all of them extreme skiers and snowboarders high on the adrenalin of leaping off cliffs, full of Red Bull and Vodka and with levels of testosterone that could fuel a rocket launch. The girl was receiving a lot of attention, which she loved. Her father, looking like a bear in a mountain cave, had other ideas. As he pounded his Casio Keyboard into submission, he glared at any of the lads that got too close, even swiping a huge mutton-like hand at them as if they were bees buzzing around a hive.

For most working musicians, it is covers or nothing. The exception is covers of blues songs. Thankfully the people who go to blues venues usually prefer musicians to play these their own way and not just copy the originals. In this, America and the UK are reversed; it is sadly common to hear blues bands in the UK playing Peter Green's solo in *Need Your Love So Bad* note for note. I've never heard a band in America do it that way. It seems weird to play a blues song exactly like someone else, kind of getting away from the point. Oh...oh... I just remembered something ...I was at a blues jam in London, and this guy got up to play *The Thrill Is Gone*, the BB King classic. He was quite a good guitar player, but had a very strong French accent. The poor guy could not understand why everyone was laughing at him as he sang: 'De Treel Ees Gone...'

Anyway. There are different types of 'cover' bands. Most just play a selection of whatever is or was popular – you'd think that after 40 years, *Brown Eyed Girl* would be growing stale, but definitely not. But other bands specialise. At some point in the distant past, someone realised there was a good living to be made playing in a 'tribute' band. And so every successful band now has many clones playing their songs. I don't know of any band that pays some kind of royalty, license fee or commission to the real artistes, although perhaps some do. Yeah, that'll be the day.

Many of them are very successful, touring the world, tour buses, big trucks, 5-star hotels, backstage catering and laundry services – the lot – even playing more and bigger venues than the originals. There is a seemingly insatiable demand for them, especially when the original band has croaked or split up in such a spectacularly acrimonious way that they will *never* play together again.

There are countless pub-versions of bands that are still touring. AC/DC has hoardes of tribute bands playing all over the world in everything from sweaty pubs to big venues. One of my favourites is Thundherstruck, an all female version from Los Angeles, but then I may just be a dirty old man. And there's the wonderful Hayseed Dixie, who play AC/DC in bluegrass style. Abba will never set foot on a stage again, so to feed the huge demand for their music is Bjorn Again, a franchise, with European, Australian and American versions. They have performed something like 5000 shows in 70 countries. This is big business.

The best of these bands are meticulous in replicating the stars. I played on the same bill recently as a Fleetwood Mac tribute band and very good they were too, even looked just like them, hair, everything. I seriously wondered if the drummer had a nose job to look the part. Tribute acts are unique to the music business; you don't find comedians dressing up as Billy Connolly or Ricky Gervais and telling all their gags. Perhaps there is a rich seam waiting to be mined.

Most tribute bands are pretty boring. Three songs and, yes, you get it. Tribute bands usually play all the right notes but they don't have anything like the charisma or feel of the real stars. Nowhere is this more obvious than Beatles tribute bands, of which there are many.

There's a lot that sets the Beatles apart from any other band. They wrote so many more good songs than anyone else – most bands have built careers on only four or five 'hits'. The Beatles have such clever arrangements, the interplay of the guitars, how the parts fit together and don't clutter the songs, the way they enhance them. The thing with Beatles' songs is that they are so melodically strong many people don't notice the incredible musical depth of the playing behind them. I have often played in bands when someone has suggested doing a Beatles song and I always try to talk them out of it simply because they are far too complex to play properly.

Another thing that makes the Beatles unique seems obvious, but I have never seen it mentioned in any of the books about them. To be a star you need to have an immediately recognisable voice. It is the one factor that major record labels are looking for and will spend big money on promoting. It is exactly the same as in the movie business where film stars must have their own 'trademark' voice. Almost all top bands have only one recognisable singing voice and on that rests their success. The other guys in the band are sidemen.

The Beatles had four distinct voices, each one of them able to front their own band. You know each voice the moment you hear it. Doubtless some academic will correct me, but I can't think of any other band that can be said about. Perhaps CSNY, but they were really four solo artistes brought together for the gig, so it's not the same. The Beatles were a proper band that grew up together and learned their craft over countless all-night gigs in little clubs. These songs that sound so simple are very complicated, and most of the Beatles tribute bands I have seen destroy the music.

There is an exception. The best tribute band I have ever heard, and that is possibly the finest in the world, is the Bootleg Beatles from London. They do an astonishing job of singing in the 'voices' of the Beatles and in capturing their unique harmonies. But what really sets them apart is that they play every note live. The Bootlegs refuse to use 'samples', backing tapes, or any of the keyboard-operated crap most tribute bands need.

Many Beatles songs have string and brass sections on the records, the iconic Sergeant Pepper album being a great example. The Beatles never got around to playing most of these songs live. The Bootlegs tour with their own brass and string players who get really involved in the music. The warmth of these instruments brings the music to life, there is no comparison between the Bootlegs and bands that use electronics as a cheap and easy substitute. Musically, it is fascinating to hear real musicians play these songs as they were intended to be heard. Bearing in mind that Sergeant Pepper is widely regarded as the finest and most important album ever made, it is invaluable from an artistic and cultural point of view that musicians who are contemporaries of the Beatles are performing it live properly with the real instruments. They are only a 'tribute' band in the same way that the LSO might be called a Mozart tribute orchestra.

I've only played in a couple of tribute bands. One was a Stones clone, and I got to do Keef's parts. I loved it – it is amazing how much he actually plays, the whole sound of the Stones comes from him. All these rhythmical accents and things he does.

I've also always liked Rory Gallagher, and when a pal who owns a rehearsal studio called to say he knew someone who needed a bass player for some Rory tribute gigs, I jumped at it. A couple of phone calls and I was all set to audition for them.

Rory, who very sadly passed away in 1995, was one of the most loved and highly respected musicians in the world, and rightly so. Phil Hoolihan, the 'Rory' in the band, sent me a list of songs to learn for the audition and I got stuck in, learning them as close as possible to how Rory's bass player Gerry McAvoy had played them. I love his style of bass playing, nothing fancy, a good solid foundation that allowed Rory to play brilliantly.

When you audition for a band, you should never need to ask if you have got the job. You should know by how you all play together if it is going to work. You can also watch their eyes, the wee glances at one another. You'll know.

I had a pal, a bass player, who auditioned for Hall and Oates when they were about to do a world tour. He'd been a sideman with a couple of well-known songwriters when they had toured and that had opened the door for him. Hall and Oates knew what they were doing when they were auditioning musicians, and picked a brand new song that he wouldn't have been able to learn first. That way they'd get a good idea of how quickly he'd pick up new material. The only problem was that in his previous gigs my pal had been told exactly what to play. He had always been happy to do whatever the writers wanted; he was very respectful of their vision.

So when he plugged into his amp at the Hall and Oates audition and cheerfully asked them what he should play, he genuinely thought he was being professional. The confused silence shook him, and he began to shake as he struggled to figure out tasteful bass parts on the spot. Busking is a skill, but confidence is the most important part. You have to be able to ride out any mistakes you make. It was obvious from the puzzled looks of the other sidemen, guys with the thousand-yard stare of old road dogs, that his fumbling attempts ensured he would not be called back. He never played bass again.

As soon as I started playing with Phil's band, Defender, I knew it would be good. We met in Berkely studios, a great rehearsal room in Glasgow, the best in Scotland. It is a long way from the basement sweatboxes of the old days – it's even air-conditioned. And of course no smoking allowed. It is a good size, so even though the band was louder than they really should have been, it wasn't too deafening. We sounded great.

Phil is a huge Gallagher fan, and we got on very well. I had toured America with the String Band at the same time as Rory was on tour there and got to know him. He'd invited me onstage to jam with him at a gig in Long Island. Unfortunately I let myself down. We'd all drunk far too much before the show. Rory could handle Irish Whiskey. I couldn't. He had given me his beautiful old Strat to play and we battered out some 12-bar tune. I was so drunk I stepped back and tripped over a monitor speaker. In those days, thank fuck, there was no gap between the crowd and the stage and I fell on top of the front rows. They gently pushed me back to my feet. My face still turns bright red when I think about how near I came to wrecking Rory's guitar. Any time I feel like drinking I remember that awful moment. No kidding.

I didn't want to mention I had known Rory, in case they thought I was bragging, so I didn't. After playing the songs they told me I was exactly who they were looking for. I was very pleased because at the time they were exactly what I was looking for too.

They were doing some shows in Norway a couple of months later, then some UK gigs followed by a festival in Ireland. I told them I'd be very happy to do them, especially the Oslo dates because I could ski during the day. When I said that, the drummer and singer gave me a puzzled look. Somehow I got the impression that they would be spending the day in the bar. But the band was good fun, and I respected the way Phil must have spent a great deal of time figuring out Rory's parts – not an easy task.

I had a trip to America booked and headed off, arranging to start rehearsals with the band in January. As soon I came back, and tired from the flights, I headed for a rehearsal room outside Glasgow. This one was very different. It was in an area clearly familiar with the mellow delights of Buckfast wine, roll-up cigarettes, and vomiting contests on the pavements. The studio must have been the only one left in Scotland that allowed smoking. Or perhaps just didn't give a shit. By the time I had plugged in my bass, my head was reeling. The band all had lit cigarettes on the go; I could hardly see the walls for smoke. Phil even had a spare burning in an ashtray at the side of his amp. The room was sealed to keep out the local burglars. It was crammed with overflowing ashtrays. It stank. There was no way to catch a breath of fresh air. The rehearsal was due to last from 6pm until midnight. This was not going to be easy.

If you are a smoker you may not understand how ill smoke can make a non-smoker. You might think all the legislation banning it is an evil conspiracy, but if you do ever manage to quit, after a couple of years you may find that your body seems to become allergic to smoke. It's very weird. I used to smoke 40 a day, had a hell of a time stopping, but now I have been off them for over 20 years I can't stand being near a lit cigarette. It's as if your lungs go mental at the slightest sniff of burning tobacco. Come to think of it, I don't remember ever seeing Rory with a cigarette in his hand.

As the rehearsal went on, I felt worse and worse. I had only a few hour's sleep after the flight from America and with each song felt more and more tired. The drummer and singer were gulping down superlagers and chain smoking. In the tiny room the band was defeaning; the drummer was hitting his kit like a one-man demolition company. I began to make mistakes.

When there is only bass and a guitar in a band there is nowhere to hide. The drummer heard me flagging. I felt lousy from lack of sleep and the smoke; I couldn't concentrate. And the volume of the drums was killing me. I began to worry. I was meeting the editor and a photographer from a magazine the next morning before dawn. They were doing a special feature on a book I had written about climbing and all that malarkey. The rehearsal wasn't due to finish until midnight. I'd be lucky to get four hours sleep before having to climb a bloody big mountain.

Rock bass playing is very physical and needs strong hands. I was pounding out the notes as best I could, but my concentration had gone, I couldn't remember the parts, and was late on a couple of chord changes. At the end of one song the drummer glared at me.

"Ah fucking heard that!"

When the *drummer* in the band notices you've played a wrong note you realise you're really playing badly. He gulped back yet another Super-Lager, tossed the can on the floor with the others, opened a fresh tin, took a deep pull on his cigarette then turned to me. His eyes seemed to be focused in different directions.

"You're fucking not fucking playing the fucking way you fucking did last time!"

He was right. I wasn't.

As the rehearsal went on, thick tobacco smoke filled every corner of the room and the drummer played louder and louder. I was holding back; instead of driving the songs as I should have been, I was trying to breathe and worrying about climbing an ice-covered mountain next morning. My playing got worse. Then the looks, the little glances between each band member. By half past ten, they knew and I knew this was pointless.

I called Phil the next day and told him I was sorry, but I just hadn't been able to function with that amount of smoke in the room. And I reckoned that drinking large amounts of alcohol at rehearsals was wrong; with each can of beer the drumming got louder and louder. The drummer was a good guy, but I couldn't work in that atmosphere. Phil was very nice, said he'd realised what was happening and that next rehearsal would be different, but I called off. I promised to do the Norway gigs if they needed me, but said I reckoned they'd be better with another bass player. One that smoked.

A month or so later I bumped into the band in the State Bar, a Glasgow pub famous for its weekly jam sessions. The drummer was very apologetic about the amount he'd been drinking, said he'd been going through a rough time. We talked for a while then the house band let us get up and play a couple of Rory's songs.

The drummer was very loud, so Phil turned way up too. So did I. Fuck it, why not? I had seen Rory Gallagher close up often enough to know he actually played fairly quietly. But the drummer was hitting the kit as if it had attacked him. The bemused crowd stared at us. A couple had their hands over their ears. We were playing Rory's songs, but the way the Keith Moon and the Who might have done them. Or perhaps Motorhead.

I loved it.

29

WE ARE *NOT* THE INCREDIBLE
STRING BAND 1

I was at a party and I heard former String Band member Malcolm le Maistre singing some songs that the folks were loving. It got me thinking. Malcolm has a distinctive voice, and for some reason he has managed to hold onto it. Most singers lose a lot of quality and range after they hit 50 – isn't life cruel? Wouldn't it be so much better if our bodies worked perfectly until, say, 60 or 70, then we simply dropped dead, cold before we hit the deck, as if a switch had been pulled? The tortuous, slow, gnawing decline of the human body must give Satan his biggest laugh.

The Incredible String Band could and should still be touring; they certainly had a big enough following. Most of their contemporaries, Joan Baez, Bob Dylan, Fairport Convulsion, Pentangle, CSNY and the rest are still selling out all over the world. Sleepy old Leonard Cohen did a 270-gig, two-year tour when he was almost 80. Even Joe Boyd, a former manager of the String Band, is on the talk circuit with an acoustic guitar player. And why not? There's a massive worldwide audience of older people who still love live music. What band are they going to want to see? *X-Factor* winners? A musically-savvy generation that grew up with the Stones, the Beatles, the Who, Zep and the rest is not going to queue all night to buy tickets to see freakin Jedward.

The two main musicians in the ISB, Mike and Robin, were extremely talented. Still are. They were never guys who readily followed advice or the opinions of others, and working together was difficult for them. They were either never interested in the commercial practicalities of running a successful band, or they were very naïve in the ways of the business world. Perhaps that was part of their charm. In some ways I didn't really fit in with the band – when I played with them I spent hours trying to talk the manager into opening a chain of Incredible Coffee shops – this was long before Starbucks.

I say this uncritically; I talk to Mike and Robin regularly; I will always be indebted to them for letting me play in their band when I was young, and love them both dearly. I admire them for playing from the soul; it is a rare thing these days not to bow to the forces of capitalism when one really good tour could rake in a nice retirement fund. They did do a sort of reunion tour around 2000, but their choice of material was not quite what loyal fans were expecting. Mike and Robin… well… they always had their way of doing things.

And so I was very interested when I heard Malcolm sing at the party. Malcolm played with the band for about four years, and wrote strong songs for the albums. He is also good at chatting to audiences. The people of a certain age who are willing to go to gigs on cold winter nights want a lot more than 15 tunes thrown at them. They like chat. The biggest selling acts these days are not bands; they are stand-up comedians. I find this very interesting. Many of them tour the same venues that bands used to play in, and some effortlessly pack huge venues that only a few bands could sell out.

The thing is, if you are at a comedy show it is all about the intimacy and the atmosphere. If you watch many of these guys on TV, they aren't very funny. And there's a fair chance you will have seen them on TV so you'll have heard their material already. You can happily listen to *Dark Side of the Moon* over and over again, but jokes? But if you are in the room the warmth they create is what makes the show. I love comedy shows; I love the banter.

So I asked Malcolm if he would be interested in doing a show at the Edinburgh Fringe Festival that would be half music and half chat. The idea would be that we create a relaxed feel, as if all of us in the room were sitting around a kitchen table, telling stories and singing songs. Malcolm was intrigued but very cautious – he has been running a theatre company for 20 years and has appeared in many shows at the Fringe. He knew only too well that almost all of them lose money, there's just so much competition – we would be up against 40,254 performances of 2,453 shows in 259 venues, to be exact. Selling out a show is a rare thing.

The way the Fringe works is that the artistes hire the main venues. They pay for room rental, commission on all tickets sold, advertising, inclusion in the Fringe brochure – expensive and an absolute necessity – and other things. Next time a performer gives you a free ticket for his show at the Fringe you should be aware that he has almost certainly paid for it. Just thought I'd mention it.

There are always shows featuring the top comedy acts in the world – the Fringe has more comedy acts than anything else, possibly because it's the cheapest form of theatre, you only need a microphone, a few people at the front from out of town to take the piss out of and maybe a heckler or two.

It's great that so many people enjoy simply listening to someone telling funny stories – it is so much more personal than some drunk, stoned, skinny rock star yelling *'ello Edinburgh, is you ready to rock!* The beautiful old city is packed to bursting point all through the Fringe, even in these austere times. But selling out is still an Everest to climb; oh, did

I mention that already?

Malcolm invited me through to his home in the armpit of beyond. It was in deepest West Lothian somewhere, in an area famed for UFO sightings, although you would think that with the galaxy to choose from green men from some distant constellation might pick more picturesque places to visit. Perhaps they thought no-one could possibly be living there, or maybe they just like shopping at Spar. Even the normally reliable woman on Tom Tom had no idea where to find it, gave up somewhere in the woods near Avonbridge. That's a place where a farmer grows scrap cars. I passed his scene of pastoral beauty three times trying to find the correct turn off.

Malcolm's long-time partner is a very enterprising woman called Mary, the daughter of a Lancashire hill farmer. Ee, by gum, they know what's what, lad. While Malcolm had been pursuing an artistic career for the last 30 years, Mary had quietly been making sure he eats properly and pays the electricity bill on time. This may sound patronising, but it is amazing how many musicians have returned from world tours to discover the gas had been cut off because they forgot to pay by direct debit. She is a kindly soul, and for many years has quietly been running a training programme for young people who found themselves homeless and out of work. She never talks about it, but she has helped a lot of people.

She's been the generator behind Malcolm. Many people buy run down houses and do them up; Mary found an abandoned and crumbling stone-masons' village, complete with former school building, the lot. They realised it could be beautiful; seemed a tragedy that it was falling apart. She and Malcolm discovered it had special architectural significance and have spent the last 20 years restoring it – backbreaking work. She's expert in ferreting out obscure Government grants, and even found some environmental scheme that allows her to recruit a voluntary army of students from all over Europe to help with the heavy labouring work, building paths, walls and so on. Many of them come because, correctly, they realise that a working commune in Scotland is an ideal place to find hippy chicks and spend a few blissful weeks getting laid. And so Malcolm watches in amusement as temporary romances unfold every summer, and does his best to get the volunteers digging ditches at least a few hours a day in return for a mattress in the barn and homemade soup in the kitchen.

Following exact and painstaking directions, involving turning left at specific trees and right at derelict barns and crossing tumbling streams, I finally found his house, and stunning it was too. A beautiful stone-built cottage, but about four times the size of what you are probably imagining. Spread over two sprawling floors, it had several bedrooms and from the gasps of pleasure coming from one of them a couple of young folk were having an energetic lunch break.

Malcolm took me into the kitchen and introduced me to his three spaniels. I am kind of wary about dogs, I always have been, but Malcolm's were lovely. Crazy, leaping about like demented little things, wonderfully friendly. Maybe it's just yob dogs I don't like – pitbulls and other slavering hounds. The kitchen was packed with students and migrant workers from many countries, many of them holding hands and gazing deeply into one another's eyes. It is a sure sign of approaching old age when every twenty-year-old girl seems heart-achingly beautiful, even the wee fat ones. But they were. Several languages were being spoken over the lentil broth and home-made bread. It tasted great.

I find Malcolm very easy to talk to; he is exceptionally bright and has well-researched knowledge of many subjects, most of which I know nothing about. Everywhere I looked I could see his books. Thousands of them. His American mother was a successful author, she even wrote some sort of porn novel. Malcolm looks like an absent-minded professor, wears glasses, is balding with most of what's left in a long ponytail. His clothes were purchased at South Kensington market round about 1968, and I am sure he was wearing the same brown corduroy trousers the first time I met him back in the 70s. He doesn't really look like someone who played some of the biggest venues in America and Europe when he was young.

He is vegetarian, hates any kind of ill-treatment of animals, will talk for hours about caring for the environment, even keeping used tea bags in a wee tin thing. Generally speaking, I'm not in the habit of releasing toxic waste into my local rivers, or radioactive gases into the atmosphere, but keeping a recycling container for tea bags is far beyond my level of commitment to the cause. He showed me trees he was growing from seedlings he'd gathered in the forest. Not just any old trees, but proper brands like willows, and ash, and elm and things. Over the years he has gradually created a whole wee forest at his back door. They are his children. Like an ageing professor he can be a little grumpy, and gets exasperated easily, but he is easy to like. He also writes very good songs, about interesting things.

He took me through to the back of the cottage where he had a recording studio buried beneath mountains of books, sheet music, magazines and partially restored ancient furniture, most of it liberated from skips in posh suburbs of Edinburgh. He waved out a young couple that were locked together in a voyage of panting discovery and we began playing our guitars. It felt great. We played a few old String Band songs, and some other ones that he'd written.

I was very excited at the prospect of playing original songs again instead of covers. We played well together; we knew right away that the show could work. He was up for it as long as I understood, very clearly understood, that he couldn't put any money into it, not a coin. Rebuilding a village, as he was, takes a lot of money, every penny he had, even with half of

202

Lithuania helping him, or at least when he could stop them shagging each another for an hour or so.

I told him about the wee fat roadie I had seen at the Fringe and how the crowd had loved his tales, even if they did seem like bullshit. Then we both remembered Stan, the former bass player in the String Band. Before he had joined the ISB, he had worked with all sorts of people, including Muddy Waters, Noel Redding and Mick Jagger; a lot more than the wee fat roadie. If we could get him on stage with us he would surely have loads of stories to tell. We wondered what he was up to these days?

That's when the fun started.

30

WE ARE *NOT* THE INCREDIBLE
STRING BAND 2

After the String Band had split up I hadn't spoken to Stan in over 30 years, but it only took seconds to find him on the miracle that is Facebook. I know FB or, Spazbook as some cruel people call it, has its critics but I think it is wonderful how we can type in an old pal's name and they pop up in a flash. Although I imagine young people may have a torrid time with it, as dumped girlfriends take revenge, and drunk lads shoot their mouths off about their soon to be ex-boss. Thank God there was no FB when I was young. I dread to think of what I might have said on it.

I fired off a message to Stan and he replied. He was living in New York City, had been for years. Was I ever over there? *Must meet some time, lol.*

I love New York City and had loads of air miles that had been piling up for years. I realised I had enough for a free trip including a hotel for a few nights. Idly I tapped away on my computer to see if I could actually use them – airlines usually have so many 'blackout' dates that you're never able to cash in their damn miles. Surprise! February was a quiet month; for once the dates were available. Glasgow was dark and damp, cold and wet. New York was freezing but snow was forecast to fall on Central Park soon. Have you ever been in Central Park as the snow gently drifts down from above? It is the dog's bollocks. I don't think the tourist brochure puts it quite like that but New York in snow is a sight to see. A few weeks later I found myself waiting to meet Stan at a hotel on 55th Street.

I recognised him the minute I saw him, and he greeted me with a huge smile. We talked about old times, all the gigs we'd played together with the String Band, we couldn't remember how many, but maybe 200. Was it really that many? And the good people we had lost along the way, as Bob Marley's song goes. But Stan knew I hadn't just come to share war tales, and I got down to it.

I explained that Malcolm and I were putting a show together for the Fringe. I told him we'd like him to play lapsteel guitar and tell 'road' stories. Was he up for it?

He loved the idea but was worried about what the founder members of the band, Mike and Robin, might think. He liked them both and didn't want to upset them even though he hadn't seen them for years. He didn't want them to think we were cashing in on the band's name. But yes, as long as they weren't pissed off about it, he'd fly over to Scotland in August to rehearse and do the show with us.

This was exactly what I had hoped. We shook hands and I agreed to e mail him the songs we'd be playing so he would have time to figure out parts. I was very pleased. I had a terrific five days happily wandering around favourite places in Manhattan: the Park – in the snow it was lovely – the Natural History Museum, Bleaker Street, Washington Square, walking across the Brooklyn Bridge, all those things. I even jumped on one of those open-top tour buses and settled back to listen to the tour guide. He was a troubled soul.

"On our left is the Dakota Building, where John Lennon was shot on that terrible day in 1980. I bet we can all remember where we were *that* day". He paused for effect.

"And now on our right is the Cathedral of St. John the

Divine, the fourth largest church in the world. That's right, folks. In the entire world, and it's right here on Amsterdam Avenue, New York City. Construction on the cathedral began with the laying of the cornerstone on December 27, 1892. Which is over a century ago," he added, for the benefit of a party of people from Arkansas.

"The foundations were completed at enormous expense, largely because bedrock was not struck until the excavation had reached 72 feet. The walls were built around eight massive 130-ton, 50-foot granite columns, sourced from Vinalhaven, Maine and said to be the largest in the world. But I could spend all day telling you about Manhattan's old buildings. I'm guessing what you really want to know, is where in the city do you get the cheapest ham and eggs? Am I right?"

He continued, telling us about his favourite diner on East 42nd Street, full breakfast under six bucks, and then switched to a different subject.

"Would you like to buy clothes that belonged to the stars? When Woody Allen and Madonna give clothes to a charity shop, which one do they go to? Well let me tell you which one."

He spoke with enthusiasm and I was enjoying it, even if the other passengers seemed a little confused. Then his voice dropped, and he sounded very somber.

"And if you stay on the bus to Downtown, we will pass Ground Zero. Where on that awful day the world changed. My brother was a cop there, and he saw it all. They were jumping out of the building. Landing at his feet. Have you ever seen what happens to a body when it falls from the 90th floor onto concrete? Have you any goddam idea of what that looks like? Right there in front of him. Well that's what my brother saw, and he hasn't been the same since. When those rag heads flew the goddam planes into…"

I thought it best to get off at the next stop.

Stan, Malcolm and I kept in touch by e mail. Stan was insistent that we make it clear that we were not some sort of Incredible String Band reunion. Malcolm and I both agreed that neither of us wanted this – we didn't want to annoy Mike and Robin. But we couldn't escape the fact that we added up to half the final line up of the band, and people were bound to mention our connection. Stan was quite agitated about this and sent me another long e mail. I needed to do something to calm him or he would pull out. I called him.

"Ok Stan, how about we call the show, *We Are NOT the Incredible String Band*?"

He laughed. That was a good sign. And so that became our name. Or the name of the show. Or both. I let Stan decide.

I did all the stuff you need to do to organise a show at the Fringe: booking the venue, the dates, the times, the adverts, all the wee bits and pieces. I started rehearsals with Malcolm. We recorded the songs we planned to do then e mailed them to Stan. Isn't technology fab? Stan would reply, with often animated, and always detailed comments running to hundreds, perhaps thousands of words telling us songs we should check out, arrangements to which we should pay great attention. He was taking this very, very seriously. Eventually we kind of stopped reading them. It would all work out when he arrived at the end of July.

I asked him to send me his road tales; he had great stories. He had toured with so many people, managed Art Garfunkel and Janis Ian, worked on television as a talent handler, looking after Al Pacino, De Niro, all the big names. His stories were long and rambling with the main points coming in the middle and needless explanations afterwards. But there was so much good material. He is a very likeable guy. He told me he was nervous about telling his stories on stage but if I could rewrite them in a way that got to the point in half the time he'd give it a go. So I did.

The summer soon came, or at least summer as we know it in Scotland. It's usually three or four days we remember. The emails flew back and forth. At last the morning arrived when I had to pick Stan up. I drove to Glasgow airport and managed to stop my car about five miles from the Terminal building. Ever since those guys tried to drive right into it with a car full of bomb, they have tightened up security so much it feels like you are entering a military installation. Stan was there, gazing around, looking for me.

He was here, we were going to do this.

31

WE ARE *NOT* THE INCREDIBLE STRING BAND 3

Malcolm, Stan and I had finally agreed on the songs we would play, and the tales we'd tell. It hadn't been easy though. Stan was self-conscious about his playing, and didn't want any other musicians in the band. Malcolm and I wanted a few more to add some extra sound layers, harmonies, that sort of thing. Malcolm was very keen on a female double bass player he'd written some songs with; she could play well and had a nice singing voice. Stan hummed and hawed but agreed to meet her and see how it sounded, which was just as well since Malcolm and I had been rehearsing with her without telling him. Fortunately he liked her and we were now a four-piece band, but no more or Stan would *catch the next fucking plane home, ok?* That would have been bad; we really needed Stan's road tales in the show.

I'd given Stan a room at my house in Glasgow. He had originally planned on staying with Malcolm, thinking the Scottish countryside would be such a nice change from the honking traffic of Manhattan, but he found it hard to cope with the writhing Eastern European workers groping one another in every corner of the commune. Every day for two weeks we drove through to rehearse and I would coach Stan on how to tell his stories.

He was very jittery about the whole thing, and told me a few times he'd changed his mind, he wasn't going to say a damn word at the gigs, he'd leave the chat to Malcolm and me. This was worrying; Stan's road tales were terrific, far funnier than the wee fat roadie I'd seen at the Assembly Rooms. And when he relaxed he told them well.

We had lined up a few warm up gigs before the Fringe shows. The first was at a cute little village called Carradale, in southwest Scotland, headlining a small folk festival. Scotland has so many of these beautiful wee places tucked away off sleepy B roads that are perfect for cycling on, they make you feel as if you are back in the 1920s. And there are lovely forests and lochs and sparkling wee streams and hundreds of beautiful soaring mountains, proper ones. Stan loved the drive; he was in a good mood.

Carradale is near Campbeltown, so everyone knew Paul McCartney, and had lots of stories of their own about when he lived there with Wings. When he found this out Stan began to twitch nervously. The festival was being held in the village hall just like so many of these halls all over the country – it brought back a lot of memories from my young days with Powerhouse. I just hoped I wouldn't meet anyone from then.

Malcolm likes to play acoustic, he's not very comfortable using amplifiers and stage gear; he gets a bit flustered. The problem with working without backline amps is that you then completely rely on the soundman to send a mix back to the monitors or you can't hear what you are playing. So I had insisted that we use some stage amps. That way we could get a good sound on stage that we were in control of and just have vocals coming through the monitors.

We set up our gear, tuned our guitars, plugged into our amps and played a few songs. It sounded good. We had put in a lot of rehearsal time – most of the bands I had been playing with in recent years had been thrown together and we just busked all night, making it up as we went along. It felt very nice knowing exactly what we would be playing for a change.

Doors open.

We waited in a room behind the stage, pacing the floor, bobbing from foot to foot, peeking out to see if there would be a crowd. It would be awful if the place was empty.

Within minutes, the hall was packed.

This was good.

Malcolm hands were trembling before we went on; he always gets very nervous, even though he's played thousands of gigs. I get the same way when I am flying; the flight is fine, it's all the palaver checking in and queuing at security checks – I get agitated because I keep thinking the plane will fly off without me. I also get like that when I am skiing and looking over the edge of something silly; I suppose it's all part of the buzz.

Somebody announced us. We walked on stage: a huge cheer.

It sounded so good.

It was time to play.

We started with an old String Band song. The crowd stood and clapped and cheered. I felt a surge of relief. I introduced the band, talked a little about the dear old ISB. Then it was time for Stan to tell the first of his road stories. I knew if he kept calm and didn't speak too fast, he'd be fine. I smiled at him, *come on, you can do this.*

He took a deep breath and stepped up to the mic, then told his tale about how he'd been asked to pick Jack Bruce up from Kennedy airport many years ago. Stan had found him in Arrivals, and noticed he was dressed in flowing, flowery hippy clothes. So he thought he'd perhaps shake him up a bit. At the time there had been riots in Harlem, so Stan had driven Jack past smouldering rubble and burnt out scenes of carnage.

"So whaddya think of Noo Yawk?" Stan asked him.

Jack idly looked out the car window at what might have been a mugging in progress.

"Hey it's just like home. I'm from Glasgow."

The crowd laughed their heads off. Stan smiled, a huge grin. I could see the tension leave him and knew then that the show would be fine.

Our next warm up gig was at Malcolm's commune, playing to the young migrant workers. They seemed to enjoy the music ok, but I think the stories went over their heads; most of them only spoke a little English. Apart from that, they were too busy doing the warm up work for the night's boffing, and lay around in each other's arms, fondling one another, like it was West Lothian's Woodstock.

And so to the next gig: Dunfermline folk club. The large back room of a pub, a fiver to get in. Now I hadn't played in a folk club since I was very young. Even the String Band never played them; we only ever did medium to large venues. But I had fond memories of these places. They used to be so cool, a great place to hang out because it was gang-free. In the 60s and 70s, Glasgow was full of marauding lunatics who enjoyed slashing innocent people; the genteel academics who pontificate about this being something to do with deprived backgrounds missed the fact that some nutters just love the thrill of violence, much like an extreme skier or a bungee jumper.

These guys loved Tamla Motown music long before Northern Soul, as it became known, finally reached the famous Wigan Casino, and the only clubs in town bounced and punched to the Four Tops, Isley Bros, Sam and Dave, and the rest. I loved the music, but not enough to risk having my face rearranged in a permanent sort of way.

The few folk clubs in Glasgow were peaceful oasis of art students, beautiful girls wearing flared denims and white cotton tops with hair tumbling onto their breasts, and thoughtful musicians who played acoustic guitars. If you could play *Anji* by the legendary guitarist Davy Graham, you were made. If you had managed to learn *Black Mountainside* by Bert Jansch – the song later 'borrowed' by Jimmy Page – then your hard work might be warmly rewarded by one of the lovely hippy chicks. So I was looking forward to this gig, what would it be like?

Of course, nothing like the old days. The people were all very nice, very friendly. But also very old. I felt like I was playing in the Happy Duck Rest Home for the Bewildered. And something I had forgotten: in the old days anyone could get up and play something. I used to go round folk clubs and do a couple of instrumentals – I was never much of a singer – anything that would get me on a stage. The club still encouraged people to get up 'from the floor.' When I was young that was simply an expression, but judging by the frail years of the people here it could be worryingly true.

There was a fiddle player who played some jigs, well sort of. He was in his 90s, so I think he had to be careful not to play faster than his pacemaker or things might have got out of hand. It was great to see someone that old still playing though, even if his hands were a tad brittle. And a guy who unfortunately was blind, but could sing in a weird Cornish accent all 22 verses of a song about…I don't know, some traditional ballad. I have no idea what he was warbling on about. It must have been an amazing feat of memory, although I doubted if anyone would have noticed if he changed a few verses. There was an obnoxious drunk who sang some of Robert Burns's baudier songs, droning on and on and would not shut the fuck up. And a sweet old lady that crooned about fishing for mackerel and how her troo luv was gone far to sea. She also sang in that strange Cornish accent that folkies sing in, even if they come from the East End of Glasgow.

It wasn't really what I expected, but they seemed to like us ok.

And so to the Fringe.

On the first morning of the show you are allowed a very quick sound check at the venue you are playing. I drove through to Edinburgh with Stan, who was gaining in confidence every day. Apart from selling out, which I may have mentioned already, the most difficult thing about playing at the Fringe is finding somewhere to park. Most of the buildings were built long before cars were invented, had no stage access areas, and the stern traffic wardens have absolutely no mercy, no matter how much gear you have to unload.

Malcolm had enlisted a few of his volunteer workers, and I managed to grab a metered parking bay only about quarter of a mile from the gig. This is a wonderful feeling. Finding a parking spot in Edinburgh is like winning a wee prize on the lottery. I put a suitcase of coins into the machine and we started *humphing* – that's the Scots word – our amps and instruments to the backstage door.

The gig was in the Gilded Balloon, one of the three top venues for the Fringe, in the wonderful old building of Edinburgh University, which has been *influencing the world since 1583*, according to its website. The whole place was converted to accommodate shows of varying sizes that run all day. We had the prime time slot, 8–9pm, for three nights, Thursday, Friday and Saturday, but there are shows that start as early as eleven in the morning. I often go to early shows and remember seeing a guy doing stand up at 3 o'clock in the afternoon; I was mighty relieved we weren't on at that time, there were only three people there. Mind you, that comedian – Eddie Izzard – has done pretty well since. If you catch enough early shows you'll see someone who goes on to be a star. The Fringe festival is very exciting that way.

We had half an hour to set up the amps, play a few songs to check mic levels and all that stuff. The first show of the day was due to start at noon – I think it was a children's puppet theatre or something – so as soon as we had done our quick run through we had to take our gear off stage and stash it out of sight until tonight. One of Malcolm's workers, a guy from Belarus called Dimitri, took charge, assigning tasks to each of the volunteers: one of them would look after the amp for the double bass, another would set up my amp and Stan's lap steel guitar amplifier.

And so to the next essential job facing any Fringe performer. Handing out fliers. Selling out is extremely difficult — you can see where I'm going with this, heh heh. If you are to have any chance of filling your venue you need to roll your sleeves up and get out on the streets. Edinburgh is a heaving mass of humanity during the Fringe – I can understand why locals get pissed off, although many of them cash in by renting out their flats in August for enough money to pay their mortgage for another year. If you want a crowd you have to be prepared to earn it, get out there with leaflets for your show and badger as many people as you can to come along.

Most performers either do it themselves or employ street teams. I love this sort of thing; I've always been a salesman. Malcolm wouldn't do it, he gets nervous enough before a show, but had brought along a lovely Swedish girl and her new special friend from the commune to help. Malcolm's son Frey was with them, ready to steer as many people as he could to the show; he works in performing arts and has taken part in many shows in the Fringe so he knew the script. Dimitri and his girlfriend also took a huge stack of leaflets and we positioned ourselves in key spots outside the Gilded Balloon. Stan didn't fancy handing out fliers so disappeared into the throng with his camera – back home in Manhattan he is a photographer and he wanted to take pictures for a book he was planning. Or something.

At last, eight o'clock.

We were sitting onstage as the crowd filtered in, finding seats. We chatted to some of them, we wanted the show to feel very relaxed. Most were avoiding the front row because so many shows at the Fringe are stand up comedy and the front row is always the target. So we reassured them we wouldn't be picking on anyone, wouldn't be doing any of that 'is there anyone from out of town' stuff. The front rows quickly filled. It was looking good...

We didn't quite fill the place the first night, there were a few empty seats at the back. The show went great though, and some old friends appeared that we hadn't seen for years. Next day we spent even more time handing out fliers. The Swedish girl and Dimitri were great, wouldn't let anyone pass without giving them a flier for the show and telling them how good it was. The second night looked completely packed. Did I mention how difficult it is to sell out at the Fringe?

On the third night, just before the house manager did his speech about switching off mobile phones and where to find the exits, he turned to us and made the official announcement we had hoped to hear.

"You have sold out."

We knew we had a good show; the crowd gave us a tremendous reception. My son came through and filmed us so we would have a wee souvenir. There was no time to set up multiple cameras, or special lighting, there were other shows immediately before and after us, so we were only allowed ten minutes to set up and take down our stuff. Malcolm and I thought he managed to get a very good result bearing in mind how difficult that was.

Stan had to go back to New York. It had been great playing together again after all these years, and we had a nice dinner before he left. Malcolm and I reckoned that we could keep the show going, we had joked onstage that the five gigs we had done had been more of a commute than a tour. So I began to plan a small-venue tour of the UK, and a few nights in Dublin at the theatre I'd done with Marsha. When word had got out that three ex Incredible String Band members were playing together I began getting e mails from people in America that were keen to bring us over to play some shows. This is what I hoped would happen.

I e mailed Stan, and asked him if he would like to do some proper tours, but it was clear that he was feeling nervous again. When I mentioned that the film my son had shot looked really good, he had a palpatural. How dare we film him and even think of letting anyone see it without his editorial consent? He demanded that we send it to him right away so that he could go over it and tell my son what to use and what must be deleted.

I tried to explain that this was only a dvd for our own use, that my son didn't have the time to spend editing it, it was what it was, but he wouldn't listen. Artistes can be very highly strung. For some reason he seemed terrified that I would be selling the dvd on Amazon. I couldn't understand why this would bother him – it wouldn't affect him and anyway, the film was good. Maybe he'd played a few bum notes, but who cares? But the more I tried to reason with him, the more agitated he became. I lost patience and we fell out; it was obvious we wouldn't work together again.

It was a pity and I was annoyed. We could have had a great time touring.

I didn't break my promise, I didn't sell the dvd on Amazon.

I just put it on Youtube.

Heh heh.

32

THE COFFINS

Wee Joe Bone sips his Costa coffee and recoils.

"Sugar. When it's that size I need a lot of sugar."

He stares at the giant cup, then drops in a couple more. Coffee wasn't always his drink of choice.

He's in a good mood today. His band, the Coffins, or the *mighty* Coffins, as they are becoming known, has just released a cd. It's not really a finished product, it's a collection of demos. It's rough, but a lot of people have been asking for it, and they have managed to put this together on a budget of not a fucking coin. The 'launch' was on Saturday night at a Glasgow music pub and they packed the fucking place.

Joe is grinning. It was so busy there was no room to set up a table to sell the fucking cds. The place was fucking bouncing. And even though their manager decided to quit after the gig – fuck knows why – Joe is going to keep on grinning. The drummer has just quit too, he's been offered some sort of a job in Vietnam or Thailand or one of these places. Already he's trying to sell his kit through Facebook. He's going there because it's a great country to ride his motorbike. Ah well, it's his loss; Joe has another drummer lined up. No setback is going to stop the Coffins. No fucking way.

The Coffins are not a boy band. The name is a good clue. They are an 'unsigned' band. They face the same cliff face as all unsigned bands. To attract the attention of a record label, the kind that has the clout, money and speed dial numbers to move a band from obscurity to national radio play, you need to be noticed. To do that you need to pull crowds of people who want to hear you play. If you can do that then the record labels will flock to you. In every town in Britain, unsigned bands are playing free every night of the week, all of them clamouring for attention. Very few will make it. Unsigned bands spend a great deal of time and effort trying to convince the big labels to send one of their talent scouts to check them out, but they are usually wasting their time. If a band is creating a buzz, then the talent scouts will know about it without being told. It's their job.

If a band is pulling lots of people in their hometown, if they have built a large following, the labels are not slow to realise that this could be duplicated nationally and internationally. They will approach the band, sign them, and start them on their climb to success. Many disgruntled musicians bitch about record labels, and often have good reasons, but they overlook one simple fact. The labels *want* their bands to sell millions of cds, even more than the bands do – their jobs depend on finding new talent.

Right now the Coffins, like millions of other unsigned bands around the world, are doing whatever they can to get heard, grabbing as many gigs as they can, sending out messages on Facebook to as many people as possible, trying to pack the next gig. It's not easy – there are so many shit bands yapping about themselves that the punters get fed up. They've heard all the talk before, been suckered into paying five quid for tickets too many times.

Occasionally labels will listen to demo cd's but the way to get signed is simple: nothing puts them off more than a band playing to an empty room and nothing impresses them more than a queue outside a gig. The Coffins had a big queue. Joe is *very fucking pleased, by the way.*

The world is full of musicians who played in bands, enjoyed the lifestyle too much, and ended up alcoholics. It's a well-travelled road. Joe did it the other way round; he started off as an alcoholic and cured himself by playing in bands. The Coffins have kept him sober.

"I realised one day that I could either drink, or play in a band, but not both."

Joe is in his 40s now, and it took him a long time to reach that understanding. Before the Coffins, he was "basically a drunk, a party animal." He's lost count of the number of times he'd been in rehab; he does recall that he has seen prison cells 14 times, always for drunk and incapable, that kind of stupidity. If the Coffins do make the big breakthrough, if they do get to tour the UK, he'll drive past every jail he's been in and wave. He's looking forward to it.

Glasgow has a badly deserved reputation for alcohol-fuelled violence. If scientists ever get round to investigating it, they may find many people here have the same genetic defect as the Apache Indians, the firewater drives them nuts. Joe grew up in Possil, an area where violence was lurking on every street corner. He personally knows six convicted murderers. Fortunately, alcohol didn't make him violent, he "just loved to party. I get the same buzz now when I play with the band." Music has saved him. But it was a near thing.

If you have ever spent a few minutes with rock climbers and mountaineers, you'll know they take great delight in telling tales of near-death in the mountains. They love sitting in a bar somewhere in the Scottish Highlands, or Kathmandu, or Sheffield – where the 'right hard' climbers live – swapping stories of how they spent the night dangling on a bit of string from some desperate ledge after something had gone horribly wrong. Climbing books are full of these yarns. Alcoholics, too, tell of the times that they were almost killed, but through *the drink*.

Joe shrugs and grins : "These stories become part of your

banter, the things you laugh about later."

Like a reckless climber, Joe has many tales of stupidity. The time as a young man he staggered onto a busy road and was hit by a car. Bones shattered, he has metal rods and plates holding his small skeleton together. Three months in hospital – it should have been longer but his doctor spotted him on his crutches, getting rat arsed in the pub across the street. Told him to leave – if he was fit enough to stagger to the pub, he was fit enough to fuck off home.

Or the days when he used to be a pool-hustler. His father had started him off young, taking him to play snooker in the kind of places where it was wise not to bump into anyone. Joe had a natural talent for the game, switched to pool, and by 18, he could beat anyone. *Fucking anyone.* He used to visit bars all over the country with pals, who would set up the big bets by playing the local hot shots and getting beaten. Then they would point to wee Joe, who looked about 14, and tell them that the boy could beat them. Joe always won.

One time, in Newcastle, he couldn't resist playing one of his trick shots to end a game. The local big man immediately knew he'd been conned, was not happy about losing a week's wages. Joe realised from the way he was staring at him that it was all going to go bad. So he bought a bottle of cheap champagne, shook it up. He held the cork in, then pointed the bottle at the guy's head. Joe's aim was perfect, when he released the cork it flew straight at the man, hitting him smack between the eyes. He dropped like a corpse. The man's friends thought he had been shot, and all hell let loose. Joe managed to escape, but it was a close thing; the pub was wrecked and skulls broken.

He's always been a survivor, has now stayed sober long enough to breathe a sigh of relief, but even when he was drinking managed to hold down some well paid jobs – he reckons that alcoholics, because their addiction is so demanding, sometimes make better employees than normal people.

"If a normal person wakes up with a hangover, they might take the day off. But an alcoholic can't do that, he knows he must make money for his next drink..."

So despite being hit by fast moving traffic, chased from bars, falling asleep in a ditch in sub-zero temperatures – the police doctor who examined him couldn't believe he hadn't frozen to death although Joe laughs that the alcohol in his blood acted as antifreeze – and even surgery for bowel cancer, wee Joe battled on.

He doesn't realise it, but he has a certain charisma.

When he was young, after only 6 months training as a commis chef, he discovered he was a good cook, and managed to charm his way into a job as head chef at one of those theme English village pubs that serves dinners by the truckload during the tourist season. He could work long shifts under pressure and they paid well, they were desperate to keep him, but he wandered off drunk one day and didn't return.

When the money ran out, he met someone on a small building site on the south coast that needed a caterer for their hungry Polish labourers. Joe set up a portakabin doing good old-fashioned Scottish fry-ups. They wolfed them down. There was good money in it. Then his contact told him the site was being expanded and would soon have 200 workers – 4 large catering companies had tendered for the contract to feed them. *Eh, would Joe like to know their prices?* Joe undercut them, was soon making a fortune and could have made a lot more. But one day he woke just too hungover, desperately needing a drink to get back to some sort of normality. Joe could never have just one. His career in catering ended that day, as so many days had ended, comatose. The Coffins now play a song about it, *Bloody Mary Massacre*.

The Coffins have a gig in Dunfermline, the birthplace of Andrew Carnegie who made a pile of money in the steel industry and then used it to build libraries and universities and useful things like that, even that hall the Beatles played in New York. Dunfermline is an historic sort of town, but also has the world's largest warehouse – Amazon's million square feet – providing jobs nearby. It is also close enough to Edinburgh to have commuters buying their dream home in one of the new housing estates, far cheaper than similar gaffs in the capital city. It is the sons and daughters of these new suburban dwellers that the Coffins hope to convert to their cause on Saturday.

Their bassist, a young lad called Mikey, can't do the gig. Like so many young musicians he plays in several unsigned bands in the hope one of them will make the big time. He's a good player, in demand, and he promised that he'd do another gig. Joe doesn't want to cancel, would I be able to cover for Mikey? I'd have to learn 13 original songs I've never heard before for the one-off gig, and there would be no money in it. Of course I immediately said yes.

I like The Coffins.

A few days later, we're in a skanky back-alley rehearsal room in Glasgow. There are so many of these places; it is beyond me how they stay in business. Some of them are awful, smell really bad, with scaffy old equipment and the abandoned sweaty dreams of countless forgotten bands. Others, like this one, have what any bass player needs to make a god-awful noise: a huge Ampeg amp sitting proudly on top of an 8 x 10 cabinet, like a prize fighter flexing his muscles. It is far, far too powerful for this small room, it's utter madness, a bit like trying to drive a full size Porsche round a Scalectrix track. Nobody in their right mind needs a bass rig as loud as this in a rehearsal room no bigger than a kitchen, but here it is. Lots of young musicians want to rehearse with gear that make the Who look like a church band. Hundreds, thousands of watts of thumping power, big enough to play Glastonbury. If you want to make money, buy shares in a hearing aid company.

When a band gives you their CD to learn, it's always difficult to decide what to copy note for note, and what not to worry about. You should, of course, play exactly what is on the record but it is not always as simple as that, especially if time is short, as it was. Mikey's bass parts are straightforward enough, but in some places he wanders off down a side alley; there's nothing wrong with that, it's just the way he feels the song. But it can be hard to remember exactly where this happens and to duplicate what he might have been thinking about. And so this was the other reason I wanted to do the gig.

When I was a young musician, I only had to play a song once and I had pretty much nailed it. Perhaps the twiddly bits might take a couple of run-throughs, but most of the time I was gig-ready very fast. I could easily busk anything I hadn't memorised. When you are young, your brain is so wonderfully efficient, but it gets worn out like all your other bits. I wish elderly politicians would accept that. Wasn't that why the good Lord invented Viagra – so war-mongering old men wouldn't have to get their kicks by running for President?

I'm not getting any younger and I'd noticed recently that it was taking me much longer to learn songs, or at least to remember the changes, the structure of songs. I suspect most older musicians will know the feeling. But unlike some, I won't ever resort to using a music stand – I mean how insulting to the crowd is that? It simply tells them you couldn't be bothered learning the tunes. If you see a rock player using a music stand, suspect gayness. If he is also using reverb then that proves beyond any doubt that he prefers the company of young boys. At least that's what I tell my guitar-playing pals in America when I want to wind them up. Never fails.

The Coffins' songs are all based around exact riffs, so I can't just busk along with a convincing smile. The guitar player, Bil 'Deadbolt' Gilchrist, a mental health worker from grim Airdrie where I imagine they need a hell of a lot of them, starts about half the songs, so I wasn't worried about playing these, I could just jump in as soon as I heard the riff. But the bass starts the other songs and I had better make damn sure I remembered them; I was determined not to let the band down. I liked the thought of putting myself on the line like that; a bit like rock climbing, standing below some mental cliff and willing yourself to climb up it. I think I might have been dropped on my head when I was young.

So after one quick rehearsal we were off to Dunfermline. The gig was at a former working-mens' club down a muddy lane. A local music shop had taken it over and were using it as a rock venue. They were putting their heart and soul into it. They deserve medals.

I've always found it interesting to play in places that are really not far from the big cities and see how quaintly some of the locals dress. Only in little towns like this will you find someone who is still wearing drainpipe jeans and trying to look like John Travolta. Or a lovely barmaid floating around in a see-through, black lacy chiffon thing. It was below freezing outside, and when she came back in after grabbing a smoke she reminded everyone of the rivets on the nearby Forth Road Bridge; she was the star of the night. Some of the fashion-sense of Glasgow had reached this rural outpost though: there was a girl wearing pink pyjama bottoms, in the style of the ladies of Govan and all females under the age of 50 in Essex.

Before we played, there were three other unsigned bands eager to display their wares. The first was a punk band, with two not exactly young guys who appeared to have dined well and often at MacDonalds. After them, a young blues sort of guy, who played harmonica and wailed and breathed heavily into it. His baby had done left him and he wanted her to come back home, although if another man's wife would let him be her back door man he might get over it. Then an electro-group that were rather good, sort of a Kraftwerk kind of thing. I suspect they, like about 5 million other bands playing 'original' material, live in hope that it's only a matter of time before one of their tunes is snapped up by O2 for an advertising jingle. We sat and watched every note, and politely applauded because unsigned band night decorum demands that each band listens to the others.

At last it was time to play. Four strapping local lads – probably farmers – carry in a coffin and place it in front of the stage. As we hit the first riff of the night, Joe arises and starts singing about killing someone, his face contorted like a deranged madman. It's brilliant, I love it.

I remembered all my parts, and we played a hell of a show. The band has a compelling presence, forcing people to watch in much the same way that people gape at a road accident. The songs are about murder, drinking, blackmail; not the sort of things you are ever likely to hear on *Strictly Dancing*. One of the songs, *Bring Me the Head of a Boy Band Member* leaves no room for doubt about their feelings on pop music. It goes down very well, although I think pyjama girl was a little annoyed when Joe put on a Robbie Williams facemask.

It was about three in the morning before I got back to Glasgow, mainly because the guy who was driving us insisted on making a detour via Edinburgh airport to see a plane that Ryanair had just added to its fleet, if you can believe such a thing. He told us he spends all his spare time travelling to airports, meticulously noting the planes he has seen. He knows exactly how many Ryanair have, and is planning a trip round the UK to spot them all. He once drove all the way from London to Stuttgart and back in the same day to see a plane that was parked there. Twenty-two hours driving. And the thing I found strangest of all, he knew four other people with a similar mental affliction who went with him. He took great pictures of the band though.

When wee Joe got back to Glasgow he spent a couple of hours messaging fans on Facebook. It had been a good weekend, another one free of alcohol. On Monday he'll go back to his much quieter day job.

Joe is a librarian.

33

AL FULLER BLUES JAM

It's a hot, tropical night in Florida.

I've driven down Gulf of Mexico Drive on Longboat Key, a 12-mile barrier island with million dollar homes and secluded nature reserves that somehow separates the ocean from Sarasota Bay, then over the four bridges to the little city of Sarasota. No one is driving fast.

The sun has just settled down behind the curved horizon of sparkling turquoise water, leaving a last flare of glorious warm colours: reds, oranges, yellow and for a brief moment a shimmering green halo not far above the edge of the world. Inland, over the steamy hot town, the sky has slid into dark blue, and, yes, there's the first wee star twinkling – what is that? Venus or something? Ok, so it's not really a star, but it will do anyway. The palm trees are sighing, settling down for the still of evening.

Sunsets in the west coast of Scotland are often just as beautiful but as soon as the sun starts its curve out of sight the temperature drops faster than a whore's knickers. Warm Florida sunsets alone are worth the price of the flight.

I've parked outside the 5-0 Club on Hillview Street – one of the cool things about gigs in Florida, you can always get parked. The club has been here a long time, just across from the hospital. You can see the low stage through the front window, and there's always live bands playing. None of that karaoke shit. In front of the stage is an old wood dance floor, it can get pretty packed at weekends depending on the band, especially if local legend Twinkle is playing, or some of the guys from the old Allman Bros band, like Dickey Betts and 'Dangerous' Dan Toler; they all live nearby. Even the actual Allman Brothers played here, and the place hasn't changed much since except it now, thankfully, has air conditioning.

The room is long and narrow, stretching away from the stage right through to open air seats and tables at the very back. There is a long bar, neon Budweiser signs glowing above the counter, reflecting red and blue on the mirrors and glasses, and friendly girls who can mix, pour and serve drinks faster than anyone I've ever seen. They get to know the customers quickly, remember names and what you had the last time. Or maybe that's because I only drink coke.

I'm sitting with a pal, Howling Bob, a blues musician who, like me, has come down tonight for a wee jam with Al Fuller. Bob is about 60, has a beard, wears his silver hair long in a ponytail that drops out of his cowboy hat. He loves Florida, says he and his wife wouldn't live anywhere else in the world. He's always smiling, I've never seen him in a bad mood; he's one of those people who cheers you up the minute you see him.

He plays most nights of the week, it's his job, his work, but always enjoys playing a few tunes with Al. Hey, what else is he going to do on his night off – watch reruns of CSI? Like many musicians in the area, Bob plays with more than one band, even some nights by himself on a little cruise boat tootling around the bay serving tourists dinner while they watch for dolphins. It's all about keeping busy, making a living. He says he'll never be rich, but he doesn't need to be, he knows what's what.

Bob is well known in the area and soon a young girl asks if she can join us for a few moments. She is very attractive in that perfect young way, wonderfully slim, long brown hair with just a few golden highlights, or perhaps the sun has bleached it a little, sparkling eyes, beautiful white teeth that must have paid for some orthodontist's Merc. Her arms are long and slender, tanned golden. She's wearing faded low-slung jeans and has a tiny blue dolphin tattoo on her hip that she makes looks classy. She's a Florida girl all right, could be on a postcard, she's way out of everyone's league in this old blues bar.

She works for a local free newspaper that covers gigs and asks Bob about shows he'll be playing soon, taking notes in one of those little Moleskin notebooks that you could buy at Borders before they closed. Times are tough here too.

When she hears my accent, she talks to me. Her grandfather was *Scotch*, she says, and one day she'll go there. It's one of her dreams. She's chatty and friendly, tells me that she hasn't always been a journalist. Soon I'm getting her life story, and it's nice.

"I majored in philosophy. I really wanted to know why we are here, what the point of life is. And I discovered the answer is *we don't know*. I felt good finding that out because I figured, you know, I'd done the research. And since we didn't have an answer to that question I changed to graphic design and got a job doing page layouts for the paper. I always liked writing, when I was young I used to read books, like Stephen King. I loved Anna Rice who writes vampire books. I never read books now. I'm too busy, I don't have the time. But I read a lot of magazines. I enjoy fashion magazines."

She thought to herself one day, "wouldn't it be cool if I could get a job doing what I love doing, like writing about going out to clubs every night?" So she asked the editor and he thought the idea was way cool too. Now she writes the clubbing section for the paper and she loves it. She is ambitious and has charm; she's confident and focussed, the private school she attended in the Midwest knew their business. She's doing well, has already managed to buy her own home. The editor is leaving and she has applied for his job; who knows where she'll be in a few months?

I enjoy talking to people at the 5-0.

Al has set up his gear and is about to start playing. He is as tall as a basketball player, softly-spoken. He grew up on a small farm in Massachusetts where he rode horses every day. His mother was a music teacher and she taught him piano from when he was old enough to sit. When the cold winters came he used to watch the geese flying south and always imagined living somewhere warm one day. When he was young he gigged all over America and Europe, even played for the troops in Vietnam, but when he discovered Sarasota he knew he was home.

He's got his two regular sidekicks onstage, Ritchie MacDonald on drums, a nice guy who always has a slightly surprised expression and brings large cold pasta salads to eat in his car during breaks – drumming in this heat needs plenty calories. Burt Englesman plays bass and always arrives exactly three minutes before the first song. He's an old pro, has the long-stare eyes, toured with Percy Sledge, Clarence Carter and the Greg Allman band, he's got his routine down cold, he knows how long it takes to get here and plug in. I'm sure there's been times Al has started the count for the first song as Burt walks in; he always makes it on time. Al has been hosting this jam night at the 5-0 for over a decade, and has settled into a nice weekly routine.

It is difficult to run a jam session. Most places operate a sign-up sheet: musicians write their names on it and they are called up to the stage in the order their name appears to do two songs. This is to ensure that everyone gets their turn, no one's feelings get hurt – some people prefer this. The trouble with random jams is that a good player can be stuck with someone who hasn't a clue and the result is a mess. And every so often some drunk will put his name on the sheet, never with a happy outcome. So Al never uses a sheet; he has come to know most of the jammers – who can play, who can't and which guys play well together. He calls them up by name and usually he gets it right. He says that "sometimes I'm playing with them and thinking this is the best music I've ever heard."

I've just spotted Jimmie Fadden outside, so I nip out into the sweltering heat. Some white-collar Floridians bitch about high humidity, but I love being able to go out at night only wearing a thin tee shirt. I haven't seen Jimmie for a while and he shakes my hand, he's a friendly guy, makes you feel really welcome. He's with his lovely French girlfriend and is celebrating ten years sobriety.

"I realised I could have a great life, or I could drink alcohol. A simple choice." He hugs his girlfriend. "It was a no-brainer."

Jimmie has been touring the world with the Nitty Gritty Dirt Band for many years, but whenever he is in town loves to sit in with Al here at the 5-0. Tonight he'll blow some harp, sing a couple of songs, like *On The Road Again*. He does it well.

The 5-0 is the kind of old-fashioned place where you can expect to get to know people, once you've been a couple of times you'll always have somebody to talk to, everyone is here for the same reason, to hear some good music. Most people living in Sarasota have come from somewhere else, often alone, perhaps leaving someone, the kind of people who want to make new friends. When they ban smoking, the 5-0 will be perfect, but the air conditioning is pretty good. Like most places, it can get a little rowdy on Friday and Saturday nights if college kids hit the town with their fake id's, but during the week they never need a bouncer.

I've gone back in. Al is playing *Born Under a Bad Sign*, in that quiet, easy blues style he has. He doesn't try to sound like a black bluesman. He plays in his own way; if you had to compare him to anyone I suppose it would be James Taylor. He keeps the volume down, never plays too loud, you can always hear what's being said at the next table.

Like the guy I'm eavesdropping on. I better not mention his name, he might take offence. He is a young hot-shot management consultant, seems to make a living telling other people how to run their businesses. He's always badgering someone, trying to sell them on some big idea. I don't know him, but I've heard him talk. He's full of expressions like *outcome focused approach, discounted input margins, critical mass footfall, person centred management strategies, blue sky thinking*. He doesn't realise no one takes him seriously. They just smile and nod, then call for another round. He's harmless.

A guy comes up to me and says hi. He's from Birmingham, England, and I would enjoy talking to him a lot more if he didn't always have a burning cigarette in his hand. I suspect he used to smoke something a lot stronger, maybe still does, because he's not sure how he ended up here but he is sure going to stay, he never wants to shiver through another English winter. He used to be a roadie, worked with Robert Plant and all those guys, has all the tales.

There's a guy at another table, surrounded by friends. They are knocking back a lot of fast cocktails, making a night of it. He wrote a diet book years ago, and it sold millions of copies all over the world, been translated into many languages. He's been living high on the proceeds ever since and, judging by his bulging stomach, the kind of food that isn't recommended in his books. Hell, he's having a great life.

Al has switched to a Steven Ray Vaughn-type shuffle – if you are going to jam in the 5-0 you better know how to play one. A tall, slim guy gets up to dance with his partner, an elegant, well-dressed lady, she looks like she is used to paying her bills in advance. You know the gold Rolex on her wrist is the real thing. They are teachers at a nearby dance school, and the 5-0 is a good place to relax, try out some nifty footwork. They dip and turn and move their feet quickly in well-rehearsed patterns, it's great – like a free floor show.

There are always a lot of people who come along to jam, and Al tries to make sure they all get a turn. A lot of pro musicians stop by, many of them sidemen in big-name touring bands. The other night Brian Johnson from AC/DC got up and sang Route 66. You never know who's going to be there.

Ah, I've just spotted Nancy, who owns the Bar-B-Q on Pineapple Ave, just a short drive away near Main Street. They call that part of town 'historic' because it's been there longer than most other buildings, although not nearly as long as the average Glasgow tenement. She makes the best ribs and pork for miles and specialises in huge combos, like the Tractor Pull, which is aimed at six people although I have seen three demolish one. Eh, I was hungry that night. She often comes in with her lifelong pal, Pee-wee Herman. Maybe he'll show up tonight if he's not at his favourite movie theatre. That was cruel, I shouldn't have said that.

Al brings on his first jammer, a drummer called Lou Croes, a popular old guy who at 89 is the oldest man in the bar. In Florida being the oldest takes a bit of doing. It is probably the only State that flashes 'Silver Alerts' on freeway signs asking motorists to watch out for someone with Alzheimer's who has got hold of car keys and driven off. Bob gets up too, playing the beat up Les Paul guitar he's had since he was a teenager. It sounds great. He and Al do a slow blues, trading solos, letting Lou get warmed up; they work together well, are old pals.

Then they do a swing number to feature Lou. He used to play in big dance bands and still has that crisp, delicate touch, holding his sticks like a marching band drummer. Al and Bob step back from the mics and nod to Lou to play a drum solo. He does his thing. He's still got it. The crowd goes nuts, and the way Lou's eyes sparkle you know he loves every moment. This is what keeps him going, what keeps him alive.

Hey, there's Ryan, with the staff from Starbucks where he's been working these last six years while he's been writing his best seller; looks like they're on a mission. They're gathered round a table, hitting the tequila shots, *slam, bang, lick that salt*. Ryan is just about to leave town, he's had his goddam heart broken. When he married *that bitch* three months ago he reckoned it was for life; he truly loved her. Six years living together, twelve weeks married. What's that about? Suddenly she started working late, way too late, then finally admitted what was going on. Some guy at work, hell, what does it matter now? He's off to Colorado in the morning on the first damn plane out of here. He's not looking forward to the cold, but nothing could be colder than *that bitch's* heart. *Slam, bang, lick.*

His former workmates are all drinking with him. There's ...I better not say his name, but his thing is that when he serves a customer he must, absolutely must, state exactly what their drink is. *Here's your triple venti latte, half soy, half non-fat, no foam, extra hot.* If the customer interrupts he has to throw it away and make it all over again. A few of the people working the nozzles have similar little mental challenges; Starbucks gives them part time work but full time health insurance. In a country like America, health insurance is everything.

And – I can't say her name either. Bi polar as hell, her life can be trembling terror. When the *fear* arrives, as it always does, she huddles in the back room, rocking back and forth, out of reach. She was gently taken to hospital last time, spent three weeks there while they figured out her medication. But when she is up, she's the funniest person in the room. She's got everyone laughing:

"So this fucking troll comes in, this Longboat Key *troll* with her fake tits and teeth and botox and looks like she's never eaten a square meal in her life and she says *Young lady, I will have a decaffeinated, half shot latte, low on foam. Decaffeinated, you understand? And I am going to drink that outside. Outside!*

"So what was my response supposed to be? I figured, now you're someone who really knows what they want out of life. What was I supposed to say? I looked at her and said, uh, *congratulations*?"

Brenda, one of the older hands, laughs like a donkey on speed. She has huge bouncing breasts and is happy that everyone notices. She used to work in the porn industry, behind the camera, and if you ask her she'll tell you all sorts of stories you wouldn't want your mother to hear. *I tell you, that was before Viagra, when porn stars were something else, not jacked-up little pansies like nowadays.* Then she lets rip with that laugh again. Yeah, the Starbucks lot are a lively bunch.

There's a short break and Al changes the line up again. He nods to me and calls me up to the stage. Then he brings on Jimmie Fadden to sing and play harmonica, and a brass section I've seen around town before. I'm feeling a bit nervous; on jams like this you have no idea what you will be playing, or even what key it will be in; it could be anything, depends who is singing. They are great players, if I play a duff note they will spot it right away. Most of the time we'll be playing 12-bar stuff, what they call here a *1–4–5*. Someone will shout, *ok, play an intro on the 5*, and off we'll go.

As I plug into the little Fender amp Al has given me, he turns and whispers.

Wait to you hear this kid.

He calls out a name – *Kei Bland* – and a young boy comes up to the stage, drumsticks in his hand. He has long red hair, way down to his shoulders, and looks like he can't be more than eleven years old. Al grins and turns to me again.

"Wait to you hear this kid play drums, he's only ten. He's going places…"

We launch straight into *Sweet Home Chicago*. Jimmie is singing and playing harmonica through a little tweed amp and he's making it howl. The brass players are great, playing all the right phrases, swaying together from side to side, perfect. And young Kei is bang on, has every accent, every beat nailed, cracking that snare drum like a pro. It's amazing to hear someone of that age with such power in his playing. If he keeps his head and he gets a break or two, he'll be a star in a few years, that's for sure.

I'm standing right beside Al and he turns to me, as he always does.

"Now keep the volume down. Don't play too loud as you always fucking do."

He grins.

And so I grin back at him and nod. Then play too loud, as I always fucking do. Just a little, just enough to get away with it when Al gives me 24 bars to solo on. I know how far I can go, but I need to make my Strat wail. The crowd like that here.

Then something happens. Al cues young Kei to play a drum solo. I've rarely listened to one since John Bonham's times, I mean, who has? But this is something else. I have never heard or seen anything like it. Kei becomes like a human rhythm machine, his feet and hands a shimmering haze of motion. He never loses the timing or the feel of the music as he powers round the kit, his tiny body swaying back and forth. What he is doing is impossible for someone this age. He should not be able to play with this strength. His foot becomes a blur as it hits the bass drum pedal, the sticks like a wizard's wands in his hands – he just shouldn't be able to play that fast and that precisely. Then he throws his head back and his hair flies wild, and for spellbinding moments he is no longer a kid; he is a huge timeless spiritual presence hovering over the drums, in total control, making them do whatever he wants them to do. It is mesmerizing, like watching a shaman.

I thought of the gurus who sell the idea that there is no such thing as talent, and that with practice anyone could become a great musician. If that were all it took, there would be thousands of drummers like Kei. If he had practiced every second of every day of the 11 years of his life, he could never have become this good unless he possessed a vast well of talent.

The gurus that promise false dreams should come to see Kei; they'd have to rewrite their phoney books.

34

TWINKLE

I mentioned earlier that restaurants gigs are probably the worst jobs – it can be soul destroying to play your heart out and look up to see someone shovelling down a slobbering plate of pasta right in front of you. I've played very few restaurant gigs. I remember doing one in the grim, concrete town centre of Cumbernauld in Scotland – it was really just a posh fish and chip shop. When it came time to get paid, the waitress pointed to the manager; if we could wake him he'd pay us. He was drunk and unconscious under a table.

Another time I played a charity event at a large Indian restaurant in Glasgow. They had hired a comedian to be master of ceremonies. He started his routine, full of swearing, shagging and wanking gags. He had seriously underestimated the very dignified Indian ladies present. I have never seen a comedian die a death like it. Shocked and bewildered silence. *Who is that vulgar little man?* Not a single laugh. Only the occasional awkward cough and perhaps a fork being repositioned on a plate. Mind you, a year or so later he had made it to national TV – I guess every gig after that was a dawdle.

Anyway, I've just left Sugar And Spice, a nice Amish restaurant in Sarasota – shit, that sounds like one of those radio broadcasters. A friend called Twinkle has invited me over to her house for a wee chat – I'm going to be sitting in with her band tomorrow night. I'm really looking forward to it, because she is a great singer who almost became a huge star. If the dice had landed ever so slightly differently she could have been living in a gated mansion, although I don't think she would ever choose that lifestyle. She was signed to Warner Bros, has done back up for Rod Stewart, and sung alongside Paul Rodgers, Aerosmith and many others. So I thought I'd take along one of the ten-thousand calorie, sky-high-sugar pies made here by the good Christian folk of Pennsylvania.

I quite like the Amish restaurant, it's hard to get simple food in America, everything seems to be smothered in posh-sounding, gooey sauces that are a lost cause on my Glaswegian palate. The Amish pride themselves on old-fashioned home cookin' that suits me fine, even if they do have hymns and bible tracts all over the place. I like simple meatloaf with spuds and I've never been struck by a thunderbolt yet.

Night has fallen, bringing with it hot, humid air and the southern chirping of crickets. I'm driving up a long, quiet, dark road, and can see the far off flashes of a thunderstorm that looks like it is flickering itself out way over in the east; it won't make it this far. I have sat nav to guide me to Twinkle's house, which is on the other side of the old railroad tracks that cross Sarasota county. There is no street lighting in most suburbs in this part of Florida; without the wee woman from Garmin I'd have no chance of finding Twink's place in the dark.

Ah…here it is…this must be it…

It's one of those neighbourhoods where lower income American families live, the sort of area most native Floridians live, the ones that were here before northern white ass money started throwing condos up on anything with a water view. Old wood, screen doors and those slatted windows that slowly crank open to let in a little cooling breeze at night. It is surrounded by shady oak trees trailing Spanish moss, and built off the ground because of the summer rains. I'm willing to bet there are snakes in the space below the house – big ones – where else are they going to go to escape the heat?

Twinkle comes to the other side of the screen door, holding a big dog by the collar. She is slim, barefoot as always, and wearing a floral hippy-chick cotton dress, her long hair tumbling past her shoulders. No make up, she doesn't need it. She notices me glancing warily at her dog which is quickly sizing me up for the big feartie that I am. Southern folks like their dogs to be dawgs – you never hear a good ole boy talking about his pet poodle – and Twinkle's is a dog among dogs. It's some sort of hybrid, a cross between a Doberman and a wolf. It is big and black with dark don't-even-think-about-patting-me eyes. Its fangs could rip my arm off in about three seconds flat.

Twinkle grins at me. God, she is beautiful.

"The last house we stayed was in a bad area. Drive by shootings and all. It won't bother you none, but I'll put it in its cage."

She leads Fang or whatever its called off to a cage big enough for a lion, then comes back, tosses back her hair, and gives me a warm hug.

"It's so good to see you again. How is Scotland? You know my dream is to move there one day and open a little village bookshop? I would love that, it would be so cool. Come in, come in. Have you met Tony? My brother?"

Tony is tall, long blonde hair, a well-built guy with a friendly smile. He looks like a rock star. He shakes my hand, strong handshake, seems genuinely pleased to see me.

"Hey man, how are you? I read your book about the mountains and all. Loved it."

We go to the back porch; it's screened so the mosquitoes can't get at us. It's warm, a beautiful balmy evening, the storm in the east has headed far off, the stars are out and the crickets are making that great noise they make, the one you hear in every cowboy movie you ever saw. I love it.

Twinkle brings some camomile tea. None one of us drink alcohol; I guess we might have similar reasons for giving it up. Tony is a bass player, plays in the band with Twinkle, and when he was younger used to be in a big time heavy metal band based in New York City. These had been wild days.

"Twinkle and I have the same father, but different mothers. Our paw worked with the Allman Brothers Band, he travelled a lot, got round a lot of different women. I didn't even know I had a sister until I was well into my 20s."

He shows me one of his basses, his pride and joy, a Fender Precision that was specially modified for him. Tells me to go ahead, play it. The dog barks, something has irritated it. Tony goes over to the cage and says something then gives it what looks like a human leg to gnaw on. It quietens down. I start breathing again, for a second I thought he was going to let it out, it's a scary looking animal, like the Hound of the Baskervilles.

Twinkle grins at me. "Don't mind the dawg, he just heard a neighbour's out back somewhere. You don't like dawgs? It's part wolf. Once he knows you he won't bother you."

Tony comes back and lowers himself into a wicker chair.

"Yeah, I never knew I had a sister. I was in New York and saw an ad in Billboard. She had just been signed to Warners and there was a big picture of her. There was something about her, I realised right then I had to meet her. I jumped on a plane to Tampa, tracked her down. I cain't tell you how good it was to find her, and to discover my sister is a musician, like I am. She has this great voice, I knew right away I wanted to play in a band with her."

He pauses, sips his tea, and leans back in his chair. There is the awful sound of crunching bone from the dog cage.

"That was the first time I met my daddy. First thing he does is grab my hands. Looks at my knuckles. In them days I used to love to fight, was always getting into fights. And he says, *woah there, boy, that's teeth marks on your knuckles. That's from fighting.* Then he shows me his hands and he's got the exact same marks on his knuckles."

Twinkle notices I'm wearing boots – I've always liked them, but would feel a right idiot wearing cowboy boots in Glasgow. It's not the place for them.

"Hey, I like your boots." She says.

"What size are you?" asks Tony.

I tell him and he grins, says he's the same and has something I might like. He goes into the house and comes back with a pair of ostrich-skin boots. They are hand made and must have cost hundreds of dollars.

"Try these on, man"

They fit perfectly, far better than the cheap Chinese-made things I have on.

"Now these are boots! You keep them, Graham. I got plenty. You have 'em."

Twinkle's teenage daughter comes into the porch with a friend who is carrying a baby.

"We're going out now. Can you listen out for the baby?"

"Sure, have a nice night," says Twinkle.

She turns to me.

"My daughter's friend got knocked up and she had nowhere to go. So I've taken her in. Couldn't see her on the street. Hell, how much can a baby eat? It's no problem, she's welcome here."

Tony sips his tea, and stretches out. There's a lot of him to stretch. He's been trying to give up smoking for a long time, and he sucks on one of those smokeless electronic cigarette things that he keeps dangling round his neck.

"What are we going to play tomorrow night? It will be good to hear you play with Lenny, our guitarist. You know Lenny, don't you?"

"Yeah, I know Lenny. He's fixed up a couple of guitars for me. I like him, he's a great guitar player."

"Yeah, Lenny and I have been playing together since we were kids. We're opposites. I'm like a bear and he's calm, keeps me in check. When we were on the road, any time I was about to do something dumb, or lose my temper with someone as I often did he'd just give me one of his looks and shake his head a little. *Don't say no more, stay cool*. I always took notice. *Rolling Stone* did an article on us and said that together we made a great person. They were right."

He laughs, sucks on his electric cigarette and blows out a long stream of smokeless smoke.

"Twink and I are very alike in some ways and completely different in others. I'm a New York boy, love the city, the noise and all. Twink is like the original hippie; her friends are all called Astral or Celeste or Moonbeam and things like that. When she had some money she invested in an eco-friendly tourist thing in Puerto Rico. She really felt she was helping the local people."

Twink laughs. "I guess he's right. I grew up in the sunshine. I went to so many schools here...I would change schools whenever I was dating a cute guy who went to a different one. Florida was so good then, Dickey Betts and Dan Toler from the Allman Bros playing in the bars for fun when they weren't on tour, there was great music everywhere, Southern Rock. I love it here, this is where I want to be. I don't need to tour any more. I love playing my own music right here to the people I love."

There is a crunching noise from the dog's cage, and we eat some more Amish cake then I head home. I'm looking forward to tomorrow night. Shit, we forgot to decide what we'll be playing. Ah well, it will work out fine.

Twink and the band are playing at *Eat Here*, a new Main Street restaurant that caters to the kind of crowd that likes to have valet parking at the door and be handed leather-bound menus, but happily leave big tips. It's not the sort of place that has daily specials chalked on a board. It has a lively atmosphere, attractive young waitresses in tight black dresses, and a lot of smiling people, many of them wearing Tommy Bahama shirts that cost as much as everything I have on. I'm a bit wary because I know I'll have to play quietly, something I've never been good at.

The band are set up on the second floor, on the balcony under the stars. It looks great, playing in the open air is fun, especially on a beautiful night like tonight. Twink and Tony greet me with a big hug and introduce me to some of their friends. I'm hungry so I try something from the menu, coconut shrimp. It is really tasty and not brutally expensive.

"Ok, Graham, we'll do our first set then we'll call you up? Ok? What will be play?"

We decide to do *Honky Tonk Woman*, and *Rock And Roll*, by Zeppelin. I'm sure we'll get away with playing a couple of loud songs. What the hell. Twink writes out a set list and I tell her I'll bring my little amp in at the break. I'll just go tune my guitar in my car meantime.

"Oh, Graham. I forgot to mention, the guys tune down a half step. Ok then, I'll call you up at the start of the second set."

The car park is just out the back door. I like playing the Keith Richards parts on things like *Honky Tonk Woman* so I need to change the guitar to open G tuning. A lot of people don't do that, especially here: I don't think I've ever heard a band in Florida play the song with the guitar in the tuning Keef uses or that jagged style he plays. I am sure we all know that he likes a wee refreshment before his gigs, so I think part of his sound is the variation in timing and the accents he does as the mood takes him; it's a feel thing. American guitar players are usually very controlled, great technically, but they perhaps think too much about their Mixolydian and Minor pentatonic scales instead of just grabbing the song by the balls and getting stuck in.

I jump in my car and tune down the whole guitar a semi tone, then the fifth and first strings down another tone. It sounds ok but even though I'm using medium gauge strings, they sound slack. There's nothing I can do, ideally I would put on heavy strings but there's no time and, anyway, I'm only going to be playing two songs. It'll be fine, I go back in and watch the first set.

The band is great. They are playing original songs from Twinkle's Warner Bros album, and they sound terrific. Tony and Lenny, both real big guys, are wearing black jackets and white shirts; they look good, like they are meant to play together. Sitting low at the back is Troy, their seen-it-all drummer. They switch to a Foo Fighters song with Tony singing, and Lenny somehow plays the guitar parts perfectly and without deafening everyone – not many guitar players can make a band sound full with only bass and drums, especially at low volume. He's got a really nice touch, very controlled, precise. I'll need to watch my volume.

Twink is joking with the crowd, like it's a party, everyone is in a good mood. Tony sings a song he wrote that warns *Mister don't you mess with my sister.* He seems to be making the words up as he goes along; it's fun, the crowd know it and join in. She and Tony suddenly decide to do an acapella version of *Truck Driving Man.* The bear and the gentle hippy may be opposites, but they obviously share the same musical genes, their voices mesh perfectly. Everyone listens. It's terrific, what good live music is all about. This feels like a proper gig, not a hungry restaurant.

Over the years I've seen Twink sing many times and tonight her voice has never sounded better, she seems to be home at last. Everyone stares at her as she rocks back and forward, at the way her long hair falls over her slim arms, at the way she sways on her bare feet. Sarasota loves Twinkle.

It's Lenny's turn now. He switches guitars and plays *Black Mountainside*, the Bert Jansch tune, then drifts into one of his own songs, a kind of blues thing, very swampy, very atmospheric. He's using what is called DAGDAD tuning, the strings tuned down, as mine are for *Honky Tonk Woman*. I reckon he must have heavy strings on the guitar and just hope mine holds up ok. I'll be on soon.

At the break, Tony tells me to set up my amp and guitar so I bring them in from the car. It's hot and humid in the night air, and the stage lights make it even hotter. Better check my tuning once again. Yep, fine. *Relax and enjoy this, it'll be fun.* I prop my guitar against my amp and go back to my table. At last Twink gets up to sing again.

"And now we're going to bring up an old friend from Scotland…"

It's my cue, and I step up beside Tony, switch over the standby switch on my amp. Troy hits the bass drum, snare and cowbell then I pick the first notes of *Honky Tonk*, playing the fourth and third strings together with my fingers.

SHIT!

There's a fan blasting freezing air straight at the stage and it's been blowing on my guitar. The sudden change in temperature from sweltering to cool in a heartbeat has knocked it out of tune. I have to stop the song, I've no choice. I very quickly re-tune as best I can and start again. I feel a right prat. Not to worry, Keith has often played out of tune, it's all about feel.

Once we get going, there's no stopping us. I'm playing through my little 5E3 amp; it has a lot of balls and I'm driving that thing like we were playing a stadium. Lenny is filling in loads of wee phrases; Tony is pounding the bass. Twink is singing like she means every word; I've seen Sheryl Crow sing this with the Stones but nowhere near as good as Twinkle.

Everyone looks up from their lobster and cutlets, drinks forgotten, glasses in mid air. Even the young waitresses in their cute little cocktail dresses stop and stare. I'm chugging out Keith's oh so horny chords, my wee tweed amp sounds as if it it's about to come. Twink screams the end chorus like Aretha Franklin and Lenny throws out a last howling solo, then we finish, holding onto that final G chord. The crowd are on their feet, yelling. Before they get a chance to sit, Troy cracks out the drum intro to *Rock And Roll* and we're off again. While Lenny plays the intro I quickly tune back up to normal tuning and – this is so damn good…Twink has the place going nuts. What a voice, what a fantastic rock voice. It's brilliant.

At the next break I'm having a quiet coffee with Twink and Tony. We're still sweating, still on a high. She can hardly sit still.

"Hey, sorry about my tuning going out there, I didn't realise you had cold air blowing onstage."

Tony pats my arm and grins.

"Hey, man, don't worry about it. It was those pussy-gauge strings you're using!" He laughs. "Man it rocked, it was great. I loved hearing you play that English way, like Keith Richards does. It gave me a hard on!"

Twink smiles. She looks round the room, everyone knows her.

"See what I mean, Graham? Why would I want to tour when I can play here in my hometown, to people I love?"

She grins at Tony, squeezes his hand, then speaks, her voice soft.

"I remember when I was on tour with the Dickey Betts band. All over America, two years on the road, living on the bus. The first year was fine, I had everything under control, just did a line or two, maybe a little tequila. But the second year it all got bad. By the end I was in real trouble, was a mess.

Doing coke and booze all the time. In six months I had no money, they cut off my electricity and I was on the street for not paying my loan. I knew I couldn't go on taking drugs and drinkin'. I couldn't go on *needing*. I dropped to my knees and I said *Lord just take it away...*"

35

JIM WARD, BUSKER

He slouched back in the doorway of the crumbling dark Glasgow tenement, digging into the white cardboard carton of greasy fried rice and…maybe it was chicken. It might have looked a mess, but it was his Sunday dinner. His hair was pointing in several directions, his shirt hanging loosely over his thin bones. He would be somewhere between 45 and 55, and looked it. Life had thrown him some heavy punches, but he wasn't complaining. In a few minutes his belly would be full, then he'd go next door to the pub. This was where he earned one night's pay a week. He worked a few of these places, as the resident guitar player. During the day he played tunes in the streets for change. It all added up to enough to pay the rent on his high-rise council flat. This was his life.

When he was young, for a while he might have hit the heights and no one would have been surprised or grudged him success. He had played alongside some guys he'd grown up with in the same windswept housing estate and had become big names, guys that knew he was a far better player than they could ever be. He had a touch, a feel for the guitar that no one can learn, that can't be taught. But he lacked the killer instinct, the brashness and confidence to stand squarely in front of a record label manager and demand to be picked for the first team. He just didn't shout loudly enough.

So he'd been left behind.

Maybe, too, he'd cared too much. When he was playing in young pop bands perhaps he had concentrated on the music too much instead of simply performing and looking good. It was way too late now, the years had gradually taken their toll, his face was lined, greyish. He should have quit smoking a long time ago, but it cleared his head. Each hand-rolled smoke gave him a little island to hop to, resting places to reach to help get him through the day. Without them, each day would be too long a journey. Without cigarettes he couldn't settle, they helped stop him thinking too much.

His meal finished, he crushed the cardboard tray, smoked his little roll-up, and then walked into the bar. Some heads quietly turned, watching him. They knew who he was, what he could play. In the corner were the bass player, the singer and the drummer, all older guys, the other musicians in the band, getting ready. He walked over to them, nodded hello, pulled his battered Stratocaster over his shoulder, flicked the glowing red standby switch on his ancient Twin Reverb amplifier and, *1-2-3-4*, swung straight into the sweetest blues you ever heard. He stood straight now, with dignity, the stoop gone, his eyes closed as he squeezed out each and every beautiful note, and the years fell from him.

As always, they played a few tunes then opened up the stage to jammers. In bars all over the world, blues jams attract musicians, some for all the right reasons, some for all the wrong ones. Older guys, too jaded with the hassle of playing in a full time band, too soured by arguments, or just tired of lugging around their gear and standing on a stage for hours on end playing for too few people and too many drunks. Not wanting to quit altogether, some of them still love to play a few songs, play their favourite guitar licks, enjoy the simple pleasure of making music with other old-timers. It's either that or take up golf; no, it's an easy choice.

Sometimes it's pro musicians passing through town and wanting to hook up with local players, often after meeting them on Facebook. Or young hot shots, like the one playing right now, trying to show up the old master. The kid has plugged into an eBay-bought effects board filled with pedals: digital delay, tube screamer, compressor, wah-friggin-wah wah; all the things that naïve players think are a substitute for good fingers. The young guy is full of arrogance, he's stabbing his toe at one footswitch after another until his guitar is a screeching mess, and he's running a furious cluster of notes together in a distorted blur. The old guitar man grins, he knows the kid is just trying to learn some chops, trying to build some confidence. He doesn't want to destroy him, so he just smiles and nods appreciatively then plays a few beautifully phrased notes, letting them hang softly on the air, a gentle invitation to the kid to learn one simple truth: guitar playing is all in the hands.

And in Glasgow, because it is Glasgow, there's always the guy scowling at the stage. The sour guy that plays harmonica, or bass, or something, and rates himself way above anyone else. But he has slagged off too many jammers, he has built himself a name on criticising others. No one has heard him actually play. He doesn't dare get up and take part; he dreads being found out. And so he stands there, week in, week out, hating the jammers for having the nerve to take part, knowing that he probably is far better than most of them, but that he will only ever play in his dark little flat when his wife is out at work.

Then sometimes, some new player in town joins in quietly, and something happens, the band notches it up a level, and everything just comes together beautifully. The old guitar player loves that, lives for these moments. He knows that really good players just play what they play, they don't try to impress anyone or worry about what they can't play. And they leave plenty room for everyone else.

Tonight is a good night. Alan Nimmo, one of Britain's top bluesmen, has stopped off halfway through a big tour to sit in with the band. He and the old guitar player are really rocking it up. It's great to watch. Outside, the cold north winds are swirling through the dark streets, chasing discarded food cartons along the gutter. Another bitter winter will soon grip the city, but in here in this hot Glasgow pub, for a few songs at least, life is good.

Long months passed and I hadn't seen him since that night. I wanted to play with him, perhaps at the blues jam, but definitely when he was working on the streets. I've never done any street busking, I've always been lucky enough to be able to make enough money without relying on passers-by throwing coins into a hat at my feet. There's nothing wrong with that, the streets of ancient Greece and Rome probably had buskers. It's an honest way to make a living. And Jim Ward is a great busker.

He plays instrumentals by the Shadows, note for note copies. He does it really well, takes a lot of time recording bass and drums backing tracks on his home studio. So I called him, asked him if I could sit in with him next time he was heading for the city centre.

"Sure, as long as you can play these songs. You know they are a lot more difficult than they sound? Have you listened to *Wonderful Land*? It sounds easy but it has chords all over the place and three key changes."

We decided on half a dozen Shadows songs I should learn, and arranged to meet the next night. He wanted to be sure I could play the rhythm guitar parts perfectly.

"I work at this, I like to get it right. There's so many crap buskers, guys turning up with some old guitar they found in a skip, three strings on it, just making a noise. They're just beggars."

So I found the Shadows on YouTube and spent the next

afternoon working out the chords and the rhythms. Modern pop music often relies on three or four chords, sometimes using verses of varying length to create a sense of dynamics. I'm thinking about songs like *Valerie, Sex on Fire, All Those Things I Have Done*. They are great songs, no doubt about it, but it is interesting to listen to something like the Shadows and hear the way the chords closely follow the melody line. If any young guitar players are reading this, I'm just making the suggestion.

I drove to Jim's flat. He had just finished giving a guitar lesson and he lit a cigarette then asked me what I wanted to play first. I picked the one he'd mentioned was tricky, *Wonderful Land*. I was confident I had nailed it but, of course, I'd missed a passing minor chord. But apart from that, I had it. A few hours hadn't been long to work out the chords – I had looked them up on an internet site but they were wrong – but at least the structures of the songs were easy to remember, and none of them lasted more than two and a half minutes. So many songs, from Hank Williams onwards, were that length; I often wonder who worked out that was the perfect time for the hits of the day?

We played one called *Atlantis*, and talked of how great it sounded when the Shadows played it on their final tour, which I'd watched on YouTube. Then we went through a few more. For once, the weather forecast was fantastic and so I asked Jim if it would be ok to play with him next morning.

"Sure, but I have to get there early. Busking has changed in the last years. You don't need a license and these days there are Eastern Europeans everywhere. Last time I was in town there were at least a dozen playing accordions. If you don't grab a pitch first thing, you've no chance."

We arranged to meet in Sauchiehall Street. I was looking forward to it.

Next day the sun was scorching, absolutely lovely. Glasgow is a different place when it is hot and sunny, makes you wonder how many aches, pains and moans are caused by the weather. Jim had grabbed a prime spot in the middle of the pedestrian area and set up a battery-powered amp for his guitar and a little cd player for his drum and bass backing tracks. I brought an acoustic guitar that would be loud enough without an amp.

"Can I get you a coffee, Jim? From Costa over there?"

"No thanks. I have a wee flask. You have to be careful how much you drink when you're busking 'cos you can't go off to pee or you lose your pitch."

The street was quieter than I thought it be would on such a lovely day, but I guess that's the economy we live in. It was still early so we played through the songs I'd learned. I forgot a couple of chords but recovered by the time we got to the same part again. And sure enough, people started dropping coins into Jim's hat. Mainly pound coins, but one old soul put in a few pennies. Jim politely thanked everyone. Every time we finished a song, Jim carefully checked each string then looked up from his tuner.

"The tuning has to be absolutely precise. There's a lot more to these songs than people think."

After about 20 minutes or so we finished our wee set list.

"That sounded great, Graham. Well done. That was good, having an extra guitar gives it that bit extra, like the original songs."

I was very pleased.

"What's the most anyone has put in?"

"A woman came out of Marks and Spencer one day and put a £20 note in the hat. I was delighted – if someone gives me a fiver I'm over the moon. You have to take the money out quickly, a couple of times junkies have grabbed the hat and run off with it.

"Anyway when I picked the note up there were four more twenties. A hundred quid. From that one person. That was a great day.

"Another time this guy came up to me with a big movie camera. He was making a film, wanted me to play as someone was walking past. And then he asked if I could write a couple of songs in the style of the Shadows for the film, that way he wouldn't have copyright problems. So I did. I got a thousand quid for that. But these things don't happen often. People usually just give you change."

I decided to go off for a coffee; my brain doesn't really function in the morning until I give it a wee jolt of caffeine.

"Are you sure I can't bring you one?"

"No, no you're fine. I have my flask."

I came back after half an hour. The weather was beautiful, after weeks of rain it was finally summer. Everyone in the street was smiling. I watched Jim for a while, then a couple of jakeys, as we call aficionados of Buckfast wine in Glasgow, staggered up to him.

"Hey pal, can you give us some Pink Floyd? *Another Brick,* can you play that?

I saw one of them eyeing up the coins in Jim's cap. They hadn't noticed me standing some way behind Jim. I reckoned if they grabbed the hat and ran towards me I could trip one up and deck the other before they realised what was happening. I'm not a fighter, and didn't fancy the idea at all, but it would be the last thing they'd expect. I couldn't let the bastards rob him. I braced myself, making sure they didn't notice I was watching every move.

Jim started playing the riff from *Another Brick in the Wall.* This pleased the jakeys. "Haw that's magic, wee man."

Then they lurched off somewhere else. I breathed a big sigh of relief. I'm way too old to hit anyone, even if they deserve it.

I picked up my guitar and we played our songs again. I had the chords and changes nailed now, and was enjoying being able to relax while I was playing them. The Shadows were famous for the little tight dance-type steps they did when they played. So I had a go at that. People stopped and watched us, grinning and even dancing a wee bit; although these songs are almost half a century old, everyone seemed to know them. Just goes to show. After we finished *Dance On* I turned to Jim.

"I was trying to do the wee steps, Jim, but it's difficult enough when playing rhythm guitar. I don't know how Hank Marvin managed to play the songs perfectly and do the moves at the same time."

"I know and he made it all look so easy. Hank Marvin was some guitar player, very underrated for a long time. I think people realise now just how good he was."

And so the morning passed. I loved it. We played our half dozen tunes, then I would have a wee break while Jim played instrumentals by 60s surf bands, such as *Walk Don't Run*, *Perfidia*, as well as other Shadows songs, every one note perfect. People stopped, smiled, and listened.

About one o'clock, I told Jim I had to go somewhere, and thanked him. He picked up his hat and began counting the money in it.

I handed him a £20 note.

"Here Jim, let me put this in. I really appreciated you letting me play. It was great fun."

"No, not at all…I can't take that, I was about to give you half the money we got…"

36

KETTLE OF FISH

I t's the wee things people say to you about your playing that makes it all worthwhile. The little compliments that mean so much, the thanks for making a night special. All those years of toil and practise at last bearing fruit.

I was sitting in with a great band called Kettle of Fish at a steamy open-air bar in Siesta Key, Florida. They have the best musicians in the area, and I was well chuffed when Dana Lawrence, the band's front man, invited me along to play a few tunes. Jimmie Fadden from the Nitty Gritty Dirt Band plays drums with them whenever he is in town, although he is often on tour all across America. It says a lot for him and the band that he spends his few nights off playing with them.

Tonight the drummer is a local guy, Garrett Dawson, a terrific player, he works hard, sweats buckets, and really listens to what the guitar players are doing, adding accents when it will emphasise what they are playing and not, as most drummers do, just when they happen to feel like it.

There's a big difference between bar-type bands in the UK and America. In the UK, bands usually only play one or two sets at most. Many young bands only play 30 mins for their night's work, don't have enough songs to do any longer, and share the stage with 2 or 3 other groups. In America, most bar bands think nothing of playing a 4-hour gig. Dana has a huge set list, pages and pages of songs he can play if anyone has a request, as well as writing a lot of good stuff himself.

I've always reckoned American guitar players are usually technically far better than British players because they play such long gigs and have to be very inventive to come up with fresh ideas, especially in their solos. And so American guitar players usually study musical theory with the devotion of monks. One of the guys Kettle of Fish often have sitting in with them is Greg Poulos; his mastery of obscure scales and modes is something I've never seen in a British guitar player. When he plays, his guitar solos are a thing of beauty and wonder. On the other hand, British players make up with feeling and guts what they lack in blinding technique; Eric Clapton could only have been born in the UK just as Steve Vai could only be American.

Anyway, I'm feeling seriously honoured to be playing with the band. The bass player is a great musician, Berry Duane Oakley jr, the son of the original Allman Bros bass player. The other guitarist is Thorson Moore who not only plays beautifully, he looks like he should be on stage with the Eagles or Kings of Leon. All the Florida girls talk about Thorson.

I never get nervous no matter how big the crowd is, but when I am playing with really good musicians I can get scared. I know they will spot any weakness in my playing and I'm afraid I'll be found out. I remember once playing in London with the String Band and just as I was about to go on being told Jimmy Page was out front. I didn't stop shaking until the encore. Honest.

An old pal in the UK, former international rugby player John Beattie, once gave me great advice. He was telling me how it felt to play against the mighty All Blacks, and how you can't allow yourself to be intimidated, you'd be flattened. He said you just have to go for it, put everything you've got into it and what happens is what happens. I knew Dana and Thorson are nice guys, and even if I did play a bum note or two they wouldn't mind, but I didn't want to look like a pillock. So I thought of what John had said, didn't allow myself to worry about how good these guys were. I just concentrated on playing what I could play and put every ounce of energy into getting that over to the crowd. By the time we'd finished the first song, I was dripping with sweat, the crowd could see I was working hard and we had a great gig. I loved it.

There was a table beside me with three young girls, probably there to see Thorson. They were beautiful, as wonderfully beautiful as only 21-year-old American girls can be. Blonde, golden tans, slender, dazzling smiles...thankfully I'm not one of those sad bastards that lust after young girls, I've reached an age where I see them in a detached sort of way, only as creatures of perfection. They were cheering every song, and throwing high fives at me, all that kind of American stuff.

"Hey, you rock! You're great!"

I smiled modestly.

"You're fantastic on that guitar! We love you. We want to adopt you into our family."

What hair they had, what sparkling teeth.

I grinned at them. "That's really nice of you. Thanks."

"We do, we want to adopt you! We want you to be –"

Such warm and lovely smiles. So beautiful.

" – our *grandfather*..."

37

MIDDLE OF THE ROAD 1

S ome bands are a pain in the arse. Musicians, especially those that insist on call themselves *artists*, can be highly strung, as we know. Inevitably there are fall-outs, bitter disagreements and disputes. You would think that as they aged, musicians would mellow and work together, perhaps happily doing reunion tours in their mature years, celebrating the wonderful times they had when they were young, and might have enjoyed a lot more if they hadn't been so distrustful of one another.

I just read a wee article in Rolling Stone magazine, saying that Black Sabbath are going to tour again but that the drummer is refusing to play unless "a signable contract is drawn up that reflects some dignity and respect towards him as an original member of the band". I mean, come on, Bill, you are almost an OAP, you're getting to play huge stadia with Ozzy, don't you think you just might be a little over sensitive?

This is the terrible thing about bands.

The falling out.

The feuds.

Something like a third of marriages end in divorce. Actually I just guessed that statistic, because it doesn't really matter – divorce is far more pleasant than a band split. The life-long hatred that some musicians harbour for one another makes most marriage break-ups seem like harmless little tiffs. It is almost certain that most bands will fall out sooner or later; making music is a very personal creative thing and even little squabbles can be magnified out of all proportion. When an artiste has invested their entire soul into writing songs for the next CD release and it's not really what the rest of the band fancy playing then there can only be one heartbreaking outcome.

Perhaps a band member was sacked just before the group went on to become stars – this is every young musician's greatest terror. Every time their hit songs are played on the radio it opens a wound that time can never heal. No girlfriend, no woman could ever inflict that kind of pain on their former partner. The world is full of bitter ex-members of bands who will never again speak to their former closest friends. Many divorced couples find a way to have some kind of truce; will perhaps even share some enjoyment recalling happier times. But when a band breaks up...

Sometimes a band will have had enough of one member's personality traits: it may be a singer's demands for the best hotel rooms, or private transport for his entourage that has to be paid for by everyone else. Or it might be as simple as growing sick of the same old jokes and farting on the tour bus, or the only person in the band who still likes to make the same old jokes and farts on the tour bus.

I know a guy who has some unfortunate inability to digest boiled eggs, they make him fart uncontrollably – I promise I'm not making this up. So of course he thoroughly enjoyed eating a few before a long trip. On one journey across France his bus-mates counted 68 parps in one hour. That kind of thing is hilarious once, but can soon become tinder for a massive fire.

It's the Shakespearean hatred that former band members can have towards one another. Guys that conquered the world, who started as spotty school kids with a playground dream and became million-dollar industries employing armies of happy, willing workers and providing entertainment, inspiration and comfort to millions of people – but when that oil tanker runs aground it can never be refloated. It can be an argument over the silliest thing, but when the final harsh words have been spoken there is no turning back.

Happily, some bands are terrific fun.

For many years I had been pals with John Beattie, a former international rugby player who had played all over the world for Scotland and the British Lions before having to retire through injury. John loves rock music, especially Status Quo and AC/DC. He is a great guitar player; he has very strong hands and when he plays his Gibson SG through a Marshall amp it can have the power of a steam train.

We had first met when we played together in a band featuring a Radio Clyde DJ called Tiger Tim that a successful businessman had put together as a wee hobby. In England, I don't think many people would have heard of Tim, but in the west of Scotland he was a star and could pull in big crowds. We landed some good gigs but the band split up because we were all too busy doing other things, like making a living. John was busy coaching rugby and building a career as a journalist: he is now a top presenter with the BBC.

After a gap of about 15 years, John was desperate to get out playing again. Then someone offered him a last minute gig at a big venue after an international rugby match and he called me to help put a band together. He knew James McPherson, who had been a star of the Scottish TV show Taggart, and was a good rock singer. We arranged a rehearsal and James brought along one of his neighbours, Tommy Cunningham, the drummer with Wet Wet Wet.

The rehearsal room was pretty crappy, manky in fact, but the only one we could find at short notice. We played through a few songs, no problem, just good old school rock. John had also invited Jackie Bird, a TV newsreader who had been a professional singer in her early 20s and she sang a few songs, very well as it happens. She's one of those people who enter a room and somehow fills it with her presence; she is very charismatic.

The gig went very well. We could have done with some more rehearsal time, but we all enjoyed playing so much that the crowd responded to that. I think bands often over-rehearse; there's just no atmosphere. Semi pro bands usually make this mistake – they think that the punters are impressed by hearing songs done exactly like the originals. This may be true for tribute bands, but if people want to hear perfect copies of chart hits then they can listen to them on their iPods. Many semi-pro bands stand very seriously onstage, thoughtfully and meticulously playing the parts they learned in their bedrooms. When most people go out to a bar or wherever, they want a good time, they don't want to see a bunch of grim-faced muzos showing how well they can regurgitate the solo from *Thriller* – especially these awful covers bands that place music stands in front of them like they are the friggin Philharmonic Orchestra. I'll happily play with any band except, of course, one with *Project* in its name. Or *Fusion*. And definitely not with one that uses music stands. I mean, give me peace.

Word seemed to get around after the gig and we were soon being asked to do more, some of them surprisingly big. We were happy to have a good time and belt out some old classic rock and the crowds seemed to like that. We never seemed to have time to rehearse, and played maybe once a month, so it was always fun when we did. Michelle McManus, who had won *X Factor*, did quite a few gigs with us, and we often had guests from the BBC getting up to sing a song or two with us. Tommy went on tour with the Wets, and we had drummers sitting in with us who had played with Deacon Blue, Rory Gallagher, and Jim Prime. It was all very relaxed, great fun.

I enjoyed playing guitar beside John, we got on well together. Alan Thomson, a terrific bass player who had worked with John

Martyn, Rick Wakemen, Pentangle, and loads of other people, played regularly with us when he wasn't off on tour somewhere. James McPherson had to go off to do a six-month theatre gig in England, so we brought in Scott Wallace; he loved playing the big venues, it made a welcome change from playing his regular gig in Coatbridge. He's a great singer, the star of the show, really knows how to get a crowd going. We also had a girl called Andrea who worked beside John at the BBC and was far more attractive than the rest of us. She was a terrific singer and also gave the crowd someone nice to look at.

We played some big charity gigs including events after international rugby matches, when Scottish team members Kelly Brown and Chris Cussiter would join us for a few songs. I'm still playing with John as I'm writing this; only last night we sold out a gig in Melrose to over 1200 people; we have a great time.

John also got us gigs at the BBC, usually for Christmas parties and that sort of thing. I think we played the last gig at their famous old Queen Margaret Drive building, and the first at the new, purpose-built studios beside at Pacific Quay in the centre of Glasgow.

I made an arse of myself there.

I had just got back to Glasgow after being in America for a while, during which time a Continental Airlines pilot managed to crash-land a jumbo jet on the Hudson River. We were playing on the top floor of the new BBC building and I was looking out the window at the River Clyde, watching the sunset. Suddenly a plane came flying down into the water. I screamed like a schoolgirl, yelling to call the cops, a plane had just crashed. How was I to know that while I had been away some company had started flying seaplanes in and out of Glasgow?

And then...

Alan couldn't play with us that night so I switched to bass. I set up my gear and plugged in my wireless transmitter. John liked us to both go right into the crowd during the gig, get them dancing. I started to tune up but nothing was coming out my amp, although I could hear a terrible rasping, farting sound every time I played a note. Suddenly it dawned on me that the building's hi-tech internal speakers were picking up the low signal from my bass, and I was about to blow the whole system. I very quietly plugged in a normal lead before anyone noticed. I was in a sweat all night, expecting to be handed a very big bill. I don't think I've used the wireless system since.

One night we were playing a charity gig at a big venue, the Old Fruitmarket in Glasgow. There were a couple of other bands on, including Middle of the Road. I had known Ian, the guitar player, since I was about 14 when I first saw him carry his guitar along the street, and it was good to play on the same bill as them. Like most chart bands of the 60s/70s, they had been through their share of traumas and had fallen out and so, just like the Searchers, Ten Years After, the Stranglers, and doubtless many others, there were now two versions of the group on tour. Ian McCredie and his brother Eric played in one version, while the band's former singer Sally Carr regularly toured Germany and the Continent with Ken Andrew, the band's original drummer. It seemed very sad, especially since none of them appeared to have made any money out of their hits, even though they had sold an estimated 40 million records.

Ian's version of the band was excellent, they had a very good female singer from London who had done a lot of session work. After the gig, we chatted for a while and I had pretty much forgotten about it until a year later when we were asked to do a big corporate gig in Glasgow, one of those 60s-themed events. The organisers wanted a well-known band from the 60s on the bill and we suggested Middle of the Road.

By then Eric, the bass player, had sadly died, but Ian and the band's singer wanted to do the gig and suggested using our drummer with me playing bass. They also wanted to use our keyboard player, Tom Urie, who is a popular actor in a Scottish

TV series called River City. Tom is a pro musician and confessed that Middle of the Road had been one of his favourite pop bands; he was delighted to be playing a gig with them. They sent me a cd of the songs and I learned the bass parts exactly – Eric had been a clever musician, his playing had been very melodic. As is so often the case, old pop songs have a lot more going on than just a catchy tune. There was only time for one very quick rehearsal then the gig.

When you are on stage with someone like Ian, who had been a pop star, the difference between him and the average semi pro musician is immediately obvious. Backstage he was like any 60-year-old man, but the second he stepped in front of the crowd he was transformed, he seemed to have the energy and charisma of a teenager. I remembered Stan, from the String Band, telling me that when he was a talent handler for a TV show in New York, he'd noticed the same thing when he was looking after Al Pacino. Pacino had been shaking, apparently terrified of the large crowd out front. Stan had felt him grip his arm as he slowly walked him to the studio floor; it was like leading an old man. But the instant the cameras were on him, Pacino became the huge star everyone recognised.

I enjoyed the gig playing with Middle of the Road – remembering watching Ian play in church halls when I was a boy, and how I used to stare at his hands, and try to figure out the chords he was playing. It felt good to be playing the band's hits with him.

But as much as I liked him, and his new singer, there was no escaping the fact that Middle of the Road's distinctive sound had been the voice of the original singer, Sally Carr. I wondered what her version of the band was doing, and if there was any way they could patch up their differences. Perhaps I could reunite them? And then I noticed that her keyboard player was Shug Devlin, an old pal who I'd played with in Kim Beacon's Band. I decided to send him a Facebook message...

38

MIDDLE OF THE ROAD 2

It took a while for Shug to get back to me. Two years, to be exact. He said he'd been living in Germany for a long time, making a living, *you know how it is*. And yes, he'd been playing with Middle of the Road, the version featuring Sally Carr, the proper one. Shug told me they mainly played big 60s pop fests with loads of other bands from that era; it was a lot of fun. We kept in touch and I mentioned that I was writing an article about bands falling out. He put me in touch with Ken Andrew, the other original member of the group.

Ken is a filmmaker. He'll never retire, loves what he does, lives quietly near Edinburgh, and enjoys life; he's bursting with enthusiasm. His busiest time of the year is the Edinburgh Festival when he films the Military Tattoo. It's a big job that takes up several months a year. The rest of the time he loves doing tours with Middle of the Road in some of the places they had a massive following: Norway, Italy, Spain, all over Europe.

Ken and I sent emails back and forth while I was writing the article. I watched early clips of the band on YouTube; they were a terrific pop band, perfect for the market they were aimed at, and Sally Carr was very sexy in an innocent kind of way, as if she had no idea of how good she looked. She also had that very Scottish voice which gave the band its unique sound. At the time that MoR were having one chart hit after another, almost all British singers were trying to sound American; Sally made no attempt to disguise her accent.

I noticed that the band's records had acoustic guitar on them but when they played live now they didn't use one, and mentioned that to Ken. He suggested I might like to sit in with them some day, playing acoustic; it had been a big part of the band's sound. I thought about it for about two seconds. *Absolutely*. It suddenly occurred to me that I might be one of very few people who would have played in both versions of the same chart band, but not in the original.

Ken sent me a live recording of a recent gig and I sat down to learn it. I also listened to the original tracks to see what the acoustic guitar was up to; I already knew the bass parts to most of the songs from playing in the other version of the band, so it didn't take long to figure out. There were some interesting wee twists and turns in the chords – it's really only when you take these songs apart that you realise how cleverly they'd been put together.

Ken asked if I'd like to do a couple of gigs in Italy, but I had a gig with John Beattie so I had to turn it down. He then suggested coming on a small tour in Germany. He reckoned it would be terrific because it would be just like the old days – they'd be playing three gigs in the same day, in Friedberg, Oberhausen and Werne.

I couldn't wait.

First we had to have a rehearsal. Ken wanted to make sure I had learned the parts properly, and to play with Sally, see how it sounded. So we arranged to run over the set at Sally's house, a lovely detached villa in the countryside overlooking the River Clyde and the Kilpatrick Hills.

I arrived a few minutes early at Sally's house. Ken was picking up the guitarist in Glasgow, but had been delayed. Sally was very friendly, still very attractive, with a lovely warm smile. She made coffee and we sat in her upstairs lounge, watching dark clouds swirling and brooding over the hills. It was grey and cold out there, drizzling, threatening to pour at any minute. Scottish weather, especially over hills and mountains is very moody and can change faster than a bipolar actor. There are terrific old Scots words to describe it. *Dreich, glowerin*, getting *drookit* – none need translation. It looked like a storm was heading our way.

Ken called. He was going to be about an hour late. I was enjoying talking to Sally, about the days when Middle of the Road were at their peak, they'd been so busy, they'd never had time to think. The more she told me the more I realised: their story is bizarre.

They had originally been a Glasgow-based club band called Los Caracas. I remembered seeing them on Hughie Green's *Opportunity Knocks*. The show regularly attracted 18 million viewers, about 3 million more than *X Factor* does nowadays. They won four times and gave up their day jobs. It was a clever move. Not quite so wise was their choice of management. They had stacks of offers but instead of signing to a top London company, they were talked into working with a couple of South American characters who worked in a Glasgow casino.

They offered them a gig on a Caribbean cruise ship that they were told would lead to South American dates, fame and glittering riches. Only one thing, the name would have to change; they couldn't go to South America with a Spanish name This was perhaps not an obvious career move, especially since Opportunity Knocks had made Los Caracas well known in the UK, but the managers were very persuasive. They decided to call the band Middle of the Road.

After the cruise ship dates, their managers arranged some gigs in Italy, which they promised would be a stepping-stone to South America. Not long after arriving in Italy the managers disappeared and they were stranded. Not a coin. They managed to find a gig in a restaurant and set about earning the fare back to Scotland. As it happened, an A&R man from RCA decided to have dinner there and loved the band. He immediately set up a recording session in Rome.

The band had always been very strong on vocal harmonies and RCA initially used them as a backing band for Italian artistes. They even recorded a song – honestly – backing Sophia Loren. As we chat, Sally laughs and even that sounds musical. She and Sophie became pals. *I've got a picture somewhere… yes, here it is.*

Sophia Loren was, of course, a goddess in Italy and suddenly Middle of the Road were attracting a lot of attention. RCA began looking for a song for them and came up with one written by an English guy who had released it on the Phillips label without exactly becoming the next Elvis. The band thought the song was a joke, but once they had recorded it, there was no doubt it had something very catchy. It was called *Chirpy Chirpy Cheep Cheep.*

As is often the case, luck played a big part. RCA were a massive record label and just at that moment had a big convention in Rome with execs from all over the world in town. They dropped by the studio, listened to *Chirpy*, realised it would sell barrowloads, and released it worldwide. It became one of those holiday hits, helped by the top UK radio dj of the time, Tony Blackburn. It was right up his street and he gave it a lot of airplay – he had 20 million listeners, more than a third of the country.

In June 1971 it went to the top of the UK charts, stayed there for 5 weeks and was the third best selling single of the year. In case you were wondering, *My Sweet Lord* and *Maggie May* were the top two. But times were changing. In 1971 Britain pretty much ruled the world with rock bands like Zeppelin, the Who, the Stones, Rod Stewart and the Faces, Pink Floyd and the emerging David Bowie releasing *Hunky Dory*. Middle of the Road had several more huge chart hits, but they were never regarded as 'cool'; they were never going to make a *Sergeant Pepper* album. Overseas they did very well though, constantly touring in Europe, Brazil, Malaysia, Hong Kong, South Africa, New Zealand, Australia and Japan. They even played at the 1972 Munich Olympics. It was a terrific life.

Sally has no idea how many millions of records they sold. She laughs: "I've no idea who got all the money either – certainly not us…"

Ken and Kenny, the other guitarist, finally arrive and we set up.

Sally asks me: "Is there anything you want to go over?"

"No thanks, I'm happy playing the set."

So we did. Straight through. Perfectly.

It's always a wee bit nerve-wracking playing with a new band, you know they'll be listening to every note you play. But I had learned all the songs and practised them so I had them down cold. When some people get on in years, as I am now, they do things like Scrabble and Crosswords to keep the brain ticking over. I like to memorise songs. I had written them out just in case I forgot anything, but deliberately left my charts in my guitar case. I wanted the band to know I'd done my homework. I could see Ken giving a wee look to Sally and her nodding with a little smile, yes it sounded good.

"That was great, Graham, I'd forgotten how much we used an acoustic guitar in the old days," said Ken.

I was like a wee puppy dog.

"OK, folks, I've made soup. You all ready for a bite to eat?" said Sally.

While we ate, Sally mentioned how she loves good Scottish soup. During the week, she works as a volunteer in Paisley, making soup for homeless people. I wondered how many of them realised who was ladling out their Scotch broth. She has had a tough time of it over the years, losing her son in a terrible motorbike accident in 2001. Despite the awful pain that never leaves, she has managed to stay cheery and lights up the room; she's one of those people you meet who are instantly likeable.

Ken emailed me next day, saying how pleased he was that it sounded so good. He told me he would get back to me soon with the arrangements for flights to Germany for the gigs I'd be playing on. I was in Florida when he sent an email with my ticket details and I flew back to Scotland with a couple of weeks to spare so I could do one more rehearsal with the band.

A few days after I got back, I received this email from Ken:

I'm afraid we have had to cancel all engagements for the foreseeable future. Unfortunately, Sally was rushed into hospital last night in a coma.

39

STEVE ARVEY

He's from Chicago, or someplace like it. He's a very interesting character, probably has attention deficit disorder, and is definitely one of the most versatile and talented musicians you could hope to meet.

He plays anything from steely cigar-box slide and clawhammer blues to smoky jazz and plays them well. He has extraordinary stage presence, stares out at the crowd with a slightly puzzled look as if wondering what they are all doing here. No one leaves, no one even goes to the bathroom when Steve is playing one of his searing, agonizing guitar solos, different every time, he figures them out when he gets there. He's toured a lot, released a few albums, played all over Europe too. I think he's big in Italy. I am amazed he's not as well known as Seasick Steve, or someone like that.

We're talking on the telephone.

"Hey man, howya doin? Ya back in town? Come to the Clam Factory on Friday. You know it? On Cortez? Course ya do. Ya gonna sit in on a coupla tunes? Great man. See, ya got good tone, man. Good *tone*. Yeah, not many people got good tone. That's what gitar playin's all about. Good *tone*. See ya Friday..."

So I see him on Friday.

"Hey, howya doin? Now tell me, what keys ya like to play in?"

"Whatever...I suppose A, G, C, E, D, B...you know, the usual?"

"Great man, ok. We gonna do *Sweet Home Chicago*. Ya know that?"

"Yeah, of course, no problem."

"Ok then, *Sweet Home Chicago* it is. In the key of *F*...."

40

LITTLE MISS DEBBY AND THE
SCUMBAG BOOGIE BAND

For centuries, the ancient town of Paisley in the west of
Scotland was a spiritual place, the home of thoughtful
and studious monks. Then came the industrial revolution
and the narrow cobbled streets were soon packed with men
and women bustling to their jobs in factories, shipyards and
even building cars; not very good ones, but better than some.

In the 1930s, the company J & P Coats employed 28,000
people in what was the largest textile factory in the world,
exporting the reinvented ancient Persian design which became
known everywhere as the Paisley pattern, except I guess in
Persia. It was used in many products, from fashionable shawls
to really cool Fender Telecasters played by Eric Clapton and
Jimmy Page.

There were plenty of jobs until the 1980s. Then J & P
Coats became one of the first big companies to discover the
financial savings of employing children in far off villages, and
set up factories in Brazil and India. Since then many other
factories in the town have nailed *Closed* signs on their gates;
even Paisley's most loyal citizens would probably admit it has
been dying a slow and painful death. There have been brave
attempts to revitalize the town, but sun tan parlours and Pound
shops are no substitute for industry. The busiest place is the

Sheriff Court, where a grumbling procession of unemployed thieves and junkies keep defence lawyers fully occupied. It is a tragedy.

Little Miss Debby is a blues singer, in the style of Janis Joplin. She's tiny, under 5 feet, and always wears a hat to add a wee bit so she is not lost in the crowd. Every Sunday night she sings with the Scumbag Boogie Band in the Patter Bar, a tiny pub in the soot-blackened buildings near the old train station. I love the name of her band, and she'd asked if I fancied sitting in with them. Of course I would.

Exactly a week earlier I had been in Florida, playing in a classy bar/restaurant called Ocean Blues, backing a great singer originally from New Jersey, a young girl called Boochie. If you had spilt a drink the chances are it would have landed in the lap of a millionaire. The menu offered Southern dishes: flapping-fresh grouper, steak tacos with something called *pico de gallo* on them, pulled pork, fried sweet potatoes – very tasty. There were lots of fancy sounding dishes – I think they call them entrees. They give the band a good feed so I'd turned up hungry, set up my amp then got my snout into the trough. Yum yum.

The well-stocked bar had everything: Pom Tini martinis, Sauvignon Blanc, Pomegranate Margarita, sparkling beers from every corner of the world; anything the discerning drinker might desire. The Diet Coke was perfectly chilled. And no one was pished.

Ocean Blues is a very friendly place; the regular crowd mainly successful retired folk, happy, rich, with perfect teeth, their veneers costing anything up to 20 grand a grin. Most of the good people here looked like they had been diligently working out with personal trainers and even the ones who liked their grub a little too much managed to look classy, knew just the right Armani clothes to hide the extra pounds.

You can see faces that are suntan-etched with wrinkles like

a Shar Pei but that have perfect gnashers and breasts, as many of the good ladies of Sarasota do. Some of them have spent more on their bodies than a house in Paisley would cost to buy. They were great to play to, applauded every song, and gave young Boochie plenty of cheers.

The band played at a respectful volume, even me. I have a terrible habit of playing too loud. The drummer, as we so often find, is usually the person who drives the level up, but he was restrained, considerately tapping his snare and hi-hat so that we played nice and quietly – the energetic people dancing right in front of the stage were able to chat about their stocks and shares without raising their voices. I think he even used brushes in a couple of songs, for crissake.

We were playing through nice new shiny Fender amps, sparkling microphones, and the semi-circular stage was polished wood, clean and gleaming. The room was no-smoking, but very few smoked anyway, and for the occasional stranger who might like a Marlboro they had a thoughtfully positioned sitting area outside, shaded from the baking mid-July sun. Even half an hour before sunset it was hot and steamy Florida-style, but the club had softly-humming air conditioning so I hardly broke sweat. In front of the band was a Tip bucket, already full of dollar bills, even a couple of twenties. Everyone was having a nice time. I was very happy to be playing there with Boochie and the band.

The noisy crowd at the Patter Bar was just as friendly in a less restrained, Paisley kind of way, and preferred what teeth they had to have a natural look. They were drinking pints of Export beer, and wolfing down bags of crisps. A few ladies were painfully thin, while others were, eh, more fulsome, but every roll of wobbling flesh was their own. Every so often they would take a crumpled piece of roll-up paper from a green Rizla packet, build a little smoke then shuffle outside into the drizzling Scottish rain to drag some brown nicotine deep into their lungs.

One guy wearing a big hat kept squeezing past the band to get to the toilet, far more often than I would have thought was medically necessary. An old man with huge leathery hands, like a former welder, sat grinning and nodding his head in a corner, tapping his walking sticks on the floor in time with the music.

The gig was going well, although the band was louder than I have ever heard anyone play in such a small area. Tanks rolling into battle would have made less noise. The drummer was hammering the kit as if trying to beat it into submission, like it was a wild dog that would attack him if he didn't batter it senseless. The bass player and guitarist knew exactly where to find the volume controls on their battered old amps and turned them as far up as they would go. The windows were rattling.

I'd plugged into my amp and we blasted out Rock N Roll, the Led Zep song. Debby has a strong, Janis Joplin type voice and held her dented, rusty old mic against her mouth as she screamed above the cacophony.

It was great.

We were set up on the floor, there was no stage, and everyone was dancing all around us, hurtling around, yelling if they needed to say anything to the person they were nearest to. They were having a great time. I was wearing earplugs, and even then I felt like I was in the middle of an explosion, but everyone seemed to be used to the volume. Maybe Florida has made me soft.

After a while, Debby invited another drummer up to jam. He looked very thin, frail and grey. I turned my amp down, he looked like he would play much quieter. But he hit the kit like a man possessed and we thundered into Honky Tonk Woman. After another couple of blitzkrieg-level songs, Debby said it was time for a break. She pointed to a small table at the back for the room. The buffet was ready. Food, or 'purvey' was laid out on paper plates. Time to eat.

Debby came back with a plate heaped with a couple of sausage rolls and sandwiches – *pieces* as they are known in these parts. She pushed them towards me.

"You want one? Spicy chicken tikka. It's great. Tasty."

I haven't been able to eat anything spicy for years; I lived on curry for too long when I was young. Getting old is such fun.

"You want something to drink?"

I can't drink either. Even if I could, the last time I did, many, many years ago, the smallest amount gave me a splintering headache. I thought I was having a brain hemorrhage. I felt like the life and soul of the bar. Ah well.

Ocean Blues also has open jams that attract a lot of blues players, many of whom have adopted 'blues names': Manatee Mike, Phil the Hat, Howlin' Bob, Kid Red. They all seem to have them. Paisley musicians also have blues names; like the recently departed Willie-Jukebox-Mathews, so called because of the thousands of songs he knew by memory. Debby told me her friend and rhythm guitarist called John the Haun might be coming.

"John the Haun? Why do they call him that?"

"It's because of his haun – his hand. When he was two years old, he grabbed the bar on an electric fire, burned all of the fingers on his right hand and they've been disfigured ever since. When he plays his tiny pinkie keeps catching on the strings. By the end of the night there's blood all over the guitar. He keeps asking the doctors to cut off the wee finger thing he's got but they keep trying to rebuild it. He just wants rid of it so he can play without it catching on his guitar strings."

In Florida a 60-year-old is regarded as young; in Paisley, tragically, many 60-year-olds are long dead. They all still miss the former guitarist with the band, Denis McBride.

"They called him the Eric Clapton of Paisley. He could have done anything, he could have played all over the world but he didn't want to leave here, content to play to his friends. The cancer got him. He was only in his 50s."

She talks about other local musicians she has known, and mentions Jimmy Dewar, who lived in Paisley. Jimmy was the bass player and singer with the Robin Trower Band, who played all over the world, gold records, the big time. Jimmy's son had died of alcohol poisoning before he was 30.

"The saddest thing I ever saw was watching Jimmy Dewar being helped in and out of his own son's funeral. His son had the same talent and beautiful soulful voice as Jimmy but was heartbroken; he'd watched his father fall from fame to a broken penniless man in a mental institution here in Paisley. Jimmy died not long after, then his heartbroken wife. They fought for years for royalties, many signed away under drunken promises."

Someone passes our table and leans over to tell her something. Debby roars with laughter. Despite everything, she laughs all the time, it seems nothing can get her down for long. Like so many women in Paisley, she's a single parent. She brought up three girls alone. She's loved watching them grow up, jamming with local musicians when she got the chance.

"Now they, and our friends' children, come to jam with us". Debby laughs. "We all look after each other here. We're like one big family. People come and play a few songs, nobody's got jobs. We're all unemployed or on the long-term sick. This is how we pass the time."

Time to play again. Another guitar player joins us, an older guy with the nickname Pockets. I don't ask why. He doesn't hold back, plays like he is on the big stage at Glastonbury. The volume goes up again, but nobody minds. Debby told me earlier that everyone is deaf, and I'm beginning to think she's not joking.

After a few more songs, the bass player is beginning to look agitated. He snarls at Debby.

"Is there no fucking bass players here tonight? I need a fucking smoke!"

"Right, on you go, away outside and have one." Debby turns to me.

"Can you play bass for a wee bit? He's worried the off-sales down the street is going to close in a minute and he needs to buy his carry-oot."

I know Floridians call the off sales a liquor store, but I've never been asked to cover for someone who is rushing off to one. We batter into another couple of rock standards...I can't remember what they were because at that volume it didn't seem to matter. I love it.

Finally the gig is over.

"It's a great wee shop this", says Debby. "We don't get money, but they give us plenty food and drink. That's what we play for."

She laughs.

"The drink; we play for the drink."

AFTERWORD: WORLDS APART
Cameron McNeish

It may be a little odd to have a mountaineer write the final word in a book about rock and roll but there are connections, believe me.

My first experience of mountains came as a youngster when I saw a couple of climbers emerge from a mountain corrie in Glen Coe. I was about twelve at the time and on holiday with my folks, but the transcendent vision of those climbers remains with me to this day. I was captivated by their lean, swarthy looks, the casual way they had a rope coiled over their shoulders, socks at their ankles, unshaven, wild. To my young eyes they looked like Gods coming down from Parnassus, and I wanted to be one of them.

But I didn't know much about Parnassus. I didn't know what lay up there in the hills, beyond the tree line. There might have been dragons for all I knew. I was just aware, in that split second of time, that I wanted to be a climber, although their world of rock and heather and crags and summits was unknown to me, as mysterious and enigmatic as the dark side of the moon.

Within a couple of years I was captivated by another group of young men. The Beatles, the Rolling Stones, the Dave Clark Five, the Searchers and many others were my icons of the glorious Sixties and while I knew their songs, could whistle their tunes, could grow my hair like them I had no idea of the world they inhabited. I hadn't the foggiest notion of sound checks, dodgy roadies, record deals or the incessant travel in broken down vans.

In due course the mountains opened up their secrets to me, and I have continued to enjoy a wide range of rock & roll, blues and folk, but the dark side of that musical moon has remained largely mysterious, still enigmatic. Until now...

Rock and Roll Busker is not just about playing packed stadium gigs, signing autographs and hanging out with rock stars. It's about the whole gamut of experience that makes up the role of a working musician; the highs and the lows, the heartless rejections and the cruel betrayals; the humour and the dreams and above all, the persistent, irresistible, deep-rooted love of the music.

Musicians and mountaineers are usually two different breeds; Graham Forbes is both. I've been on hills with him and you can sense his connection to the land, but whenever he is hillwalking in his beloved Scotland, cycling the backwoods in Florida, rock climbing in Spain or dropping over the edges of insane ski runs high in the Italian mountains, he always has his iPod. While some people seek silence in the hills, Graham loves listening to music; he feels that mountains and music combined have a special magic not to be found anywhere else.

It's that profound magic that he describes so well in this book, the magic of rock and roll, the musical mystery tour that has shaped his life. I'm delighted that he's decided to share it with us.

Cameron McNeish, author, broadcaster and ageing folkie.

ROCK AND ROLL MOUNTAINS
Graham Forbes

There has truly never been a book like this...inspired.
Banff Book Festival Canada

His irrepressible, self-deprecating sense of humour shines
through in every page – in between the hair-raising ice climbs,
the snatches of mountaineering history and more personal
musings. An enormously amiable and entertaining read.
The Scotsman

A breath of fresh air; enjoyable, honest and the literary
equivalent of a two-fingered salute to the fuddy-duddy
mountaineering establishment
TGO Magazine

Rock star on the rock face...a Scots climber with a rock 'n'
roll attitude...ice climbs, night climbs, the lot...
Daily Mail

Extreme sport, fear and survival...a real page turner, written
with humour, emotion and raw observation.
Scots Magazine

There has never been a book about mountains quite like it...
reels off funny anecdotes and one-liners at an electrifying
pace.
Glasgow Herald

They toured the Highlands in search of gigs, girls and
booze...a roller coaster that takes you from hard rock to a
hard place – and back again.
Daily Record

A belter!

An exhilarating book!

ROCK AND ROLL TOURIST
Graham Forbes

An incredibly entertaining book – would make a great road movie. I highly recommend it, really makes you feel you are on the tour bus.

Gerry Ryan, RTE Dublin

Funny in the *Spinal Tap* sense, such as when in Florida the fattest lady he has ever seen offers him her body at a BB King concert. But music is his primary interest and his love of rock 'n' roll is warming.

Daily Mail

Some gloriously written tales of excess, sadness and glory (think Bill Bryson or Nick Hornby, but without the smugness). The kind of book you'll read aloud to people. Excellent.

Guitar & Bass Magazine

A cracking book

Glasgow Herald

A glimpse into the life of a touring band...the humour, stories and tales of life on the road, from Jerry Lee Lewis to Aerosmith. Forbes manages to capture the special relationship between the band and the crowd. An entertaining mix of travel, rock music and humour.

Bass Guitar Magazine

Engrossing...a funny, engaging book of surprising substance.

The Skinny

I've loved reading Graham Forbes – a real adventure guide
for the imagination even if you have never made a journey...
all you need is the right size bag and fresh underwear

Sue Marchant, BBC Cambridge

A brilliant read!

Billy Rankine, Rock Radio

This is where armchair traveller becomes armchair rocker!
Graham took me to countries and concerts I never even
dreamed I would go to – a fantastic Rock 'n' Roll journey!

Carolyn Stewart, Radio U105 Belfast

A cross between Bill Bryson and Billy Connolly, Forbes is the
perfect commentator on a music travel tour. His passion
shines through the narrative, and he guides us, with friendly
hands through the intricacies of rock and roll.
With humour that never fails him, Forbes' book is an
engrossing, informative read. Taking us effortlessly from a hot
and humid Florida night, with steamy, intimate blues, to an
enchanting Edinburgh 'in the chill of a starry winter evening'.
It is the perfect book for budding armchair travellers.

Lifestyle Magazine

Travel guide with a difference. Graham brings out the best in
Rock. A compulsive read – hard to put down.

Pam and Peter Jay, Gulf Radio, Qatar

There is much here to remind us to keep an open mind and
just keep going – it's never too late to learn.

Robert Gwyn Palmer, *Birmingham Life*

A jobbing musician, Forbes travelled the globe in the company of an array of stars and entourages who have their own take on the world. He writes as much about people as he does places – and not just those with their names on the ticket stub. Forbes' account of a young Polish girl's first day as part of Rod Stewart's road crew is full of charming detail. A sideways view of the rock business, offering countless new perspectives.

Record Collector

A welcome departure from the generic pontificating of a lot of music literature, Glaswegian-born Forbes writes candidly about the experiences and passions he shares with a bewildering assortment of musicians along his travels. From Aerosmith in Florida to Wet Wet Wet in Stirling, the balance between travelogue and musical tenacity is so precise that *Tourist* could quite easily be deemed The Rough Guide to Rock and Roll.

The Isolationist

Tall tales, mishaps and adventures are brought to life through the author's wry observations, with some weird and wonderful insights.

The Times